# ENCYCLOPEDIA
## of the
# UNSEEN
## WORLD

*The Ultimate Guide to*
*Apparitions, Death Bed Visions,*
*Mediums, Shadow People,*
*Wandering Spirits,*
*and Much, Much More*

# ENCYCLOPEDIA
## of the
# UNSEEN
# WORLD

CONSTANCE VICTORIA BRIGGS

**WEISERBOOKS**
San Francisco, CA / Newburyport, MA

First published in 2010 by
Red Wheel/Weiser, LLC
With offices at:
500 Third Street, Suite 230
San Francisco, CA 94107
*www.redwheelweiser.com*

Library of Congress Cataloging-in-Publication Data
Briggs, Constance Victoria.
  Encyclopedia of the unseen world : the ultimate guide to apparitions,
death bed visions, mediums, shadow people, wandering spirits, and much, much
more / Constance Victoria Briggs.
     p. cm.
  Includes bibliographical references.
  ISBN 978-1-57863-465-1 (alk. paper)
  1. Future life—Encyclopedias. 2. Spiritualism—Encyclopedias. I. Title.
  BF1311.F8B75 2010
  133.903—dc22

                    2009049349


Cover design: Stewart Williams
Text design: Donna Linden
Typeset in P22 1722 amd Perpetua
Illustrations on pages 48, 79, 123, 180, 221, 225, 230, 242, and 252 © Miss Mary LLC; Illustrations on
pages 14, 22, 32, and 59 © The Peppin Press; Illustrations on the cover and pages 11, 17, 18, 26, 29, 30,
35, 38, 41, 42, 44, 50, 53, 57, 60, 64, 66, 68, 73, 74, 80, 82, 84, 87, 91, 95, 97, 99, 103, 105, 107, 111,
113, 114, 120, 128, 131, 133, 134, 139, 140, 143, 147, 149, 150, 155, 156, 160, 164, 170, 172, 177,
183, 185, 187, 192, 197, 200, 204, 207, 210, 213, 232, 236, 240, 244, 248, 254, 256, 260, 263, 265,
267, 271, 273, and 276 © Dover.


Printed in Canada
TCP
10 9 8 7 6 5 4 3 2 1


The paper used in this publication meets the minimum requirements of the American National Standard
for Information Sciences—Permanence of Paper for Printed Library Materials Z39.48-1992 (R1997)

*To my father, Wilfred, who from the other side*

*validated everything I have learned.*

*Thank you.*

# INTRODUCTION

*The Encyclopedia of the Unseen World* is devoted to explaining the fascinating yet sometimes complicated subjects involved with life after death and the spiritual world. I feel that when we are seeking answers to questions such as the existence and state of our loved ones that have crossed over, it is particularly important that we understand the meaning of terms that have now become mainstream. I also believe knowing what others have experienced and are still experiencing is vital to our own spiritual growth, knowledge, and understanding. By gaining knowledge about the spiritual world, we can understand better what is ahead for each of us.

It is interesting to note that even though there are now studies being done to prove that there is a spiritual world, that there is indeed life after death, the information being discovered is basically the same as that which has been revealed to us for centuries by the ancients, whose firsthand accounts sparked whole religious movements on the one hand and disdain and disbelief on the other.

This book takes us on a journey through time, as we meet people that have received communications from the spiritual realm firsthand. We learn of people from ancient times through today that have actually crossed over to the other side and back in out-of-body experiences, and realized that they were seeing and reporting the same things as those that have journeyed into the next world and back in modern near-death experiences. We meet people that in the face of skepticism and ridicule stood up and said, "Yes, it does exist, I have seen things, felt things, and heard things that prove that we are not alone and do not cease to exist once the physical body perishes."

A relative of mine, once he found out what the subject matter of this book is, asked me if it was scary. It is not scary. Only Hollywood can turn something this interesting and enlightening into fear. It is, in a nutshell, comforting to know that there is more to our existence, to our universe, to our being, than what we have been taught. It is not scary to step outside of our limited knowledge of things and explore. It is not scary to think that one day I will be able to once again meet people that I once knew, but who are no longer residing on earth.

The book is written in easy to understand terms. It is sorted in an A-to-Z format with highlighted cross-references. I have tried to include a variety of beliefs surrounding the spiritual world, from ancient times through today. I have incorporated people that have had experiences with the other side across the ages, so that we get a better view of what has been happening in this area of belief worldwide and for so long. Unfortunately, because of space constraints, the stories are only touched upon, but they are enough to get you started on your own spiritual path, your journey into the world that Shakespeare once called the "undiscovered country." That country, by the way, is no longer undiscovered.

I also use the terms "spiritual world" and "other side." Both are terms for the nonphysical world where souls exist after the death of the physical body.

Once you finish here, you can use the references in the back of the book to continue your research.

Good luck.

I wish you well on your journey of discovery and enlightenment.

ENCYCLOPEDIA
of the
UNSEEN
WORLD

"The dead don't bear a grudge nor seek a blessing. The dead don't rest uneasy. Only the living."
—Margaret Laurence, *The Stone Angel*

# A

## Acheron

A river located in the Epirus region of northwest **Greece.** In Greek mythology it is a river connected to the spiritual world. The word *acheron* when translated means "river of despair." In ancient Greece it was believed to be one of the five underworld rivers, through which the souls of the dead were transported by **Charon** (ferryman of the dead) to **Hades**, ruler of the underworld.

## ADC (After-Death Communication) Project, The

Headed by Bill and Judy Guggenheim, this is an in-depth project on the subject of communication from the spiritual world. Bill and Judy Guggenheim are the co-authors of *Hello from Heaven!,* which contains 353 after-death communication accounts. The ADC Project was started in May, 1988 and was the first thorough study on the subject. During their research, the Guggenheims interviewed two thousand people living in the United States and Canada. They were able to compile 3,300 accounts from people who had been contacted by a loved one from the spiritual world.

## Addictions

A strong dependence on a substance (or practice) that may have negative effects upon the participant. People that have serious, problematic addictions on earth and do not overcome them may still have the addiction after they pass on. Those existing in the spiritual world who passed on with this type of addiction may find themselves either earthbound or in the lower realms, unable to move on until they let go of their habit. This addiction can pose a severe problem for a person after death because it can hinder their spiritual development. People that have had near-death experiences have reported witnessing addicts who have crossed over. One observed a person in spirit attempting to inhabit the body of a living person who had the same addiction. Once a person in spirit lets go of the addiction, they are then able to move on with their spiritual journey and move into a higher spiritual dimension.

## Adjusters

A name for guides in the spiritual world that greet the newly deceased persons arriving from the physical dimension. According to a number of sources, ancient and modern, when we cross over to the other side, there are guides to greet us and help us adjust to our new surroundings. These guides can be any number of people or entities, including loved ones from our most recent incarnation, loved ones from previous lives (that we have forgotten while on the earth plane), or even angels and beings of light.

## Advanced Souls

Souls that have had a number of physical incarnations on the earth or elsewhere. In the spiritual world, advanced souls are often assigned to be spirit guides to help those still existing in the physical world. In addition, advanced souls may incarnate on earth to assist humanity in spreading goodness and light to the world. When on earth, advanced souls quietly go about their business doing good work and finding self-fulfillment in improving the lives of others. Advanced souls are apt to focus less on institutional matters and more on enhancing individual values, and tend to possess great patience and tolerance. They also display extraordinary coping skills and wisdom. Even from childhood, these souls have an air about them that makes others feel that they are somehow wiser than their time on earth would allow. Advanced souls are not motivated by self-interest; they often disregard their own physical needs and comforts for those of others. At death, an advanced soul that has had many previous lives knows immediately that it has been set free from the limitations of life in the physical realm, and that it is returning to its original home.

## Aeons

The Aeons are great spiritual beings in ancient **Gnosticism**. They were believed to be the first beings created by **God** and number somewhere around 365. According to ancient

Gnostic beliefs, some of the aeons turned away from the Supreme Being when they became fascinated with human sexuality. This belief parallels a story in the **Bible**'s **Old Testament** (Genesis 6:1-4), which speaks of angels becoming attracted to human women and coming to the earth to take them as wives.

## After-Death Communication

A communication from someone that has crossed over to the spiritual world. In most cases the recipient is a family member or friend. In the spiritual world, people's thoughts are so powerful that they can communicate easily with each other, as well as with people still existing in the physical world. When offering a communication to someone still in physical life, the person in the spiritual world often intends to comfort the individual or bring closure to unfinished business.

This communication is achieved through the use of telepathy. Research shows that the communication can come in a number of different ways and may occur in the waking state, the meditative state, or the dream state. Common forms of communication from the other side are:

**Auditory Communication** (hearing a spirit's voice). Verbal communication may be received in two ways, outwardly (hearing through the ears) or inwardly, as a thought coming into the mind.

**Visual Communication** (seeing the spirit). A person on the other side may appear to one or more living persons. Visual communication is spontaneous and can occur anywhere and at anytime. The deceased can be seen either fully or partially. When appearing fully, the spirit of the deceased usually appears solid and often with light surrounding it. Usually, the deceased person appears younger and in better health than before he or she crossed over. The living person may see an image of the deceased in the form of an outward vision (as if the experiencer is watching a film) or an inward one (as if the living person is having a daydream). Bedside visual visitations are common; spirits often appear beside the bed or at the foot of the bed.

**Dreams.** The deceased person may appear to a living person in a dream. It is believed that this is one of the easier methods of after-death communication for a person in spirit. Usually, the recipient of the dream is certain that the contact was made and is able to rest easier because their grief and worry over the deceased is assuaged. The dreams are often experienced as real events, as if the dreamer were there with the deceased, and sometimes the dreamer is given a message. In addition, the deceased may interrupt an ordinary dream. This interruption can be likened to the dreamer watching a movie that the deceased suddenly appears in.

**Feeling a Presence.** In this case experiencers feel the presence of their loved one. They have the feeling that the deceased person is in the room with them or that they are being watched by their loved one. This feeling is often accompanied by a feeling or sense of tremendous love and tranquility.

**Touch.** In some instances people can feel a touch, such as a caress, a kiss, or even a hug, from the deceased loved one. The touch often comforts the living person's grief over the individual's death.

**Apports** (appearance of favorite items). An item that the deceased person loved or admired may be shown to the recipient in a vision or a dream, or the solid item itself might appear where the recipient will notice it in waking life.

**Smell.** Here the experiencer smells a distinct fragrance—such as the scent of perfume, cooking food, air fresheners, or soaps—that is associated with a deceased loved one.

**Telephone Calls.** Sometimes a person in spirit will use the telephone as a means of communicating a message to loved ones left behind. This call usually startles the recipient, who sometimes quickly hangs up. Usually the person on the telephone sounds far away.

**Electronic Manipulation** (e.g., lights going on and off, televisions turning on automatically). It seems rather simple for those on the other side to make their presence known by making electronic equipment, such as lights, computers, televisions, and radios, go haywire. In addition, the deceased may leave an audible message on a tape recorder, answering machine, or even computer (a form of communication also known as electronic voice phenomena).

People respond in a number of ways to after-death communications. If someone has had experience with such phenomena or are at least aware of the possibility that the loved one who has crossed over may contact them, this communication is perfectly normal. For others it may come as a shock and may even be a frightening experience. However, the after-death communication is a gift to the recipient and is usually viewed that way by those who experience it. More often than not, the person that has crossed over is trying to comfort their loved one and convey the message that they survived death and are fine. They are trying to convince their loved ones to not worry about them, and to reassure the living that they are in a better place.

The return communication tends to be problematic for many recipients. Often people feel the need to contact a third party, such as a medium, to relay a message to the deceased. However, a third party is not needed to relay a message to the person in spirit, because the person is still alive in every way while in spirit form. Their hearing, sight, and personality are all intact. Only their form has changed. Those of us living in the physical realm cannot see and hear those in the unseen spiritual world; because most people's spiritual senses are not developed, we cannot perceive those existing on the other side. This makes communication between those in spirit and those in the physical virtually impossible. However, the person in spirit can still hear and understand the messages spoken out loud by their loved ones. Therefore, if a living person has a message for a relative or friend that has crossed over, talking aloud is a simple way of conveying the message. In addition, if a living person has a question for someone that has passed on, an answer may come in one of the communication forms listed above. Therefore, one must be receptive, keep watch, and have a mind open to the possibility of communication from the spiritual world.

## After-Death Experience

A term sometimes used when referring to a near-death experience.

## After-Death Vision

A vision of a deceased individual. After-death visions have been reported since ancient times. According to historical accounts, those that have passed on sometimes visit the dying to bring them messages and/or comfort. An after-death vision is given by the deceased to the recipient to reassure them that the deceased survived death. The vision can be that of an apparition, in which the deceased may appear fully formed, or be seen in the mind's eye (as if the recipient is watching a movie of the deceased). These visions often occur soon after a person crosses over into the spiritual world at death and more often during the first three months after the death. The vision can be seen by one or more persons in the same or even different localities and sometimes occur simultaneously. An after-death vision can be experienced by anyone.

## After-Death Visitation

A visitation from a loved one that has crossed over into the spiritual world. After-death visitations most often occur soon after a person's death, but can also happen years later. They often happen to let a loved one know that the deceased is still in existence. The deceased may also come to bring a message or warning to a living individual. These visitations can occur when the recipient is in a waking or sleep state. In the sleep state they may be confused with a dream. One can discern the difference by how real the dream seemed. There is often a sense of feeling that the visitation was real and a message was conveyed. The visitation may also come in the form of an apparition.

## Afterlife

A general term used to refer to the continuation of existence after the physical body has permanently died. The term afterlife is also another name for the spiritual world. The afterlife is essentially another dimension where living beings that are involved with the cycle of spiritual advancement and reincarnation are able to study, rest, and learn in preparation for their next incarnation. It is said to be a place of emotional and spiritual euphoria, where all enjoy a state of perfect health. Any unhappiness, problems, difficulties, and ailments a person suffered during their physical lifetime are gone. Although the afterlife is said to be in close proximity to the physical world, it cannot be perceived by the physical senses.

Just what goes on in the afterlife has been a matter of debate and speculation throughout the history of humankind. Finally, in the modern era, due to a great deal of study, research and comparisons with stories of near-death experiences, out-of-body experiences, and ancient writings, a picture is beginning to be painted of this mysterious otherworld.

The afterlife is evidently a place of learning, growth, and activity. It is a busy existence, and the goal is for beings to evolve and grow spiritually. It is a time of analyzing one's spiritual development and soul's journey. There, we are able to review our life as we lived it during our most recent incarnation. We also remember and examine our past lives, lessons learned, and missions fulfilled. Important decisions are made, such as whether or not to continue incarnating on earth (or another world) or move on into the higher spiritual realms.

Exactly where a person goes within the afterlife realms depends upon the kind of person they were and the kind of life they lived while on earth. Inhabitants of the afterlife are called souls and/or spirits. Popular terms used when referring to the afterlife are *the other side, spiritual realm,* and *astral plane.* In certain religious beliefs the afterlife is known as heaven and paradise.

**Living in the Afterlife.** According to the majority of the world's religious and spiritual beliefs, the kind of existence experienced in the afterlife is one of peace and love. Most believe that this is the life that awaits honest, loving, kind people who cross over into the afterlife. It is a world of happiness, recreation, spiritual growth, and learning. There, people are involved in activities that they take pleasure in, and they associate with people much like themselves and that they enjoy being around. The skills, interests, and abilities developed in their most recent life on earth are reflected in the roles chosen after death. People in the afterlife go about their activities much as we go about ours here in the physical world.

In the afterlife, there are opportunities in art, science, music, and many other interests. Much of the information mentioned here has come to light in our modern era and was derived from research of the afterlife and near-death experiences, as well as out-of-body experiences (also known as astral projection). In addition, information about life after death can also be found in ancient scriptures and writings including the **Bible,** the **Koran,** the **Egyptian Book of the Dead**, the **Books of Enoch,** and the **Tibetan Book of the Dead.**

In the **Books of Enoch**, there is an account of the biblical prophet **Enoch** visiting the spiritual world and witnessing many amazing sights. Among them were spirits, whom Enoch referred to as angels, studying and working. 1 Enoch states:

*The men (angels) brought me to the sixth heaven, and there I saw seven groups of 'angels.' Some of these 'angels' study the movements of the stars, the Sun and the Moon and record the peaceful order of the world. Other 'angels' there, undertake teaching and give instruction in clear and melodious voices. Others are responsible for recording the fauna and flora in both the Highland and the Lowlands. There are 'angels' who record the seasons and the years, others who study the rivers and the seas, others who study the fruits of the lowlands and the plants and herbs that give nourishment to men and beasts. And there are 'angels' who study mankind and record the behavior of men and how they live.*

The beauty of the afterlife is said to be unimaginable. In addition, living conditions are similar to those on earth and include such aspects of earth life as homes to dwell in, places to go, and friends to see. There are also many places for learning and mental and spiritual growth.

**Location of the Afterlife.** For thousands of years people thought that the afterlife realm was somewhere up above the earth and that the soul ascended to this place after death. Evidence shows that this is not the case. According to modern afterlife research, the afterlife exists in the same space as the physical world. It is another dimension that overlaps with the physical plane. If we were to open our "spiritual eyes," we would be able to see into this world. Occasionally, we can get a glimpse into it by happening upon a spirit from the other side. What separates the spiritual world from the physical is the fact that the former is a different dimension vibrating at a higher frequency.

## After Life

A 1998 movie by Japanese director Hirokazu Kore-eda, starring Arata, Erika Oda, and Susumu Terajima. The film has an afterlife theme about death and memory. The movie tagline asks, "What is the one memory you would take with you?" In the film, after people die, they spend a week with spiritual counselors who help them choose one memory. They de-scribe the memory to the staff that works with a crew to film it and screen it at the week's end. As soon as a person views their memory, he or she vanishes into the afterlife, taking only that single memory with them into eternity. In the film, twenty-two people, including an elderly woman, a rebellious high school dropout, a teenage girl, and a seventy-year-old war veteran, arrive in one week and are assigned to three counselors and a trainee. In preparation for the movie, Hirokazu interviewed five hundred people, from all walks of life, about their memories. These interviews are interwoven throughout the film.

## Afterlife Communication
See **After-Death Communication.**

## Afterlife Experiments, The

A book by Gary Schwartz (who is also the co-author of *The Living Energy Universe*). *The Afterlife Experiments* documents groundbreaking scientific experiments that lend testimony to the existence of life after death. Session transcripts take the reader into a controlled laboratory environment where contact with those in the spiritual world is made. In these experiments, mediums and "sitters" worked together to establish a connection with the spiritual world, which they did on a consistent basis.

## Age of Souls

Metaphysical and New Age thinkers, as well as a number of spiritual groups and religious teachings, hold to the theory that human souls are immortal. According to some prominent psychics and people who have had near-death experiences and experienced after-death communication, people on the other side appear many years younger than they were when they were alive on earth. This is because in the afterlife people's appearance can regress or progress to their best age. This age is generally believed to be around thirty years old. Popular author **Dolores Cannon** writes in her book *Between Death and Life*, "All souls have been around for the same degree. Some of us have chosen, for our own personal reasons, to incarnate into the body more than others. That is where they get the term old or young soul." In an interview in the Internet magazine *The New Times*, medium **Rosemary Altea** writes, "I have seen young men twenty or thirty years old who had died at five or six."

## Akashic Records

A spiritual library of knowledge, located on the other side. The Akashic Records are also known as the Records of Life. They are said to hold the history and experiences of every person that has ever lived. They contain every word, action, deed, feeling, thought, desire, and intention that each individual has ever had. The records also give the account of every person's soul journey. This journey would include their past, present, and possibly their future incarnations.

Prophets, mystics, and psychics have talked about the Akashic Records for centuries. Some claim to be able to tap into these records for information. One such example is the prominent psychic **Edgar Cayce,** who first brought the term *Akashic Records* to general society. Cayce claimed that while in a trance state he could retrieve information from the Akashic Records for medical diagnosis.

Spiritual beings, such as angels, are believed to have privy access to the Akashic Records to provide humans with information needed to help with difficult problems, and to answer questions on **God,** the heavens, and the future. According to ancient Judaic lore, there are heavenly archives that hold sacred scrolls; this is perhaps an old description of the Akashic Records. These heavenly archives are said to be looked after by angels.

## Akh

In ancient Egyptian beliefs, the akh was the principal aspect of the soul of a human being or of a god. After death, the akh was believed to join the gods in the underworld. If the proper funerary rites were performed after a person's death, then their akh would become immortal. It was these rites that prevented the akh from dying a second death. The second death meant the end of one's existence forever.

## Alighieri, Dante

Noted Italian poet (1265–1321). He is the author of *The Divine Comedy (La commedia divina),* a three-part narrative poem considered to be one of the greatest masterpieces ever written. *The Divine Comedy* is a vernacular poem in 100 cantos (more than 14,000 lines). In *The Divine Comedy*, Dante explores the condition of human souls in the afterlife by going on an imaginary journey through heaven, purgatory, and hell. The journey begins on Good Friday, in the year 1300, with a descent through the subterranean circles of hell *(L'Inferno),* guided by the poet Virgil. Dante's inspiration for *The Divine Comedy* is said to come from the **Bible,** the sixth canto of Virgil's *Aeneid,* **Aristotle**'s physical vision of the universe, and Thomistic philosophy. (Thomistic philosophy is inspired by the philosophical methods and principles used by Thomas Aquinas.) In *Purgatorio,* Dante struggles up the mountain of purgatory, reaching the earthly paradise at its peak. He then undergoes the purification that will make him fit for entering paradise. In the end, the protagonist comes face to face with **God,** thus achieving the greatest desire of all souls.

## Al-Janna

Al-Janna is the Islamic name of the spiritual world. In Islamic beliefs, souls travel to Al-Janna, which is believed to be a beautiful spiritual paradise. There are eight levels of Al-Janna, most with gardens of some form or another. There the devoted enjoy delectable food, abundant fruits, spring water, goblets of silver, and an existence free from pain and sorrow. In addition, there are four rivers filled with milk, water, wine, and honey. Male inhabitants are served by *houri* (beautiful virgins), who exist to serve their masters. It is a place of rest and refreshment in which the righteous live in the presence of **God.** Another version of the term Al-Janna is *Djanna*.

## Alleviation

In the spiritual world, pain, suffering and illness as we know it do not exist. It is a place filled with love, where people are calm, content, and free of the illnesses that may have led to their death or followed them throughout their earthly life. There people can think more clearly because the mind itself is sharper and is not cluttered with the constant pressure of stress found in one's everyday earthly existence. Most people that have crossed over and returned to tell what they saw on the other side have given accounts of a place of harmony and love. It is a place where the cares of the material world are in the past.

## Altea, Rosemary

Internationally renowned medium, healer, and best-selling author (1946–). She won international acclaim with the publication of her books *The Eagle and the Rose* (her autobiography), *Proud Spirit,* and *You Own the Power.* She is also the founder of the Rosemary Altea Association of Healers (RAAH), a nonprofit organization based in England with patients worldwide. She is known as "the Voice of the Spirit World," a title she obtained by traveling extensively around the world demonstrating that we don't die and helping thousands make contact with their loved ones on the other side.

Altea was born and raised in England. As a child she heard voices and was able to see people who were deceased. Threatened by her mother, she told no one her secret. During the 1970s, however, she began working with a group of people who helped her develop her spiritual abilities. Today, Altea, along with her spirit guide, Grey Eagle, helps bring peace and joy to those who have lost loved ones by bringing messages of hope to those left behind. It is her belief that we do not die, but are transformed, continuing on long after our physical death.

## American Association of Electronic Voice Phenomena (AA-EVP)

A nonprofit educational association whose purpose is to investigate and study the paranormal communication found on audio- and video-recording equipment—communication referred to as electronic voice phenomena (EVP) and instrumental transcommunication (ITC). Founded in 1982 by **Sarah Estep,** the organization is currently under the direction of Tom and Lisa Butler (since May 2000), authors of the book *There is No Death and There are No Dead*. Currently, its membership includes people from over twenty countries who have collected pictures, recorded voice messages, and information from loved ones in the spiritual world who are trying to communicate with the living. Messages have been found on such devices as tape recorders, televisions, telephones, and video recorders.

The association seeks to assist in the understanding of this phenomenon by sharing experiences, ideas, concepts, and information with association members, as well as the general public. The association's basic theory is that we are nonphysical beings that currently exist in the physical world through physical bodies. After the death of the body, we continue on into the spiritual world.

In addition, AA-EVP seeks to lessen the grief of those that have lost loved ones, as well as find ways for us to communicate openly with the spiritual world. The messages received via EVP are thought by the association to be of nonphysical origin. For more information, the AA-EVP can be reached via its website: *www.aaevp.com*. See also **Jürgenson, Friedrich.**

## American Society for Psychical Research (ASPR)

The oldest psychical research organization in the United States. A nonprofit society located in New York City, it occupies a historical landmark building acquired by the society. It was founded in 1885 by a prominent group of scholars who collectively had the desire to explore the unfamiliar realms of human consciousness. The society's purpose is to advance the understanding of psychic and paranormal phenomena through research. Some of the topics studied that are related to the spiritual worlds include telepathy, clairvoyance, out-of-body experiences, near-death experiences, reincarnation, survival after death, apparitions, and mediumship.

## Amphitheater

According to several people who have had near-death experiences, a large, spiritual amphitheater exists on the other side. It has been variously described as an "ethereal structure," "made of crystal," and "brilliant." It is said to radiate multicolored waves of energy and be suspended in space. In appearance it resembles the amphitheaters of ancient times. Love and music emanate from it. One account describes it as having walls made of gold with jewels embedded in them. The amphitheater is also said to be a place where life reviews are sometimes given.

## Ancestor Worship

The veneration of one's ancestors. It is based on the idea that the spirits of loved ones that have crossed over after death possess supernatural powers. It is believed that these loved ones still have influence in the lives of the living and can be called upon for assistance, special favors, and guidance.

Although it is not a universal practice, ancestor worship is found in various cultures at every level of development. It continues to be an important component of various religious practices in modern times. During ancient times, it was a minor cult among the Romans. The practice reached its highest point in West Africa and with ancient Chinese. It was also well developed in the Japanese Shinto cult and among the peoples of Melanesia. In modern times, it remains an important component of various religious practices.

Ancestor worship in some cultures (such as the Chinese culture) seeks only to honor the deeds, memories, and sacrifice of the deceased. This includes making offerings in order to provide for their welfare in the spiritual world. For example, items are often placed in or near coffins so that the deceased will have their belongings with them in the afterlife. Even "spirit money" is sometimes burned as an offering to ancestors.

## Anderson, George

An internationally acclaimed psychic medium (1952–). Dubbed the **"Edgar Cayce** of our time,"Anderson has helped to bridge the gap between the spiritual and physical worlds by connecting families with deceased loved ones on the other side. In addition, he helped pave the way for other mediums in a world full of disbelief and skepticism. In 1982, Anderson was the first medium to have a cable television program, titled *Psychic Channels*. In 1987, his book *We Don't Die* was the first book by a medium to become a bestseller. In 2001, he was featured in a television special entitled *Contact: Talking to the Dead*. In addition, he has worked with the New York Police Department's homicide unit to help with unsolved murders.

Today, Anderson continues his work through private appointments, grief-support seminars, and various media, including television and books. His books include *Our Children Forever: George Anderson's Message from Children on the Other Side; Lessons from the Light: Extraordinary Messages of Comfort and Hope from the Other Side; We Don't Die: George Anderson's Conversations With the Other Side; Walking in the Garden of Souls: George Anderson's Advice from the Hereafter, for Living in the Here and Now;* and *We Are Not Forgotten: George Anderson's Messages of Love and Hope from the Other Side*.

## Andreasi, Osanna

Italian mystic and visionary Osanna Andreasi was born in Mantua, Italy to Italian aristocrats Niccolò and Agnes Andreasi (1449–1505). At the tender age of five, she reportedly began to have visions of the spiritual world that included paradise and divine spiritual beings. She even reported being held by **God.** At the age of seventeen, after many spiritual experiences and visions, she felt called by a higher source to enter into a spiritual life and became a Dominican tertiary. Her spiritual experiences included having visions of angels, **Jesus,** and God, and she fell into ecstasies whenever she spoke of God.

## Angakok

A traditional Eskimo shaman. The Angakok were believed to have had supernatural powers, including the ability to communicate with those in the spiritual world. When a person became ill, it was sometimes thought that the cause came from the loss of one's soul. Therefore, the help of an Angakok was sought. In order to cure the person, the Angakok would communicate with a deceased relative of the sick person. In addition, he was believed to be able to fly through the air in order to look for the errant soul.

## Angel of Death

An angel that escorts the souls of the dead to the spiritual realm. He is believed to come at death to take the

souls of individuals away to the life beyond. Belief in an angel of death is derived from beliefs in the "gods of death" in the various cultures and early religions. In modern times, the angel of death is

believed to mirror humankind's mixed feelings towards the subject of dying. For most people, death is still a difficult subject to come to terms with. The angel of death is the idea of death embodied as a tangible being. This being is portrayed in various ways, including an old man cloaked; a skeleton carrying a large scythe and wearing a dark black cloak with a hood; and a skeleton dressed in a gown or a white burial shroud. He is often personified as the Grim Reaper in Western beliefs.

In **Hinduism**, the angel of death is referred to as *Yama* or *Yamaraj,* which means "the lord of death." Yama travels on a black buffalo, carrying a rope to lasso the souls back to his home, called *Yamalok.* Yama's helpers are referred to as *Yamaduts.* It is they that actually take the souls back to Yamalok. In Yamalok the person's life is examined, and his or her good and bad acts are recorded and kept by the god Chitragupta (the keeper of records of humanity). Chitragupta knows all of the deeds and behaviors of each individual on earth. From these records, Yama decides where the person will go in his or her next incarnation.

The ancient Greeks believed in **Thanatos,** the god of death. Thanatos performed all of the functions of an angel of death. He was believed to come to humans at the end of their lives and carry them away to the underworld.

In the Japanese tradition, there is Shinigami, the god of death or the death god. Shinigami is the personification of death. It is believed that the idea of Shinigami was brought to Japan from Europe during the Meiji period. In fact, the term *Shinigami* is a recent term and means, loosely, "death deity." It does not represent any of the **Shinto** deities.

In the old Slavic tribes, "death" was personified as a woman wearing white and carrying a green sprout. If the sprout touched a human, they would go to sleep forever. In **Islam,** Azrael is the angel of death.

In Judeo-Christian beliefs, **Gabriel** has been called the angel of death. In Zoroastrian beliefs, Mairya is the angel of death. The Hebrew Midrash speaks of an angel of death that was created by **God** on the first day of creation; this angel is said to reside in heaven. He has twelve wings and is full of eyes. As soon as the dying person sees him, they expire. In Coptic Church beliefs, Abbaton appears when it is time for a person to die and carries them away.

In a more modern account, the famed psychic **Edgar Cayce** met the angel of death in one of his many out-of-the-body journeys. During the experience, he recognized that he had actually made contact with the person of death. He was surprised to find that Death was not what he had imagined—the Death often shown in art and media as wearing a black cloak and hood and carrying a sickle. In actuality, Death, according to Cayce, was robust, with rosy cheeks and a fair complexion. Instead of a sickle, he carried a pair of shears.

Is the angel of death real? It is more commonly believed these days that when a person dies and is about to cross over, they have an escort or guide. However, this guide is not a dark angel, or even an angel that comes to take the life force out of a human, as some have believed in the past. This is usually an angel or spirit guide (sometimes more than one) that the individual knows and has been with in the spiritual world before coming to earth.

## Angeloi

The last class of angels found within the angel hierarchy created by German philosopher and clairvoyant **Rudolph Steiner.** According to Steiner, the angeloi stand one stage higher than humankind. They are said to work directly with humans more than any of the other classes of angels. The guardian angels are said to be from the angeloi class.

## Angel(s)

Celestial beings that are superior to humans in power and intelligence. A 1991 Gallup Poll revealed that 69 percent of Americans believe in angels, and 32 percent feel that they have had contact with an angel. The word *angel* means "messenger." It was derived from the Hebrew word *malakh*, which means "messenger"; the Persian word *angaro*, meaning "courier"; and the Greek word *angelos*, which also means "messenger."

Belief in angels can be found in cultures and religions all over the world. They are believed to perform various services for people on **God**'s behalf. In heaven, angels have many functions, some of which involve the earth and humans. But many angelic functions have nothing to do with this life or this dimension. The angels that we know of are the ones directly assigned to work with this realm. They generally come to offer their help, guidance, and protection and to deliver messages for God.

In published accounts of near-death experiences, people often tell of leaving their bodies and meeting angels. These beings escort them to heaven, show them around the heavenly realm, and in some cases help them to understand why they should return to their life on earth. An example of one such account is found in the best-selling book entitled *Embraced by the Light* by **Betty J. Eadie**. In the book Eadie tells of leaving her body and seeing three men, whom she referred to as monks. These three men informed Eadie that they had been her guardian angels while she was on earth.

In addition, angels act as go-be-tweens for God and humankind, often going back and forth between heaven and earth. Angels are thought to be a necessary link between God and the physical realm and are believed to es-cort souls to heaven.

According to ancient Judaism, an-gels in the highest realms help to fil-ter down God's light and love to the lower-level realms that extend all the way down to earth. In addition, it is believed by many religions that angels assist in judging souls once the souls reach heaven. It is said that some angels help determine who will enter para-dise or heaven, and who will be thrown into hell (the lowest realms or dimensions). Angels are also sent from heaven to be guard-ians to humans on earth, helping us live out our lives, learn our lessons, and fulfill our life's missions.

While angels have so many duties relating to earth, it seems normal that they would also have many more re-sponsibilities relating to the afterlife. These duties include caring for peo-ple who have just died, bringing them comfort, escorting them through the tunnel and into the light, and com-forting souls newly arrived in heaven.

**Orders of Angels** (also known as The Angelic Hierarchy and The Hier-archy of Angels). According to Chris-tian tradition, there are nine orders of angels listed in the angelic hierarchy. These include the seraphim, cheru-bim, thrones, dominations, virtues, powers, principalities, archangels, and angeloi. Ministering angels serve and assist God. They do God's bidding in the heavens and are sometimes sent to help those in need on earth.

**Seraphim.** Powerful spiritual beings of Judeo-Christian belief; thought to be the highest order of angels in heaven. They have been de-scribed as incorruptible, brilliant, and powerful. They exist in the highest spiritual realm and, as the closest angels to the Divine, are in direct communication with God. It is said that they are so radiant that not even the cherubim and the ophanim (also very powerful beings) can look upon them. If humans stood in their presence, they would be incinerated. They control the motion of the heavens as it flows out from God. Their essence is love, and they are called *angels of love*. Through their purifying powers, they move humans to a love of God. They surround God's throne, continuously singing the Trisagion, a song of celebration. The third of the **Books of Enoch** (26:9–12) says that there are four seraphim corresponding to the four winds of the world. They each have six wings, corresponding to the six days of creation. Each of the four seraphim has sixteen faces, facing in each of the four directions. Each wing is the size of heaven. The name *seraphim* is a combination of the Hebrew word *rapha*, which means "healer," and *ser*, which means "higher being." The seraphim are represented by the serpent, which is a symbol of healing. They are also referred to as *seraphs*.

**Cherubim.** Brilliant and mighty angels who dwell close to God in the seventh level of heaven, according to Judeo-Christian lore. They are the second highest order of angels in heaven. They are sometimes referred to as *cherubs*, but are not to be mistaken with the baby angels of the same name. According to the Books of Enoch, cherubim are majestic and very beautiful. The name *cherubim* originated in **Assyria** and is derived from the word *karibu*, which means "one who prays." Cherubim emanate a subtle vibration of knowledge and wisdom that they receive from God. They are also the keepers of the celestial records, and are said to praise God night and day, continuously. In Islam they are called *el-karubiyan*, which means those "brought close to Allah." In the Near and Middle East, they were originally portrayed as mighty guardian figures. In Assyrian art, cherubim were depicted as winged creatures with faces of either a lion or a human, and bodies of sphinxes, eagles, or bulls. In the biblical book of Psalms (18:10), God is said to ride upon a cherub. In Exodus 25:18 of the Good News Bible, the cherubim are referred to as "winged creatures." The Zohar (a primary Cabalistic text that's name means "The Book of Splendor") states, "Come and see. When the sun sets the cherubim . . . beat their wings above and stretch them out, and the melodious sound of their wings is heard in the realms above."

**Thrones.** The order of angels ranking third in the angelic hierarchy. It was from the biblical prophet Ezekiel's vision that the medieval scholars derived the class of angels known as thrones. The thrones wheel around the throne of God. Their role is to inspire confidence in the power of God. They are said to dwell in either the third or fourth level of heaven found in ancient Judeo-Christian beliefs (see Heaven). They are also called *wheels, galgallin, erelim, arelim, abalim,* and *auphanim.* In the third of the Books of Enoch, they are referred to as the *ophanim.* In the Jewish Cabala they are called *merkabah.*

**Dominations.** The fourth order of angels. They are known as the channels of mercy. They are in charge of merg-

ing the spiritual and physicals worlds. They are said to receive their assignments from God directly and rarely communicate with humans personally. They are variously called *dominions, lords, lordships, kuriotetes,* and *hashmallim.*

**Virtues.** The order of angels ranking fifth in the angelic hierarchy. The virtues are responsible for working miracles in God's name on earth. They also look after the heroes of the world, and those who champion for good. They also impart strength and courage to individuals when needed. The virtues are also referred to as *the angels of grace, angels of valor, the brilliant ones, splendors, malakim, mights,* and *tarshishim.*

**Powers.** The order of angels that rank sixth in the angelic hierarchy. The powers are said to be the first angels created by God. They are guardians of the passageways leading to heaven. They also act as guides to lost souls. It is the job of the powers to bring balance to the earth. It is because of them that humans are able to maintain balance within their spirits. It is also the job of the powers to record the history of mankind. They are also called *authorities, dynamis, dunamis,* and *potentates.*

**Principalities.** The order of angels that ranks seventh in the angelic hierarchy. The principalities are the guardians of all large groups on the earth, including nations, great cities, religions, and large corporations. They are also called *princedoms*.

**Archangels.** High-ranking angels who act as messengers to God. They are thought to be the most important mediators between God and mankind. The word *archangel* is often misapplied, as it is used as a generic term referencing all angels above the last order of angels (see "Angeloi (or Angels)" below). In the angelic hierarchy, they are just one step above the angels. The archangels are said to command the heavenly army in an ongoing war with the forces of darkness. In some hierarchies they are referred to as the *archangeloi*.

**Angeloi** (or Angels). The last class of angels found within the angel hierarchy created by German philosopher and clairvoyant **Rudolph Steiner.** The angeloi stand one stage higher than mankind. They work more with humans than any other class of angels. Guardian angels are from the angeloi class. In most other hierarchies the angeloi are referred to as just angels.

**Ministering Angels.** Angels who attend to God's immediate wishes. God is said to have ministering angels surrounding his throne day and night to do his bidding. According to lore, there are many hundreds of thousands of ministering angels. They act as messengers and mediators between God and humans. They are considered by some to be a separate class of angels.

See also "Children and Angels" under **Children.**

## Animals

In many ancient cultures, animals played a large role in visions of life after death. In fact, the mythologies of several ancient cultures held that when people died, their pets were waiting to guide them into the spiritual world. It is believed that on the other side there are spirit animals from the entire spectrum of the animal world, particularly those animals that are closest to humans in friendship, such as dogs, cats, horses, and even birds. In

fact, animals not only reside in the spiritual world, but also carry their memory and feelings from the physical world.

A number of people that have had near-death experiences have reported seeing, touching, and holding their pets they had on earth, but that had died earlier. In her book *The Other Side of Death,* **Jan Price** documents her near-death experience, in which her dog that had died years earlier greeted her. Her dog communicated with her and even showed Price her home in the spiritual world.

It is believed to be the bond of love between humans and their pets that raises the consciousness of an animal, thus allowing the spirit of the pet to live on in the afterlife. It is the showing of love that helps the animal to develop a personality and cause it to become separate and individualistic. In addition, some metaphysical animal experts think that every animal, like every human, has a spiritual body. Therefore, many of the animals that are extinct on the earth can be found in the spiritual world.

Some near-death experiencers have said that during their life review, they could hear the thoughts and feelings of pets. Some psychic animal communicators hold that when an animal crosses over, their death experience is similar to that of humans. At death, the animals drift upward and have the opportunity to decide where they want to go next in the spiritual realms. Often, they stay close to their former owners for a time before leaving. In the spiritual world, animals are on a different level than human souls. In addition, there are no physical restrictions and nothing holding the animals to any place or thing. Animals are able to reincarnate with the same owner or with others. Animals in the spiritual world also have the ability to visit their former owners and loved ones in the form of a dream or apparition. They can also, like other spirits, communicate telepathically. When visiting their former owners on earth, they may come around and leave physical signs. They may also sometimes bark or meow just as they did when in the physical realm. One woman reported hearing her deceased cat meowing in the garden while she worked. He later appeared at the foot of her bed (where he used to sleep) in the form of an apparition. The animal may show itself or make its presence known in some other way, such as moving an object.

Near-death experiencers sometimes mention animals in their descriptions of the spiritual world. Birds are often mentioned and seem to be of the greatest abundance on the other side. Some of the birds sighted include bluebirds, robins, and birds with "plumage." Other animals that have been spotted include beavers, bears, deer, lions, monkeys, horses, tigers, and even squirrels. In her writings, popular medium **Sylvia Browne** also mentions dinosaurs.

## Animism

Animism is the belief that all things—animal, vegetable, mineral, and human—have spirits. The term *animism* is derived from the Latin word *anima,* meaning "breath" or "soul." Animism is one of humankind's oldest beliefs. Its origin is thought to be the Paleolithic age. It originally meant the doctrine of spiritual beings, including human souls. From its earliest beginnings, it was a belief that a soul or spirit existed in every object, even if

that object was inanimate. Each soul was believed to be endowed with reason, intelligence, and volition, identical with that of man. In a future state, the soul would exist as a part of an immaterial soul. The soul, therefore, was thought to be universal.

Animists hold that after death, the human soul stays on earth or travels to join the departed spirits of the ancestors in the underworld, also known as the Realm of the Shadows. It is believed that for eternity the human souls roam in darkness, feeling neither pleasure nor sadness. Some of the spirits of the dead may be called on to either help or bring suffering to those still on earth.

## Ankh

The ankh is one of the most famous and widely recognized images of all time. It is a hieroglyphic sign for life that looks similar to a cross, but has a loop in place of the upper arm. It is also a symbol of eternal life in ancient Egyptian beliefs. It is one of the most potent symbols represented in Egyptian art. Often the gods, as well as the pharaohs, are pictured holding the ankh. Placing the ankh to the lips or in front of the mouth was considered to be an offering of the breath of life—the breath that was needed in the spiritual world.

## Antonette, Josiane

Author, reverend, and healer (1942–). Born in France, Antonette began her spiritual journey alongside her grandmother on the island of Corsica (France). Her grandmother at that time was active in the shamanic healing traditions of the island, and she initiated Antonette into the healing practices as a child. In 1964, Antonette had a near-death experience, whereupon she learned that she could communicate with the spirit world. During the past thirty years, Antonette has taken on a number of roles, including hospital chaplain, spiritual counselor, and university lecturer. In addition, she has taught classes on both spiritual development and death and dying, in the United States and in France. After so many years of experience, Antonette is comfortable with communicating with the spiritual world, as well as traveling there either consciously or in dreamtime. She feels that she is a bridge between the two worlds and aids others on their spiritual journeys.

Antonette is also the creator of the Bernadette Foundation, a nonprofit, interfaith, educational organization founded in 1982. The purpose of the foundation is, they say, "to enhance balanced, conscious living by assisting individuals to understand their spiritual nature and their common connection with all life." Antonette's books include *Whispers of the Soul* and *Matters of Spirit*. The books relay information about what Antonette has seen and experienced in her journeys to the other side. For further information, you may view her website, *www.mattersofspirit.com.*

## Anubis

The jackal-headed god of the ancient Egyptians. His duties included watching over the mummification of a person and guiding them into the afterlife. Some occultists believe that the ancients at one time worshiped gods who came to earth from the heavens.

## Apocalypse of Zephaniah

The Apocalypse of Zephaniah is an ancient apocryphal work credited to Zephaniah, a Hebrew prophet of the late seventh century BC and author of the biblical book of Zephaniah. In the Apocalypse of Zephaniah, an angel of the Lord escorts Zephaniah through the spiritual world, where the prophet witnesses many amazing sights. These sights include a scene in the fifth heaven, where he sees angels called "lords" and a soul in torment. The book also contains a fragment dealing with burial, scenes from above the seer's city, a record of angels from Mount Seir and angels carrying off the souls of sinful men, an account of a heavenly city, and the story of an accuser and the angel Eremiel in **Hades**.

## Apparition(s)

An apparition is the unexpected sighting of a deceased person. However, there have been cases where people still alive on the planet have appeared as apparitions, due to astral travel and bilocation. In addition, the term *apparition* may also be applied to visions of angels, animals, and religious fig-ures. An apparition can appear lifelike, transparent, or a combination of both, and generally vanishes suddenly. Apparitions can be of the whole body or parts of the body and generally last less than a minute. If the appearing person has crossed over recently, then the apparition will appear more solid; if they have been away longer, it is more translucent. Apparitions of earthbound spirits will appear somewhere between solid and translucent.

According to some channeled reports from those in the spiritual world, it is not always easy for them to appear as apparitions. It requires a slowing down of their energy. The longer they have been away from the physical world, the more difficult the task of appearing becomes.

People who have crossed over into the spiritual world, but remain earthbound, often because of not being able to let go of the physical or because they feel the need to be here due to their loved ones, may appear as apparitions. These apparitions are often referred to as ghosts.

**Society for Psychical Research.** Well-organized, systematic studies of apparitions started after the Society for Psychical Research (SPR) was founded in England in 1882. The SPR was soon joined in this quest by the American Society for Psychical Research (ASPR) and by smaller research groups and individual investigators in continental Europe. Scholarly journals were established to publish ongoing research as well as theoretical speculation and fierce debates. The basic idea of these efforts was to apply scientific method to data collection, evaluation, and interpretation of psychic phenomena—an area that nineteenth-century materialistic science had ignored up to that time. See information about the ASPR's work on apparitions at *www.aspr.com*.

See also **Bystander Apparition; Collective Apparition; Crises Apparition; Ghost(s); Haunting(s); Place-Bound Apparition.**

## Appearance

Souls in the spiritual world appear much the same way as the people they were during their lives on earth. This is because the spirit body is a duplicate of the physical body. According to some credible mediums and higher intelligences, those that have had near-death experiences, and those that have had visions of loved ones in the spiritual world, the spirit person's appearance can regress to their best age. Also, often a glow of light is seen emanating from the person, as if there were a candle burning inside them. The more spiritual the person, the brighter their light. In some accounts, people witnessing higher beings could not see these beings because the light that they radiated was so bright. Some reported seeing only a faint outline of a person inside of the light.

## Apport(s)

A term for a physical item that appears suddenly out of nowhere. These are considered gifts from the spiritual world to the physical world, from a loved one on the other side to a friend or relative on earth. Objects can differ in size, may be inanimate or living, and appear none the worse from their journey from the other side to the physical world. Objects that have been known to appear as an apport include flowers, jewelry, and even live animals. In the early days of spiritualism, apports appeared, under most circumstances, in the presence of a medium that was performing a séance, and they appeared most often at the request of the medium. They have also been known to appear in situations of a haunting or in cases of loved ones from the other side attempting to relay a message to friends and family members. Some apports are thought to be created from a material called *ectoplasm*. These items are thought to come in from another dimension or the afterlife realm itself. Many believe them to be fraudulent.

## Archangels
See **Angels.**

## Archives
Ancient Judeo-Christian scriptures tell us that there are heavenly or spiritual archives with records containing the deeds and history of humankind. The scriptures also speak of specific books (or scrolls) that are read by **God** and that are protected and kept by ministering spirits. These books have become known as the *heavenly archives*. It is here that the **Book of Life** is kept. According to Judeo-Christian teachings, the Book of Life is the book in which the deeds of humans are recorded and from which God will read on Judgment Day. All sacred works are for God's eyes only. We know little about these holy records, only what the Bible and apocryphal scriptures, such as the **Books of Enoch,** tell us.

According to metaphysicians and New Age thinkers, there are spiritual records that are stored in great buildings in the spiritual realm. According to one account, the records are housed in what is called the **Hall of Records,** described as a very large spiritual library on the other side. These records are also known as the **Akashic Records.** They are said to be a complete record of humankind's history. All of God's spiritual family has access to them. It is a repository of knowledge, and information from it can be received psychically. It has been described as a library of the mind.

## Archons

A high-ranking order of angels. The Archons are guardians of entire nations. The Archangels **Gabriel, Michael,** Raphael, and Uriel are among the many angels who make up the Archons. In **Gnosticism**, the Archons are named as Jaldabaoth, Jao, Sabaoth, Adonaios, Astanphaios, Ailoaios, and Oraios. They are equated in some writings with the **Aeons.**

## Aristotle

Greek philosopher and scientist, and one of the most famous of the ancient philosophers (384–322 BC). Aristotle was a brilliant student in **Plato**'s Academy, remaining there for twenty years and earning the nickname "the Intellect" of the school. He later conducted his own school, called the Lyceum, in a spot sacred to Apollo in Athens. In his metaphysics, Aristotle argued for the existence of a divine being, which he called the Prime Mover, who is responsible for the unity and purposefulness of nature. He said the Prime Mover was a being with everlasting life and perfect blessedness, and who engaged in never-ending contemplation. He believed that **God** is perfect and the aspiration of all things in the world, because all things desire to share perfection.

## Asamando

Asamando is the name of the afterlife of the Ashanti people of Africa. According to Ashanti beliefs, Asamando is a duplicate of an Ashanti village on earth, but life there is more perfect. In Asamando, there is no drought, and there is plenty of food for everyone. However, its spiritual occupants still have to do work, such as farming and tending animals.

## Ascended Masters

Enlightened, spiritual beings that serve humanity. They have the ability to leave the spiritual world at will and go to the earth without going through the process of birth and death. In addition, they are beings that once lived in the physical plane. Ascended masters dwell in the spiritual world and have bodies of light. They have worked with humanity throughout the ages, assisting with the spiritual evolution of each person who strives to reunite with **God**. Beliefs in the masters can be found in Theosophy, the I AM movement, the Temple of the Presence, and Elizabeth Clare Prophet's Church Universal and Triumphant. In addition, there are organizations and channelers that communicate with the ascended masters.

## Ascension

The evolving of one's energy into a higher form. In religious and spiritual beliefs, the word *ascension* is associated with souls rising to heaven after death. In the modern era the word *ascension* is defined in a new way. There is the belief that some people ascend to a higher state of being and later return to the earth to become teachers and healers as **Jesus** was. It is believed that the earth will evolve from the third dimension to the fifth dimension. During this evolution, there will be a great shifting in the earth's atmosphere that causes climatic disturbances such as storms, great earthquakes, and other adverse conditions. Those who come back to teach after their ascension will pre-

pare the people of the earth for the move into the fifth dimension. The angels are said to be working with the ascended masters of the higher spiritual realms who are overseeing this change. One of the leaders is the archangel **Michael.**

## Asgard
See **Norsemen.**

## Asport
A term for an object that disappears suddenly from a room. It is the opposite of apport.

## Association for Research and Enlightenment, Inc. (A.R.E.)
See **Edgar Cayce.**

## Assumed Bodies
A term used in referring to the bodies that some beings from the unseen spiritual world take on to perform their earthly missions. Angels are thought by many theologians and scholars to be incorporeal beings lacking in substance, so they take on assumed bodies when they come to earth. Some have contended that these bodies are not real bodies at all,

but visions of bodies that are incapable of performing the natural functions of an earthly body. However, the **Bible** contradicts this thinking: In their assumed bodies, the angels ate and drank with the prophet Abraham (Genesis 18:1–8). In addition, there were angels who came to earth and had sexual relations with women, with whom they also fathered children (Genesis 6:2).

## Assyria

An ancient kingdom that flourished in northern Mesopotamia from the third millennium BC until about 600 BC. Assyrians believed in a spiritual world that consisted of gods and an afterlife. They believed that the primary god was found in the great powers of the universe and personified in the forms and images of their mythical gods. Their chief god was Anu, whose name is the Sumerian word for "heaven." Anu was the father and king of the gods. Another important god was Enlil, the air god and leader of the pantheon from at least 2500 BC. He later replaced Anu and took on the titles of "king of heaven and earth" and "king of all

the lands." Ashur was the national god of Assyria. He was a god of war and eventually assumed the role of Enlil.

The Assyrians believed that each individual possessed a sort of semi-material spirit or ghost that survived physical death. When the body of the deceased was buried or cremated, they believed that the ghost descended into the underworld.

## Astral

The word *astral* means "of the stars" or "related to a star." It refers to the subtle, nonphysical realm of existence beyond the physical world. The term *astral* originated with either Greek or Latin. Initially it was used to describe the heavens of the Greeks and the home of their gods. Today the term *astral* has a much broader meaning. It is now used in terms of our spiritual body (or soul) and the various realms and dimensions of the spiritual world. See **Astral Body; Astral Cord; Astral Plane; Astral Projection; Astral World.**

## Astral Body

The nonmaterial counterpart to one's physical body; also called the soul, spirit, etheric body, ethereal body, and in some cases the double. Other terms for the astral body include *linga-sharira* (Hindus), *ka* (ancient Egyptians), *pneuma* (ancient Greeks) and the *spiritual body*. It is an invisible duplicate of the physical body and the core of feeling and desire. It has been called "the vehicle of desire that gives personal feelings images, and emotions." The astral body is capable of leaving the physical body and traveling independently to portions of the spiritual world, as well as other dimensions. This travel usually occurs during sleep. These travels are referred to as out-of-body experiences, astral projection, and astral travel. The astral body is composed of astral material that is made up of energy. It is attached to the physical body at the naval, by a silverlike cord. It is said to be extremely brilliant in appearance, with colors of indescribable beauty. The astral body permanently separates from the physical body at death and returns to the spiritual world.

## Astral Cord

The cord that connects the astral body to the physical body. It is made of a fine substance and connects at the naval. Some people who have experienced astral projection claim that they have seen the cord. One of the cord's functions is to enable the traveling or projecting astral body to return to the physical body. It has been described as a kind of ethereal umbilical cord that is severed at death. The astral cord is also referred to as the silver cord.

## Astral Plane

Another name for the astral world.

## Astral Projection

The separation of the astral body (spiritual body) from the physical body, a phenomenon also known as an out-of-body experience. Once separated, the astral body is then free to travel and transcend time and space, covering dimensions and great distances. In astral projection the person leaves the physical body and projects their spiritual

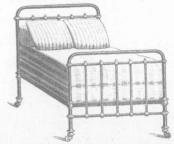

body off the earth plane and into the astral world (also known as the spirit world and afterlife realms). Essentially, when astral projection occurs, one is experiencing being outside the human body while still conscious and alive. Astral projection differs from a near-death experience in that it occurs more often during the sleep state and can happen (though very rarely) spontaneously. In fact, there are some well-known accounts of people who actually slipped out of their body without trying. Two such people are **Sylvan Muldoon,** who chronicled his experiences in the book *The Projection of the Astral Body,* and **Robert Monroe,** author of *Journeys Out of the Body*. Some people, such as **Oliver Fox,** have the ability to project at will. Projectors claim that during an astral voyage, communication with other projectors or spirits is possible.

## Astral Travel

Another term for astral projection. See **Astral Plane; Astral Projection.**

## Astral World

Another name for astral plane. It is the area of the spiritual world that humans travel to after physical death.

It is also a realm that humans can visit during sleep.

## Atman

A Hindi word meaning "the true self." It is the individual soul, the real self that continues to exist after one's life on earth is complete. In **Hinduism,** the atman is defined as the life principle, the personal soul or self, and the individual essence. An atman is believed to be hidden in every object of creation, including humans. It is the immortal part of our mortal reality. It's the part of the individual that returns home to **God.**

In some New Age thought, the atman is the supreme and universal soul from which all individual souls arise. Some call this supreme, universal soul God.

## Atmosphere

The atmosphere in the higher realms of the unseen spiritual world is said to be one filled with love and light. According to some who have had near-death experiences, it is permeated with **God**'s love, which is felt everywhere and has been said to be as important as the air we breathe while on earth.

## Atwater, P. M. H.

Near-death researcher, visionary, and author (1937–). Born in Twin Falls, Idaho, Atwater is one of the original pioneers in the study of near-death experiences. Atwater herself has had three near-death experiences. All occurred within three months (from January to March 1977). In an attempt to understand her experiences, she began researching the near-death phenomena. She began by interviewing other near-death survivors. To date, she has investigated thousands of people who have had the experience and has written several books on the subject, including *Coming Back to Life, Beyond the Light, Future Memory,* and *Children of the New Millennium*.

Other books by Atwater include *The Complete Idiots Guide to Near-Death Experiences* and *The Big Book of Near-Death Experiences*. Because of her vast knowledge on this subject, Atwater has served two terms on the Board of the International Association of Near-Death Studies. She also has a background in hypnotic past-life regressions, dehaunting houses, and mediumship, and she specializes in several divinatory practices, including astrology, numerology, dream and symbol interpretation, and rune stones. More information on Atwater and her work can be found at *www.cinemind.com/atwater*.

## Auditory Communication

An after-death communication in which the deceased is heard speaking. Often when a deceased relative dies, they visit loved ones still on earth. They may come briefly and call their loved one's name, or they may come for longer and say a few words.

## Augustine of Hippo

Early church father, doctor of the church, bishop of Hippo (354–430 AD). Born in Tagaste, North Africa, he was originally named Aurelious Augustinius. Augustine was one of the greatest theologians in the history of **Christianity** and is considered to be one of the most prolific geniuses that humanity has ever known. He was a main influence on the development of Western culture and thought. His two most celebrated writings include his spiritual autobiography, *Confessions* (a detailed account of his conversion, addressed to **God**), and *City of God*. Augustine drew from his own experience when devising ideas about the spiritual world. To Augustine, God is a powerful majestic spirit. He completely rejected the popular view that matter is evil, believing instead that all God's creations are innately good since they reflect their maker. He believed that those on earth should emulate the behavior of the angels and taught that humans should spend more time in prayer, contemplation, and worship of God, just as the angels of heaven did. He believed this to be the goal of all humankind.

**City of God.** A treatise by Augustine written between 413 and 422, considered to be his best work and hailed as a masterpiece. It is a large work: twenty-two books. The work itself has had a huge impact on Christianity, and some scholars suggest that it not only influenced Christianity, but also formed the basis of its beliefs. The book began as a reply to the charge that Christianity was responsible for the decline of the Roman Empire. Augustine produced a wealth of evidence to prove that paganism bore within itself the seeds of its own destruction. In the *City of God*, Augustine offers his viewpoint of heaven: it is a city in which heaven and earth are separated by only the thinnest of veils. Augustine describes heaven as a perfect spiritual community, a paradise, where there is peace and ultimate satisfaction, with God at its center. He writes about Creation, the fall of Adam and Eve, and the advancement of human events since then. He concludes that governments and whole societies rise and fall, but that God is continuous and never changing. People should, therefore, consider themselves a part of God's heavenly home first and members of their earthly home second. This is because our place on earth is temporary; however, God's home in heaven, God's city, is eternal. Says Augustine, "These two cities were made by two loves: the earthly city by the love of self unto the contempt of God, and the heavenly city by the love of God unto the contempt of self."

## Aureole(s)

A radiant light that encircles the head or body of an individual on the other side. This light is said to be different from light humans perceive on earth. It is a brilliant light, but not blinding. It symbolizes **God**'s divine light and the deceased's level of spirituality. The higher one is spiritually, the more radiant the light becomes. Some people are so radiant that even on the other side, others cannot look upon them. In his *Divine Comedy*, **Dante Alighieri** wrote, "They had their faces all of living flame / And wings of gold and all the rest so white that never snow has known such purity." Beings of light, angels, enlightened beings, and ascended masters dwelling in the various afterlife and heavenly realms are often described with phrases such as "white as snow," "like lightening," and "shining ones." These terms all refer to the brilliant light that these beings radiate. A variation of aureole is *aureola*.

## Australian Aboriginals

Traditional Australian Aboriginal societies share the common belief that humankind was created in a distant time period referred to as *Dream Time* (sacred time). Dream Time refers to the spiritual realm. It represents the home of the gods, psychic messages, as well as spirits and ancestors. It is a place where time and space have no meaning. At death, the soul is believed to return to the everlasting Dream Time where it existed before birth. Upon returning to the spiritual world, each individual becomes a part of the ancestors who are believed to always be with him or her. The aborigines do not worship their ancestors, but continue to view them as real people existing in another realm. They think of them as spirit guides who are forever watching over them and guiding them through life until it is their turn to join them in the spirit world, Bralgu. Bralgu is the afterlife in traditional Australian Aboriginal beliefs. Once a person dies, their soul is believed to be transported in a magical boat to Bralgu. There each soul is reunited with loved ones who have previously died.

## Automatic Art

Pictures and paintings created by a spirit through a medium; artistic expression without the control of the conscious self. It is a form of mediumship in which a person from the other side or another entity creates a piece of art through a physical being to convey a thought or message.

## Automatic Speaking

The act of a disembodied person from the other side (or some other being) speaking through a physical person on earth. It is a form of mediumship, as well as a way of communication from those on the other side. The person involved in this activity is a willing participant who agrees to step aside to allow the individual from the other side to speak.

## Automatic Writing

A type of channeling in which a person produces written scripts, received from an unseen person in another realm, without the control of the conscious self. The unseen person can include people in the afterlife or beings from other higher dimensions who wish to communicate positive information to humankind. Automatic writing is the most common form of mediumship. The writing can be accomplished through the use of paper

and pen or via electronics. See **Automatic Art; Automatic Speaking.**

## Automatism

A term used for the various forms of communication used by those on the other side to contact those in the physical realm. It incorporates such practices as automatic writing, automatic speaking, creating automatic art, moving, and other forms of channeling. One who engages in automatic art or writing is known as an *automatist.*

## Avatar

Found in Hindu lore, the word *avatar,* sometimes also *avatara,* is the earthly embodiment of a deity (human, animal, or even a mythical creature) and usually refers to an incarnation of **God** or his aspects, such as that of Vishnu. Avatar means "to appear," "to descend," "to take birth," or "to manifest."

## Aztecs

American Indian people of central Mexico. The Aztecs had a strong belief in an unseen spiritual world. They believed that after death, the soul took four years to pass through nine intervening subterranean realms. Each realm was made up of some hazardous environment or dangerous terrain that the soul traveled through before reaching its destination. There were treacherous mountains, ravenous creatures, and cold winds. The determining factors for a person's fate in the spiritual world were their social status and the manner in which they died.

Four of the realms corresponded to the four directions (east, west, north, and south). The most magnificent realm in the spiritual world of the Aztecs was the eastern paradise (also referred to as *Ichan Tonatiuh Ilhuijcan,* or "the Eastern Paradise of the Sun"). It was for warriors who died in battle, sacrificial victims, and merchants who died during their business travels. These were considered honorable deaths. It was believed that if a person died in a battle or a sacrifice, they were later reborn as a hummingbird, a butterfly, or some other winged animal that enjoyed honey. In addition, the souls of the east became companions of the sun. The western

paradise (*Tamoanchan*) was comprised of women who died giving birth (also said to be companions of the sun). It was believed that women who died in childbirth returned to earth as moths. The southern paradise (also known as *Tlalocan*) was for those who died from lightning strikes, drowning, and marsh fever. The south consisted of a beautiful tropical garden filled with friendly animals, fragrant flowers, and blissfulness. In this paradise there was no sadness or tears. The north realm, called *Mictlan,* was the place where most people went after death. It is said to be a very undesirable place.

The Aztecs buried their dead with charms and cremated dogs to assist them in their crossing over. The afterlife for babies and children in Aztec beliefs was named *Chalmecacivati.* It was believed to be an earthly realm, but void of pain and ill health.

# B

## Ba

The Egyptian concept of the soul of a human being or of a god. It is believed that the ba inhabits the body during one's life, although it is not attached to the body. At death the ba leaves the body and joins the divine spirit. In Egyptian art, the ba is represented as a human-headed bird that leaves the body when a person dies. The face of the ba was the exact likeness of the deceased person. See **Egypt.**

## Babbitt, Elwood

A noted clairvoyant and medium (1922–2000). Elwood Babbitt was born in Orange, Massachusetts, on November 26, 1922. As a young child, Babbitt could see spiritual people. For many years he could not tell the difference between a spiritual person and those in the physical realm. In fact, as a child, Babbitt would play with children that were in spirit. He was even amazed on one occasion when he walked right through a spirit friend. Elwood also had out-of-body experiences beginning at a young age. He would go to sleep and awaken outside of his body able to see himself sleeping.

In a near tragic accident when he was just sixteen years old, Babbitt found himself in the hospital, where doctors had predicted that he had only a few hours to live. That night, his grandmother, who had passed on years before, appeared before him, saying that he would be fine and that his injuries to his eyes, throat, and ears would heal. He then witnessed a large ball of brilliant glowing golden light that moved from his head though his entire body. The ball glowed and then faded away. He heard someone say the word *peace*. Afterward, he fell asleep. Babbitt left the hospital a few days later, leaving the doctors stunned. It was during this period that Babbitt realized that he had a spiritual mission. He became a trance medium who was able to speak with people no longer in the body. He became a communicator between the spiritual and physical realms and continued to do so for fifty years.

## Babies

See **Children.**

## Babylonia

An ancient kingdom in southern Mesopotamia, famous for its richness and luxury. Babylonians believed in an unseen spiritual world that people crossed over into after death. In the afterlife, Babylonians believed that each individual possessed a sort of semi-material spirit that lived on after death. They believed that when the body of the deceased was buried or cremated, the spirit of the individual descended into the underworld. This spiritual realm was also filled with a number of spiritual beings. Among them were the winged bull-men and spirit messengers called *sukalli*. Babylonians believed that each individual had a guardian spirit protecting them. These spirits mediated between them and the gods. If an individual performed an unrighteous act, the guardian spirit would leave them. If the person repented, the spirit would forgive them and return. These beliefs and others found their way into the surrounding cultures and religions.

Traces of Babylonian beliefs in an unseen spiritual world and its spiritual occupants can be found in Zoroastrianism, where Babylonian gods and spiritual beings were turned into angels. Later those beliefs evolved and became a part of Judaism and Christianity's spiritual beliefs. The Babylonians considered the seven planets to be gods, and these gods are thought to have become the archetypal seven archangels. One notorious deity of Babylonian lore was Rimmon, the god of thunder and lightning. When adopted into Christianity, he became a demon of hell.

## Bahaism

A religion founded in Iran during the mid-nineteenth century by Mirza Hoseyn 'Ali Nuri, also known as Baha'ullah. It is the goal of all Bahai followers to develop spiritually. Bahais believe in an afterlife in which the soul is immortal and continues to exist after the death of the physical body. The soul, according to Abdu'l-Baha (Baha'ullah's son, who became leader of the religion after his father's death), has the powers of imagination, thought, comprehension, and mem-

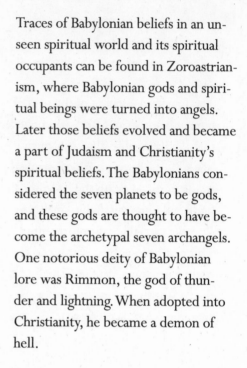

ory. At death, the soul is separated from the body and then begins a spiritual journey towards **God** through many realms of existence. Bahai followers do not believe in heaven or hell. Instead, the proximity to God is seen as a "heavenly state" and the distance away from God is considered as a state equal to hell. Because Bahais think God is omniscient and merciful, they believe that everyone has the opportunity for redemption and that in the afterlife each soul will be dealt with in a just way. Bahais have no details about how God will deal with individuals. This is indicated in their writings, which say, "The manner in which the Supreme Being, in His Justice as well as in His Mercy, will deal with every individual soul is a mystery unknown to us on this earthly plane." Baha'ullah likened physical life to an embryonic stage of a person's existence. He held that leaving the body is similar to being reborn and allows the soul the ability to embark upon a more enriching and freer life.

## Baha'ullah
See **Bahaism.**

## Bardo
A term found in the **Tibetan Book of the Dead** and meaning the in-between state after death and before rebirth. It is a stage varying from seven to forty-nine days, after which the karmic body from previous lives will be reborn. Another name for the Tibetan Book of the Dead is *Bardo Thodol*.

## Barkel, Kathleen
A well-known British trance medium (1930–). She became well known for her work at the British College of Psychic Science, where she participated in healing sessions with her husband and had voice séances with her daughter. During her séances, sitters were able to receive apports that came in the form of pebbles. Barkel's control (or spirit guide) from the other side was a Sioux chief that had lived eight hundred years prior. As he placed Barkel's hand over that of a sitter, a beautiful pebble would materialize.

## Barrett, Sir William Fletcher
English physics professor and paranormal researcher (1844–1925). Sir

William Fletcher Barrett was a professor of physics at the Royal College of Science for Ireland from 1873 to 1910. Barrett discovered Stalloy, a silicon-iron alloy used in electrical engineering and researched divining rods. In 1874, he began researching psychic phenomena, specifically mesmeric trance and physical psychic phenomena. He was specifically interested in the skills and abilities of those who claimed to be psychic, as well as the cause and effects of this extraordinary talent. Two years later he submitted his dissertation, titled "Some Phenomena Associated with Abnormal Conditions of Mind," to the British Association for the Advancement of Science, and the paper was published by the association's anthropological subsection. The article relayed Barrett's work with telepathy, and in it he said that the more fantastic aspects of physical psychic phenomena, such as levitation, could be attributed to hallucination.

In the early 1900s Barrett published a small book on deathbed visions. He was one of the first people to examine this subject. He noted in his writings that as people were close to death, they sometimes saw other worlds and saw and spoke to relatives and friends that had previously passed on.

## Bede (also St. Bede, the Venerable Bede)

Ecclesiastical English historian and Benedictine monk (672 or 673–735 AD). Also known as Saint Bede and the Venerable Bede. He authored the *Ecclesiastical History of the English People,* which was considered to be an important primary source on English history between 597 and 731. In this work, Bede wrote about the near-death experience of a man named Drythelm. The man died, but revived the next morning, giving his wife an account of what happened to him while on the other side—an account he later shared with Bede. He told of seeing a shining angel, who showed him the terrible punishments of purgatory (a concept not yet accepted by the church as doctrine), which include ice and fire. In an even darker place, he saw worse punishments and spirits who bobbed up and down in globes of fire. Those of hell attempted to capture Drythelm, but the angel guided him to a place filled with light and happiness. Drythelm wanted to stay; however, the angel informed him that the souls in that place were not completely saved, but were waiting to enter heaven itself.

## Being(s)

General term used to denote the various types of discarnate beings and life forms found throughout the many dimensions, including the afterlife. This list includes angels, ascended masters, beings of light, counselors, saints, souls, and spirit guides.

## Being(s) of Light

Spiritual beings that give help in the afterlife. They are known also as spirit guides, guardians, and angels. In many near-death experiences, beings of light have been reported. These luminous entities have been described as beings made with beautiful, vibrating or shimmering light. Some beings of light are said to be similar to crystal in color and transparency. Others are said to have the appearance of a shimmering pearl or to be composed of white or yellow and exude an unearthly radiance. One was even described as having long golden hair. Often, the being

asks the deceased person to reflect on their life, and the being assists the person with their life review. During this experience, the being of light acts as a guide to the individual, all the while showing kindness, concern, and compassion. In some cases the being of light is identified as **God, Jesus, Muhammad,** or some other religious figure that the person may believe in. In other cases, the being of light tells the individual that they must return to the physical realm, that "it is not their time." Some people are given the choice by the being of light: to return to their life and loved ones or remain on the other side.

## Belanger, Jeff

Modern American author and ghost investigator (1974–). He is the creator of the popular Internet website *Ghostvillage.com,* which he started in 1999 and which contains many of his writings on the paranormal and otherworldly activity. Belanger first became interested in the subject of the unseen world at the tender age of ten, while investigating unusual activity in a house. After graduating from Hofstra University, where he earned a degree in English, Belanger honed his journalist skills, but all the while retained his interest and fascination in ghostly encounters and related mysteries. Today Belanger is a prominent leader on the subject of ghosts, the supernatural, and the paranormal. He has also authored a number of books on these subjects, including *The Ghost Files: Paranormal Encounters, Discussion, and Research from the Vaults of Ghostvillage.com; Ghosts of War: Restless Spirits of Soldiers, Spies, and Saboteurs; Our Haunted Lives: True Life Ghost Encounters; Encyclopedia of Haunted Places: Ghostly Locales From Around the World; Communicating With the Dead: Reach Beyond the Grave;* and *The World's Most Haunted Places: From the Secret Files of Ghostvillage.com.*

## Benedict, Mellen-Thomas

Artist and near-death experiencer. In 1982 Benedict died from cancer and then experienced one of the most profound near-death experiences ever recorded. For an hour and a half Benedict was unresponsive and showed no vital signs. However, to the shock of many, he revived to find he was in complete remission from the cancer. His body was healed. The healing was hailed as a miracle. During the hour and a half that Benedict was out of his physical body, he traveled into a brilliant light and through a number of dimensions beyond the light. His experience is unique, because he seems to have traveled farther than most others that have had near-death experiences, even going farther than the void (also known as the outer darkness). In this experience, Benedict saw, in a holographic vision, earth's past and earth's future, the cosmic relationship of humans and earth, and humankind's role in the universe.

Today, Benedict is bringing the world new scientific discoveries and is working very closely with the mechanics of cellular communication and with quantum biology (research on the relationship of light to life and how our biological systems work). After his life changing experience, Benedict considers himself a bridge between the world of spirit and of science.

## Beng

A people of West Africa; also known as the Ngan or Ngen. The Beng believe that when a child is born, it is a reincarnated soul. The Beng people believe that babies enter this world with spiritual knowledge.

## Bennett, Tony

American singer of popular music, standards, and jazz (1926–). In his autobiography, entitled *The Good Life*, Bennett writes of having a near-death experience in 1970 due to a drug overdose. He writes, "A golden light enveloped me in a warm glow . . . I had the sense that I was about to embark on a very compelling journey. But suddenly I was jolted out of the vision . . . I knew I had to make major changes in my life."

## Benson, Robert Hugh

A celebrated English author and Catholic priest (1871–1914). Benson received his education at Trinity College, Cambridge, from 1890 to 1893, where he studied the classics and theology. In 1895, he was ordained a priest in the Church of England by his father, Edward White Benson (the then Archbishop of Canterbury). While in life, Benson enjoyed a career that spanned a decade. He authored many nonfiction books, a series of twenty novels, and short stories. First an Anglican and later a Catholic priest, Benson was in popular demand as a speaker in England and the United States.

After death, he authored a number of other books, which he dictated to his friend, medium **Anthony Borgia.** These books from the spiritual world include *Life in the World Unseen, Facts, Heaven and Earth, More About Life in the World Unseen,* and *Here and Hereafter.* With these books, Benson wanted to correct the teaching contained in the Christian-related books he wrote while living on earth. In his afterlife books, he talks about the Orthodox Church and faith. He also tells of life on the other side and what existence is like for those who have passed on.

## Berkeley, George

Irish philosopher and bishop (1685–1753). He is generally regarded as the founder of the modern school of Idealism. Born in county Kilkenny,

Ireland, Berkeley was educated at Trinity College, Dublin, where he became a fellow in 1707. According to Berkeley, **God** is the only other person or thing, other than souls, that exists. He believed that there must be a mind in which all ideas exist—that mind, of course, belonging to God.

## Berry, Catherine

English medium (1813–1891). Berry discovered her talent for communicating with those in the afterlife in 1864 after sitting with the famed British medium Mary Marshall. Berry's talents were witnessed by other mediums, who often sought her out to aid them in becoming more powerful. She was also gifted in automatic drawing and painting, as well as healing. In 1876, her book *Experiences in Spiritualism: A Record of Extraordinary Phenomena Witnessed Through the Most Powerful Mediums* was published.

## Bethards, Betty

Internationally known psychic, mystic, spiritual leader, meditation teacher, and healer. She founded the Inner Light Foundation in Petaluma, California. During her life on earth, Bethards aided many people in understanding and accepting the transition of death. After having a near-death experience herself, she lost her fear of dying, realizing that death is nothing more than a continuation of our existence. Bethards crossed over into spirit on July 30, 2002. Books by Bethards include *The Dream Book: Symbols for Self Understanding, Seven Steps to Developing Your Intuitive Powers, There Is No Death, Be Your Own Guru, Sex and Psychic Energy, Atlantis, Way to Awareness,* and *Techniques for Health and Wholeness*. Her Inner Light Foundation can be contacted online at *www.innerlight.org*. Or you may write to: Inner Light Foundation, P.O. Box 750265, Petaluma, CA 94975.

## Bible, The

The word *bible* comes from the Greek *biblia*, which means "little books." It is made up of sixty-six little books that were written over a period of 1,600 years, from 1513 BC to 98 AD. Some forty men shared in the writing of the Bible, which is believed by Christians to be inspired by **God**. The existence of a spirit world actually permeates the Bible.

**Old Testament.** The Old Testament (Hebrew scriptures) makes up the first part of the Bible. The Old Testament scriptures speak of Adam and Eve as immortal beings designed to live forever on earth. However, according to the scriptures, they were issued death as a punishement for an disobedient act. Later in the Old Testament are teachings about life after death. It was believed that all people (the good and the bad) after death went to a place of conscious existence, named Sheol (although certain facets of **Christianity** consider Sheol to be nothing but a grave). Books of the Old Testament referencing good people going to Sheol include Psalm 9:17, 31:17, and 49:14 and Isaiah 5:14. Scriptures referencing the bad going there include Genesis 37:35, Job 14:13, Psalm 6:5, 16:10, and 88:3, and Isaiah 38:10.

The Hebrews (or Israelites) are told that communication with the dead is unlawful and against God, that it is only God that they should seek for counsel. Neighbors of the Israelites, however, believed in life after death and believed that the dead could be contacted. King Saul of Israel went against the Hebrew belief of not communicating with the dead by contacting a medium (known as the Witch of Endor) prior to going to war at Endor. He sought to contact Samuel, a deceased judge and prophet of Israel, for counsel about the pending battle (1 Samuel 28). The medium saw Samuel clairvoyantly and materialzed him to the point where Saul was able to speak with him through her.

The Old Testament book of Daniel (one of the very last books of the Hebrew scriptures to be written) held the first definite ideas on life after death. Daniel 12:2–3 states, "Many of those who have already died will live again: some will enjoy eternal life, and some will suffer eternal disgrace. The wise leaders will shine with all the brightness of the sky. And those who have taught many people to do what is right will shine like the stars forever." In addition, the prophets **Ezekiel** and Isaiah reported having powerful spiritual visions.

New Testament. In the New Testament, John, the writer of the Book of Revelation, had a lengthy vision that involved glimpses into what he perceived to be heaven. He witnessed thousands standing before the throne of God dressed in white. In addition, the Gospel of Matthew tells how, on the Mount of Transfiguration, **Jesus** talks with Moses and Elijah, both whom had been dead for a long time (Matthew 17:1–3). Jesus also made the statement that in his father's house (i.e., in heaven) there are many rooms—a comment denoting an afterlife in a spiritual world. The most prominent New Testament account of a life after this world is that of Jesus himself appearing after death to his apostles and his mother in an effort to convey that he was not dead, but indeed alive in an unseen world.

### Bilocation

The appearance of the astral body in several places at once. This phenomenon has been reported for centuries. There have been reports from families and friends who were close to a deceased loved one receiving simultaneous visits from that loved one; those who saw the deceased were on opposite sides of town or opposite sides of the world, and both visits were completely real and completely unique. In addition, bilocation can also occur when a person is astral traveling or having an out-of-body experience.

### Binary Soul Doctrine

An ancient belief that a human being possesses two souls and that these two souls were in danger of separating at death. The idea of two souls can be traced back to the earliest days of human history. It was taught long before **Christianity** presented the world with the one-soul belief. Belief in a binary soul could be found in the first writings of certain cultures, peoples, and religions, including those of Canaan, **China**, **Egypt**, **Greece**, **India**, Israel, Mesopotamia, and **Persia**. In addition, the peoples of Alaska, Australia, the Dakotas, Haiti, Hawaii, and MesoAmerica embraced this idea. The Manichaeans, Mandaeans, Cathars, and Templars also have teachings surrounding two souls. The Greeks referred to the souls as the *psuche* and the *thumos*. The Egyptians called them the *ba* and the *ka*. To Persia they were the *urvan* and *daena*. In India they were the *atman* and *jiva*. China referred to them as the *hun* and *po*, Haiti called them the *gros bon ange* and *ti bon ange*, Hawaii called them the *uhane* and *unihipili,* and the Dakota Indians called them the *nagi* and *niya*. The ancient Israelites referred to them as the *ruah* and *nefesh*. For more information on BSD, see *The Lost Secret of Death: Our Divided Souls and the Afterlife* by Peter Novak.

## Birch, Silver

A spirit guide who was once human and passed on over three thousand years ago. He is said to be one of the greatest afterlife teachers, with the highest credibility, and one of the most influential and wise spirit guides ever to contact the earth plane from the other side. Some of the books of Silver Birch's teachings (all published by Psychic Press) include *The Seed of Truth, Teachings of Silver Birch, More Teachings from Silver Birch, Light from Silver Birch, The Spirit Speaks, Philosophy of Silver Birch, A Voice in the Wilderness, Wisdom of Silver Birch,* and *Silver Birch Anthology*.

## Bird of God
See **Birds.**

## Birds

Birds are associated with the flight into the spiritual world and the journey to immortality. They are also often associated with the journey of the human soul after death. Many myths associate birds with the arrival of death. Because of their power of flight, birds are often seen as carriers or symbols of the human soul, or as the soul itself, flying heavenward after a person dies. In addition, some cultures associate birds with birth, believing that an individual's soul arrived on earth in bird form. The mythological bird called the phoenix combined images of birth and death to become a powerful symbol of eternal rebirth. According to Egyptian legend, the phoenix burned up every five hundred years, but was then miraculously reborn out of its own ashes, so it was truly immortal.

   **The Flight of the Soul.** There are numerous mythologies that link birds to the journey the human soul takes to the spiritual realm. In some cases the bird is the guide into and through the afterlife. For example, in Syrian beliefs, eagles on tombs represent the guides that lead souls to heaven. In Jewish beliefs, the dove is a soul guide.

**The Soul.** In some cultures, it was believed that the soul, once freed from the body, took the form of a bird. For example, this belief is seen in the Greek and Celtic cultures; both believed that the dead could reappear as birds. Sumerians thought that the dead lived as birds in the underworld. In one Islamic tradition, all dead souls remain in the form of birds until Judgment Day. In **Christianity**, the dove is a symbol of the soul ascending to heaven. In Hindu myths, birds are symbols of the soul or forms taken by the soul between earthly lives. A Turkish saying describes the death of a person as "his soul bird has flown away." In some cultures, due to their great size and strength, eagles represent royal or imperial souls. This is seen in the funeral traditions of the ancient Romans. The Romans would release an eagle at a ruler's funeral. As it rose into the sky, it symbolized the ruler's soul taking its place in the heavens. Ancient Egyptians believed that the soul could leave the dead body in the form of a bird, often a hawk. They built their graves and tombs with narrow shafts leading to the open air so that these birds could fly in and out, keeping watch on the body.

**Bird of God.** The term *Bird of God* is sometimes used when referring to the angels. Throughout history, birds have been a symbol for spiritual beings. Various birdlike beings can be found in religious beliefs around the world. In Russian folklore the *Alkanosts,* winged, birdlike female figures, are known as Birds of Paradise. Native North Americans worshiped a god they referred to as *Thunderbird;* the eagle and the hawk symbolize him. In Etrurian beliefs there was **Charon,** the winged god of the dead. He had huge wings and a large crooked nose resembling the beak of a bird. He carried the souls of the dead to the underworld. In Judaic lore there was the phoenix, a bird who resides in heaven. It is charged with protecting the earth from the rays of the sun. In addition, the term *bird of God* is a term used in Dante's *Divine Comedy* when referring to the angels. The task of this angel is to act as pilot of the ferry transporting the souls belonging to purgatory.

## Blake, Elizabeth

Direct-voice medium. Blake was a phenomenally powerful direct-voice medium from Bradrick, Ohio. The voices would come through often very clearly and in daylight, and would answer specific questions accurately. Blake was investigated by the **American Society for Psychical Research** to determine whether or not she was a fraud. As it turns out, the two men who interviewed her hailed her abilities and skills with communicating with those in the unseen spiritual world. In her sessions, Blake used a two-foot-long, double trumpet. She would put the small part of the trumpet to her ear and the bigger part to the sitter's ear. This procedure gave the indication that the voices were actually coming from her own ear. The voices could be small as a whisper or very loud. Excerpts from a sitting with Blake can be found in the book *The Psychic Riddle* by Isaac Funk.

## Blake, William

English artist, supernatural visionary, and mystic (1757–1827). William Blake was born in London to James Blake, a prosperous London hosier who reared his children as religious dissenters. From childhood, William was able to see inside the spiritual world. He reportedly saw angels, famous people, and prophets. As early as the age of seven, Blake habitually saw a white-bearded spiritual person who he perceived to be **God,** peering in through his window. Afterward and for the rest of his life, he continued to see spiritual people and beings that were unseen to others. He reported seeing a tree filled with angels and angels walking amid haymakers in the mornings. However, Blake reported seeing apparitions of some very notable people, even conversing with them on occasion. In some cases he would even draw portraits of them. Some of his remarkable visitors included the prophet **Ezekiel**, Moses, **Homer**, Julius Caesar, Mark Antony, **Dante Alighieri**, Edward III, William Shakespeare, John Milton, and Voltaire. Because of Blake's willingness to speak of his experiences, there were some that thought he was delusional. However, those that knew Blake considered him to be honest and his experiences real.

When Blake's brother Robert was dying, Blake witnessed his soul ascending upward in joy. Later, Blake was visited by his brother, who brought to him information from the other side on how to improve on his engravings (his lifelong trade). Blake incorporated the technique into his work, and it helped to make him famous.

Among his many exceptional creative talents, Blake enjoyed writing poetry. He felt that his writing was inspirited from spiritual beings. In addition, he was an automatic writer. He referred to this type of writing as "immediate dictation," in which he recorded information given to him by people from the spiritual realm.

For the most part, as evidenced by his great work, Blake was a spiritual person. He believed in the Divine, he believed in an almighty, he believed in an unseen spiritual world. However, he despised traditional religions, such as **Christianity** and **Islam** and their version of God, which showed the Divine to be controlling and disallowing humans to use their imaginations and explore their passions. Yet he believed his work to be guided by God's angels and credited his creative genius to them. In fact, Blake once wrote, "It is not because angels are holier than men or devils that makes them angels, but because they do not expect holiness from one another, but from God alone."

During his lifetime, he created a large number of memorable drawings revolving around spirituality and the Divine, which included scenes from the unseen spiritual realm, the details of which he maintained were revealed to him by angels. Among his famous works of the spiritual world is a watercolor titled *Jacob's Dream*. In it angels can be seen ascending a winding staircase, leading souls toward heaven, which appears at the end of the stairs as a bright light. His other famous artworks include *The Good and Evil Angels, The Meeting of a Family in Heaven, Elohim Creating Adam, Satan Smiting Job with Sore Boils,*

*The Simoniac Pope, A Father's Memoirs of His Child, What Gleams for Joy*, and *The Ancient of Days*. Says Blake, "The man who never in his mind and thoughts travel'd to heaven is no artist." His books of poems, the texts of which he engraved and illustrated, were influenced by his unorthodox Christian and political beliefs and by such mystics as Jacob Böhme (or Boehme). He died in London, August 12, 1827, leaving uncompleted a cycle of drawings inspired by Dante's *Divine Comedy*.

## Blavatsky, Madame

Russian medium, guru, mystic, esotericist, spiritualist, and author whose birth name was Helena Petrovna Hahn (1831–1891). Historians regard her as the person that started the New Age movement. Born on August 12, 1831, at Dnepropetrovsk (Ekaterinoslav), Ukraine, Blavatsky was a woman of noble birth. She was the daughter of Colonel Peter von Hahn and Helena Andreyevna, née de Fadeyev, a celebrated novelist who died when Blavatsky was a child. As a child, Blavatsky was raised as all noble young ladies of the time were.

She was educated by governesses and instructed in art, literature, and music. She learned French, English (her native language was Russian), and piano, in a time when women still had no right to vote. However, from a young age Blavatsky stood out. Early on, it was understood by those around her that she was gifted with amazing psychic abilities. Some of the extrasensory skills displayed throughout her life included clairvoyance, telepathy, clairaudience, materialization, and astral travel. She was also extremely adept at mediumship. Her biggest accomplishment, outside of her writing, was the creation of the Theosophical Movement, also known as Theosophy. She started the Foundation of Theosophical Society in New York City in 1875. The society's aim was to advance spiritual principles and spread knowledge of Eastern mysticism, which included such beliefs as reincarnation and karma. It was Blavatsky who brought many of the mysterious teachings of the East to the West. Her writings include *Isis Unveiled* (1877), *The Secret Doctrine* (1888), *The Voice of Silence* (1889), *The Key to Theosophy* (1889), and a host of articles. She also started magazines, including *The Theosophist* (1879) and *Lucifer* (1887).

## Bodhisattva(s)

Spiritual beings in Buddhism sometimes referred to as Buddhas to be. Once mortal beings on earth, the Bodhisattvas have reached nirvana, but have put off their own salvation in order to become emissaries of **God**. In their enlightened state, they return to earth to help humans. They act as healers, spiritual guides, and teachers. In addition, they act as guides for the souls of those who are near death. In heaven, they are privileged beings that receive all the rewards of those who have reached salvation.

## Book of Life

A book believed by ancient Jews and Christians to hold the good and bad deeds of every human on earth. It was said to be the basis from which **God**'s judgment is formed. It was generally believed that after one's death, God will read this book and enumerate one's good deeds in life.

It was believed that if more good deeds than bad were found in this book, one would go to heaven; but if one's bad deeds outweighed the good, then that individual would be sent to hell. Therefore, those whose names are found written in the Book of Life would escape God's everlasting judgment. According to the Pseudepigrapha's 3 Enoch, God is assisted with the Book of Life (referred to here as the Book of Records) by Radweri'el YHWH, an angel who acts as the heavenly archivist. He is the angel who is responsible for maintaining the heavenly archives in which the Book of Life is kept. There is a passage in 3 Enoch that talks about Radweri'el YHWH's role, saying, "He takes out the scroll box in which the book of records is kept, and brings it into the presence of the Holy One [God]. He breaks the seals of the scroll box, opens it, takes out the scrolls and puts them in the hand of the Holy One. The Holy One receives them from his hand and places them before the scribes, so that they might read them out to the Great Law Court" (3 Enoch 27:1–2). See also **Akashic Records; Hall of Records.**

## Book of Death

In ancient Jewish tradition, in the spiritual world, there is a book entitled the *Book of Death*. It was believed that **God** kept the names of the unrighteous in this book.

## Books of Enoch

A pseudepigraphic work credited to the prophet **Enoch,** of biblical fame. The Books of Enoch are the lengthiest work in the Pseudepigrapha (a compilation of 52 Judeo-Christian writings that were not a part of the original **Bible**). Scholars have concluded that the original collection was written either in Hebrew or in Aramaic. Composed during the second and first centuries BC, the Books of Enoch relay the prophet Enoch's out-of-body experiences in which he traveled to the spiritual realm. There he conversed with **God** and the angels, traveled through the spiritual realm, and visited seven heavens.

In the first heaven, Enoch saw "a very great sea, greater than the earthly sea." In the second heaven, Enoch was "transported on clouds that move" and witnessed a place where he saw the rebellious angels. He also learned that two hundred angels rule the stars. In the third heaven, Enoch saw the garden of paradise and in the center, the Tree of Life, which was guarded by three hundred glorious angels. In the fourth heaven, "he saw legions of spirits, dragons, luminaries, and wondrous creatures such as the fabled phoenix flying around the earth." In the fifth heaven, he "met angelic host," the Egregoii (with the appearance of men taller than the giants of the earth) and the angels of the fall (that partnered with the daughters of men) bound for their transgressions for ten thousand years. In the sixth heaven, Enoch saw luminous angels with radiant faces. They revealed to him the motions of the stars, the phases of the moon, and the revolution of earth around the sun. In addition, he saw archangels, phoenixes, and cherubim. In the seventh heaven, Enoch saw cherubim, seraphim, and thrones. In addition, two winged men on clouds placed him at the limits of the seventh heaven. From there, he could see a divine being from afar sitting on a throne. Enoch believed the being to be God. Afterward, the archangel **Gabriel** came to Enoch to take him to the next place. In addition, Enoch saw what he believed to be angels in a special building studying time, the seasons, ecology, astronomy and humanity. In the angelic classroom, all of the angels were dressed alike and were being taught by the archangels. In addition, Enoch said the archangels kept records of the fauna and the flora found in heaven and on the earth. Other angels kept records of the seasons and years. Some studied the bodies of water of earth and still others studied the fruits, herbs, and vegetation that provide nutrition to the people and animals of earth. In addition, certain angels are responsible for observing and recording the behavior of humans.

The books contain more information on angels than can be found in any other source. It includes the names of angels, their responsibilities, qualities, and personalities. It lists the angels of hailstorms, wind, lightning, storms, comets, windstorms, hurricanes, thunder, earthquakes, snow, rain, daylight, night, the sun, moon, and heavenly bodies. The books also give information on the fallen angels, their sexual relationships with women, their corruption of humankind, Enoch's unsuccessful attempt to act as mediator for them, and the foretelling of their demise.

The experiences of Enoch described in the books are similar to near-death experiences found in the modern era, and the details closely resemble what others have relayed after visiting the spiritual world. The writings of Enoch were not included in the **Old Testament** canon because the early church doubted the authorship of the books. The books were at one time well read by the Jews and considered to be inspired canonical scripture by earlier rabbis.

## Borgia, Anthony

A medium known for his work involving Monsignor **Robert Hugh Benson** (whom he had known before Benson's death). From the spiritual world, Benson relayed important information to Borgia regarding life after death. The information turned out to be six books, in which Benson gave detailed description on what humans can expect when they die and what they could look forward to seeing in the unseen, spiritual world.

## Bosch, Hieronymus

Early sixteenth-century Flemish Gothic artist (1450–1516). His name is taken from his hometown, Hertogenbosch; Bosch spent his entire career there. Little is known about Bosch's personal life. Even the date of his birth is obscure. In addition, there are no writings from Bosch relaying exactly what his works meant or his thoughts on them. What is known about his training is but a guess.

By the time of his death, however, Bosch was an internationally known painter of spiritual visions who seemed to have an affinity towards hell, sin, and punishment. His art helped to set the mental image of the afterlife for people in his day, especially that of hell. His art, during his lifetime, could be found in the homes of the wealthy and noble.

Bosch's most famous painting is *The Garden of Earthly Delights*, a three-part altarpiece, called a triptych. Its name comes from the rich garden pictured in the central panel. The story of the painting proceeds from left to right; Adam and Eve are shown in the left panel of the piece; the middle part depicts sinful pleasure (earthly delights); and the horrors of hell—a dark, cold, yet fiery vision—are depicted on the right. Two other famous paintings by Bosch feature angels: *The Entrance to Heaven* and *The Last Judgment*.

## Bridges

In folklore and mythology bridges are often associated with the roads the dead travel to reach the afterlife. These paths are frequently referred to as "bridges of souls."

## Brinkley, Dannion

Near-death experiencer and author (1950–). His story is one of miracles, heavenly revelations, and newly found psychic powers.

The best-selling book *Saved by the Light* recounts Brinkley's first extraordinary near-death experience. On September 17, 1975, Brinkley died after being struck by a bolt of lightning during a thunderstorm, as he talked on the telephone. The bolt of lightning sent thousands of volts of electricity through his body, tossing him several feet into the air. Twenty-eight minutes later, he woke up in the morgue with a sheet draped over his body. In those twenty-eight minutes Brinkley had a profound near-death experience. During the experience, he remembers being out of his body and watching loved ones and medics as they attempted to revive him. He tells of traveling through a dark tunnel toward a spirit being, visiting a crystal city, and going before thirteen angelic instructors in what Brinkley describes as a "cathedral of knowledge." There the angels shared revelations with him about humankind's future.

In 1989, after his damaged heart stopped during an illness, he had a second near-death experience, which reunited him with his angelic instructors. This time, they told him that he was to use his new psychic gifts to help the dying. Since that time, he has dedicated his life to working with the sick and elderly and teaching people not to fear death. Through his lecture tours, books, and workshops, he has reached millions. Today he is considered an expert on the subject of grief and bereavement. Says Brinkley, "We are not human beings here for a spiritual experience, but spiritual beings here for a human experience." He is also the author of a second bestseller, *At Peace in the Light*. See **Saved by the Light.**

### *Britten, Emma Hardinge*

Spiritualist, gifted medium, and inspirational speaker (1823–1899). Emma Hardinge Britten was born in the East End of London, the daughter of Captain Floyd, a seafarer. At an early age, Britten was recognized as a talented musician, singer, and elocutionist. As early as eleven years old, she was earning a living as a musical instructor. Her musical talents led her to acquire a contract with a theater company in 1856, in America. There she performed on Broadway and elsewhere in New York City. It was there that she met Ada Hoyt, who converted her to a belief in spiritualism and also helped develop her into a medium and public lecturer. Her mediumistic talents included automatic writing, psychometry, healing, and prophecy. She was also well received as a great speaker. In one famous case the member of a famous sunken mail steamer (the *Pacific)* spoke through her while she was in trance and gave a detailed account of what ensued during the tragedy. Because of this story, the owners of the *Pacific* threatened litigation. However, the story told through Britten proved accurate. In 1865 Britten returned home to England, where she spent the next four years. It wasn't until 1869 that she returned to New York in order to confer with publishers regarding a book she was in the process of writing. During that trip over from England, she met William Britten, whom she later married. She later became known for her work as an advocate of spiritualism and eventually became the most famous chronicler of the spiritualist movement.

## *Brown, Rosemary*

A British medium (1916–2001). Brown became well known for her talents of channeling music and art from the spiritual world. She was a middle-aged London housewife when she began to be contacted by the spirits of history's most famous composers, including Bach, Ludwig van Beethoven, Johannes Brahms, Frederic Chopin, Claude Debussy, Edvard Grieg, Franz Liszt, Sergei Rachmaninov, Franz Schubert, and Robert Schumann. She was able to clearly see and hear them. She received from them dictations of new compositions that they had written in the spiritual world.

Brown wrote in her autobiography, titled *Unfinished Symphonies*, that when she was seven years old, an elderly man with long white hair and dressed in a black gown appeared to her. This man turned out to be the great Hungarian composer Franz Liszt. He said that he would be working with her when she became an adult. She described the experience of channeling as losing control of her hands and someone else guiding them. She was even able to give pieces of information about the composers from which she channeled. She said that Liszt made the arrangements for the other composers to come through. Chopin would instruct her on what notes he wanted her to play and forced her fingers onto the correct keys. Both Bach and Beethoven had her sit and take dictation. Schubert attempted to sing his compositions. As a result, Brown spent many tireless hours working with her spirit friends and transcribed hundreds of compositions. Each piece is said to have the style of the composer that wrote it. Brown wrote three books on her channeling: *Unfinished Symphonies* (1971), *Immortals at My Elbow* (1974), and *Look Beyond Today* (1986). She recorded some of the channeled pieces on an album titled *The Rosemary Brown Piano Album.*

Brown would also draw watercolors, charcoals, and oil prints from dead artists; write poems from deceased poets; write down equations from Albert Einstein, give philosophical statements from Bertrand Russell; recount psychological observations from **Carl Jung;** and even channeled and published a play from George Bernard Shaw. She received spiritual visits from other notables including William Shakespeare and Vincent Van Gogh. These visits, she said, proved that there is indeed life after death.

## Browne, Sylvia

World-renowned psychic, medium and spiritual leader (1936–). Known for her exceptional psychic abilities, Browne has appeared on numerous television shows and other media, and teaches and lectures on the afterlife and paranormal topics, often with the aid of her spirit guide, Francine. In 1974 Browne created the Nirvana Foundation for Psychic Research, a nonprofit organization now known as Society of Novus Spiritus, which means "new spirit." The organization is based upon a Christian Gnostic theology. Since that time, Browne has aided thousands of people through her books, lectures, website, and teachings. It is

Browne's aspiration to prove that the human soul survives death, that **God** is a real and loving being, and that there is a divine plan to our lives. She is the author of *Journey of the Soul*; *Conversations with the Other Side*; *Astrology Through the Eyes of a Psychic*; *Adventures of a Psychic*; *God, Creation, and Tools for Life*; *Life on the Other Side: A Psychic's Tour of the Afterlife*; and the best-selling *The Other Side and Back: A Psychic's Guide to Our World and Beyond*. Browne has appeared on national television on such shows as *Unsolved Mysteries*, *In Search Of*, *That's Incredible,* and the *Montel Williams Show*. She has also starred in the hour-long CBS special *Haunted Lives*, been a guest on the *Larry King Live* show, and had two pay-per-view specials in 1999 and 2000. To learn more of Browne and her work, see *www.sylvia.org.*

## Brubaker, Don

Author of the popular near-death experience book titled *Absent from the Body: One Man's Clinical Death*. Clinically dead for forty-five minutes after a heart attack, Brubaker left his body and journeyed to the unseen spiritual world. During this period, he witnessed the magnificence of heaven as well as the darker realms. Brubaker returned to tell of his journey into life after death and his life experience since that time. The book recounts his life leading up to his experience and after.

## Buildings (in the spiritual world)
See **Amphitheater.**

## Burma
See **Nats.**

## Busey, Gary
Hollywood actor, Oscar nominee, and near-death experiencer (1944–). In 1988, in Culver City, California, Busey nearly died in a motorcycle accident. An avid Harley rider, Busey was going between forty and fifty miles per hour when he hit a patch of gravel, which caused him to lose control of his bike. He crashed and was thrown from his bike, slamming into a curb headfirst. Not wearing a helmet at the time, he cracked his skull, nearly dying. While in surgery, he had a near-death-experience. He witnessed angels in the form of large,

golden orbs of light, exuding unconditional love. As a result of his experience, he altered his lifestyle becoming
a more spiritual individual. He now
talks about personal rebirth and near-
death experiences, and is an advocate
for wearing motorcycle helmets.

## Bystander Apparition

An apparition that appears to a person
other than the one meant to see it. The
apparition appears to the third party
presumably to alert the intended, often a loved one, to their presence as
proof of their survival of death.

# C

## Campbell Brothers

Allen B. Campbell (1833–1919) and Charles Shourds (d. 1926). The Campbell brothers, as they were known, were mediums that used slate writing and spirit typewriting. However, they became famous for their spirit portraits and paintings in pastels and oils.

## Cannon, Dolores

Past-life regressionist, hypnotherapist, psychic researcher, and owner of Ozark Mountain Publishing in Arizona (1931–). Cannon specializes in the recovery of lost knowledge. During the course of her work, she has amassed a large amount of information about the unseen realms and dimensions, taken from her years of hypnotic research as well as work in past-life therapy. In addition, she is also the world's leading expert on Nostradamus and his prophecies.

Cannon has written a number of popular books, including *Conversations With Nostradamus, Volume II; Conversations With Nostradamus, Volume III; Conversations With Nostradamus, Volume VI; The Custodians; Jesus and the Essenes; They Walked with Jesus; Keepers of the Garden; The Legend of Starcrash; Legacy from the Stars; A Soul Remembers Hiroshima; The Convoluted Universe, Book One; The Convoluted Universe, Book Two;* and *The Convoluted Universe, Book Three.*

Her book *Between Death and Life: Conversations with a Spirit* offers an incredible amount of information about the spiritual world, covering such topics as levels of existence, spirit guides, guardian angels, ghosts, walk-ins, heaven and hell, and **God** and the devil. Among its other compelling information is the assertion that the spirit can leave the body immediately before death to reduce pain. Also, there is a silver cord that ties the spirit to the physical body. In addition, it is wrong to commit suicide, and committing suicide is an error that can take many lives to correct. Regardless of the incredible variations in the past lives of the many patients she has regressed, the information they've given on the period between lives is consistent with one another.

*Between Death and Life* presents sound evidence that regression memories can provide information about the other side of death.

## Carrington, Hereward

Author and psychic researcher (1880–1958). By the mid 1920s Carrington had written many books about psychic phenomena. He wrote two books with **Sylvan Muldoon** on the subject of astral projection. The first, *The Projection of the Astral Body,* was mainly an account of Muldoon's own experiences. The second, *The Phenomena of Astral Projection,* contained a collection of cases.

## Casual Body

Indian spiritual beliefs inform us that the human being is made up of three bodies. These include the physical body, the astral body and the casual body, or body of light. It is the source of each personality that incarnates in each lifetime, causing the personality to

be and to exist. The causal body lasts throughout one's incarnations. When an incarnation is finished, the causal body reabsorbs the personality the person had during that lifetime. The causal body exists for many millions of years, as a person journeys through many incarnations. Once the incarnation cycle is complete, the causal body disappears. Humans that are liberated from the cycle of rebirth discard the causal body and move on to the higher realms. The causal body is seen as a brilliant ball of energy and light. Animals do not have a causal body.

## Causal Plane

A high spiritual level of existence. The causal plane is said to be located directly above the astral plane.

## Cayce, Edgar

One of America's greatest psychics (1877–1945). Born in Hopkinsville, Kentucky, Cayce began his amazing journey at the age of twenty-four when he discovered that he had psychic abilities. Having lost his voice due to a cold and finding no relief from traditional medicines, Cayce visited a hypnotist in an effort to find relief.

While under hypnosis, Cayce discovered a treatment for his throat. He also found that he could diagnose other people's illnesses and prescribe treatments for them in the same unique way. This was the beginning of a long life assisting and diagnosing the ailments of others. Cayce astounded doctors with his ability to diagnose and give treatment to people who sometimes lived hundreds of miles away.

While under hypnosis, Cayce found that he had the ability to leave his body and visit the spiritual world. One place in particular that he visited was the realm holding the **Akashic Records,** a vast spiritual library that holds answers to many of life's mysteries.

In his lifetime, Cayce had more out-of-body experiences—a total of 14,000—than anyone ever known. Cayce's treatments, out-of-body experiences, and predictions are recorded in his extensive collection of books, which cover a huge range of topics, including the subject of spiritual realms.

In 1931 Cayce founded the **Association for Research and Enlightenment** (ARE). It is a not-for-profit organization that researches and examines a number of spiritual topics, including ancient mysteries, dreams, philosophy, and reincarnation, among others. Cayce's readings have been preserved to assist others with similar medical or personal problems. For further information on how to obtain Edgar Cayce readings, books, and more, contact the ARE through its website: *www.edgarcayce.org.*

## Celts

In Celtic beliefs, the unseen spiritual world was referred to as the "other world" or "underworld." It was believed to be either underground or an island in the sea. There were various theories and ideas about the underworld. It was believed by some to be a great misty island, such as Avalon or Tir Na Nog. It was known by many names, including the Land of the Living, Delightful Plain, and Land of the Young. Celts believed that in this world there was no illness, old age, or death. There the inhabitants were eternally happy. Others thought it to be a universe parallel to our own, closely resembling the physical world except that everything there was peaceful and harmonious. In a second belief, some Celts thought that after a series of rebirths, in which a different inborn evil is purged in each, the perfected soul is at last let into Gwenved, the White Place, where one can experience great rest as well as earthly pleasures.

## Channeler

A person through which a person from the unseen spiritual world communicates information. People from the other side communicating information may be spirit guides, ascended masters, angels, beings of-light, famous people from history, and a loved one's friends and relatives that have crossed over.

Often deceased relatives and friends have information that they would like to share from the other side, but have no clear means of do-ing so. The channeler serves as an intermediary for a deceased person that would like to relay information to a still-living loved one. The information and scenarios can vary. The person that has passed on may want to convey that they are alive in spirit and still with the living individual even though they cannot be seen. In some cases, the deceased may share information regarding a will or a murder.

In addition, angels and spirit guides may have some information to share with a person, a group of people, or humanity as a whole, and will com-municate information through a me-dium or channeler. These messages are usually of a spiritual nature and offer help and guidance to human-kind. In recent years, there has been a steady increase in the amount of peo-ple who are coming forth as channels for those in other realms. The receiv-ing of these messages are referred to as channeling.

See also **Automatic Art; Automatic Speaking; Automatic writing.**

## Channeling
See **Channeler.**

## Chapman, George
Modern British trance medium and healer (1921–2006). He was given the Spiritualist of 1975 Award, an honor bestowed on him by prominent healer Harry Edwards (the leading

healer in the UK from the 1940s until his death in 1976).

Born in 1921 in Bootle, a town within the Metropolitan Borough of Sefton, in Merseyside, England, Chapman was raised by his grandparents after the death of his mother when he was five years old. For the first twenty-five years of his life, Chapman did not experience any psychic or mediumistic episodes. It was after his marriage in 1944, when he and his wife, Margaret, lost a four-week-old baby daughter, that Chapman first sought to find answers to the age-old question of life after death. After failing to find answers in religion, Chapman had an experience that changed his life forever.

While working as a fire officer in 1946, he began spending his free time between fire calls using an upturned glass and alphabet, which mysteriously began spelling out information. After experimenting with this communication method for a time, Chapman established that the messages he was receiving were valid. At one riveting point, he discovered that he was receiving messages from his deceased mother. He later learned that she was looking after their infant daughter on the other side. He continued his interest in mediumship and was known to practice three hours a day. During this time, he was able to leave his body and make contact with both his mother and daughter on the other side.

One important moment of his trance-mediumship career was when Chapman met his guide. The guide's name was Dr. William Lang. Lang apparently had been commissioned in the spiritual world to assist Chapman in his trance work. Lang brought Chapman the news that he was also a healer. In addition, Chapman was able to verify who Lang was through information that Lang had provided him. Chapman, along with his guide, soon became famous for their healing abilities and received healing requests from abroad. He founded clinics in several locations abroad including Germany, Switzerland, Spain, and the United States. He became known as England's most traveled healer.

### Charon

Winged god of the dead in Etrurian beliefs. He was the son of Erebus, the god of darkness, and Nyx, goddess of the night. He had huge wings and a large crooked nose resembling the beak of a bird. He carried the souls of the dead to **Hades** and was the overseer of the cities of the underworld.

## Cherubim
See **Angels.**

## Chi
See **China,** "Chi."

## Child Experiencer
A term for a child that has had a near-death experience.

## Children
In the spiritual world, there are no babies or small children, unless specific souls choose to remain in these forms. Souls have a choice of appearance once they are on the other side and may for a time choose to remain in the same form that they had on earth when they died. This means that if they died as a child, they may choose to remain in this form for a while. The aging process is different in the spiritual world than it is on the physical plane. In the spiritual world, the aging process depends on the wants and needs of each individual soul.

All souls have been in existence from the beginning of time. There are young and old souls in the spirit world, but this categorizing of souls is based on their experiences on earth (or other worlds). Therefore, a young soul is someone who has not had much experience incarnating, and old or advanced souls have incarnated several times, gaining experience, knowledge, and wisdom along the way.

The spirit becomes a baby when it chooses to enter life in the physical. In metaphysics it is thought that miscarried babies or babies who live for a short time after birth are teaching lessons or fulfilling a purpose that those around them are not aware of. Their deaths provide lessons and challenges that help the people around them to grow. It is believed that souls decide to incarnate briefly based on their free will and are fully aware of the mission before incarnating. Souls sometimes incarnate into the physical body of a baby for only a short period of time in order to aid in teaching a lesson that will help the parents or siblings grow spiritually. They may also choose to incarnate for only a short period in order to complete a karmic task. For example, they may need to complete a karmic timeline because their previous life was cut short by suicide. Once souls fulfill their purpose on earth, they leave their physical body and return to the spiritual world, where they will immediately return to maturity.

**Children and Angels.** Children are believed to receive visitations from angels more often than adults. This is thought to be due to their innocence and also their openness. Some believe this relationship with the angels begins in the womb. According to Judaic lore, as a baby is growing inside of the mother's womb, an angel instructs it on the wisdom of the Torah. Just before the child is born, an angel touches the mouth of the baby, so that it will forget what it learned. However, the impression of the wisdom is said to remain with the child during its earthly life.

Children are also thought to receive more angelic protection because they are so young and careless. As they grow and are better able to look after themselves, they require less angelic protection. It is believed that when they are very little, they have many guardian angels. In Catholicism children are taught that they have two angels, a good angel and a bad angel, one sitting on each shoulder.

Legend has it that guardian angels of children dwell in a privileged place in heaven, close to **God.** This belief stems from the **New Testament** book of Matthew 18:10, where it says, "See to it that you men do not despise one of these little ones; for I tell you that their angels in heaven always behold the face of my Father who is in heaven." Premature babies and children of adultery are protected by caretaker angels. The angel Temeluchus is the guardian angel over all children per Gustave Davidson's *A Dictionary of Angels*.

## China

During ancient times, the Chinese believed in an unseen spiritual world. The Chinese performed ceremonies to honor the spirits of their ancestors and ensure that they would have benevolent feelings toward their descendants. In old world China, there was the belief in a binary soul, referred to as the *po* and the *hun*. These binary souls were thought to split at death unless countermeasures were taken.

In some parts of the Chinese culture, it was believed that when a person died, they would go to the Fairyland of the Queen Mother of the West by "riding to the Jade Pool" or by "riding to the mountain of the Dao." The deceased were guided by Chang'e and by the god of thunder and the goddess of lightning. Souls were thought to enter this spiritual realm by its south gate. Afterward, they passed into Vaulting Mists Hall, where deities and celestial immortals, along with the great Jade Emperor, who presided over all, gathered to confer about the rights and wrongs of human conduct. After passing through the Vaulting Mists Hall, new arrivals went through the Pure Wind Gate, where a different judge examined their life and deeds from their most recent incarnation. There, demons sent by Yama (king of hell) waited to seize evildoers and take them to condemnation. The good were escorted, at the command of the Jade Emperor, into Fairyland where they would for-

ever live in paradise in the company of immortals and deities. There they engaged in nightly celebrations, where they enjoyed exquisite foods and listened to beautiful music performed by fairy girls.

Another Chinese belief in a spiritual world comes from Buddhist teachings. Although this religion is not Chinese in origin, there are still many Buddhist followers in China. The Buddhist philosophy states that a person's fate after death depended on if they lived a virtuous and good life while on earth. Buddhists believe that they could be reborn in the Pure Land, said to be to the west, beyond the sunset. This is a place where souls take refuge from the cycle of birth, life, death, and rebirth by entering this land of pure consciousness, enlightenment, and liberation.

**Chi.** One of the most important Chinese spiritual beliefs is that of the chi (or *qi*), which is the vital life force. Chi is believed to be inherent in all things. It is the chi that animates the mind and body. In ancient Chinese beliefs, the word *chi* encompassed a twofold idea, the prebirth and the postbirth chi. The Chinese during that period believed that individuals were born with a quantity of prebirth chi, which was determined by one's parents and additional factors. This prebirth chi could not be replenished. When a person depleted all of their prebirth chi, they died. However, postbirth chi could be replenished through breath, food, and sustenance. Using postbirth chi lessened the expenditure of one's prebirth chi, therefore lengthening one's life.

**Spiritual Beings.** Ancient Chinese believed in beings referred to as shen, which are immortal spirits. The Chinese refer to the shen as gods. Once human, the shen have attained salvation and immortality. Traveling between the spiritual and physical worlds, they can manifest in human or animal form, in order to bring messages, heal, teach, or offer strength, protection, and encouragement.

## Chinvato Peretav (Bridge of the Separator)

In ancient Zoroastrian beliefs, a bridge also known as the "bridge of the separator." It was believed that after an individual's death, the soul of the person stayed near the body for three days. On the fourth day, protective spiritual beings would come to escort the soul to the Chinvat Bridge. This bridge was said to be as thin as a strand of hair, sharp as a razor, and span across hell. It was a place of moral judgment, where a person's deeds, offerings, sacrifices, and prayers, as well as ethical practices and accomplishments in life, were examined. Departed souls crossed the bridge and were questioned by immortals to see if they qualified to enter paradise. If the souls were found guilty of sin, the bridge would narrow, and the offending souls would fall off the bridge to perdition. Those found worthy to enter paradise would find a wide road to the realm of light. See also **Zoroaster.**

## Christ Consciousness

A phrase used to denote the spiritual and mystical knowledge of the unity of the entire universe. To achieve Christ consciousness means to see the universe as **God** and God as the universe. Everything else is a part of this whole.

## Christianity

The religion of the Christians as originated by **Jesus** of Nazareth. The Christian religion began in ancient Judea, and its first members were Jews. It expanded into the Greek-speaking world of the eastern Mediterranean, emerging as a religion around 64 AD. The early Christians believed that man was not pure enough to enter the kingdom of heaven as flesh and blood, so all people were transformed into spiritual beings after death. Christians teach that a just and loving **God** would not have given humans life only for it to end after a short period of time on earth. Therefore, Christian doctrine teaches that the human soul is eternal.

**The Afterlife, Heaven, and Hell.** Traditional Christians believe in a spiritual world where the spirit goes and exists after death, because Jesus and the **New Testament** writers of the **Bible** mention notions of an afterlife and resurrection. In the book of Luke, Jesus tells the story of a poor man, named Lazarus, and a rich man, and the story shows people in this spiritual world, waiting in either comfort or torment for the resurrection. In II Corinthians 5:1, the apostle Paul says, "For we know that . . . when we die and leave these bodies . . . we will have wonderful new bodies in Heaven, homes that will be ours for evermore, made for us by God Himself, without human hands." And again in II Corinthians, Paul tells of an experience he had visiting heaven: "Fourteen years ago I was taken up to Heaven for a visit. Don't ask me whether my body was there or just my Spirit, for I don't know; only God can answer that . . . There I was in Paradise, and heard things so astounding that they are beyond man's power to describe or put into words."

In Christian beliefs, the unseen spiritual world consists of two realms, heaven and hell. In the modern era, the idea of heaven has changed slightly within the different sectors of Christianity. Christians still firmly believe in an afterlife or spiritual realm. However, some now reject the idea of hell, believing that hell only represents a place where the wicked are deprived of God. It is thought that existing apart from God is the ultimate punishment. This belief corresponds to some near-death accounts, which tell of a particularly bad person wondering or existing in darkness until he calls out for help or to God. In addition, heaven is now considered by some Christians to be a condition where the soul exists close to God. Christian fundamentalists, however, still believe heaven and hell are literal places. To them, heaven is still a place where the good go for their reward and eternal rest, and hell continues to be a place of punishment for one's sins.

In addition, Christian saints and mystics throughout history also spoke of spiritual experiences involving otherworldly and afterlife phenomena.

**Apparitions and Spiritual Beings.** The Bible speaks of apparitions of dead prophets. For example, in the story of Jesus' transfiguration, told in Matthew 17:1–3, the spirits of the **Old Testament** prophets Moses and Elijah appear: "And after six days Jesus taketh unto him Peter and James, and John his brother, and bringeth them up into a high mountain apart: And he was transfigured before them. And his face did shine as the sun: and his garments became white as snow. And behold there appeared to them Moses and Elijah talking with them."

In addition, Christianity has a great belief in unseen spirits such as angels, archangels and guardian angels, which are mentioned in the **Bible.** These marvelous beings go about unseen, guarding and protecting the unsuspecting. They are viewed as being pure and virtuous beings. It is thought that when people cross over to the other side, they will see angels there. The angels of Christianity are based on the angels found in the Christian Greek scriptures (New Testament) of the Bible, where they act as messengers and ministers of God. They announce the Last Judgment, separate the good from the wicked, give strength to the meek, and comfort the discouraged.

Christianity recognizes seven archangels, only four of whom are known by name. They include **Michael, Gabriel, Raphael,** and Uriel.

Angels in Christian beliefs are traditionally depicted as wearing long flowing robes and having huge wings.

They are usually depicted as being surrounded by an aureola or having a halo above their heads. They usually appear androgynous.

## Church of Jesus Christ of Latter-day Saints
See **Mormonism.**

## Cipher Test
A secret code set up by an individual before their passing. The code can be in the form of a message, symbols, or signs. It is intended to be used by the deceased person as a means of communication with loved ones or a friend still alive on earth to prove the deceased's survival after death.

## City of God
See **Augustine of Hippo.**

## City of Light
A city believed to be located in the spiritual world. It has been described in a number of near-death experiences, as well as spiritual visions and ancient scriptures. To this day it continues to be seen and written about by those that have journeyed

to the other side. It has been called by a variety of names, including the heavenly city, celestial city, and crystal city. This mysterious city is described as a crystal or glowing city in which everything, including the souls within, are made of light. In other accounts, it has been variously described as brilliant, crystalline, golden, and filled with beings of light. The city is said to radiate **God**'s love, as the light of the city is believed to be divine.

Inside, the city is said to be very much like the cities of earth, with buildings, places to socialize, work places, gardens, homes, and so on. However, the materials of which the buildings are made resemble gold, silver, marble, and other materials considered valuable on earth. Among the buildings are places of worship, crystal cathedrals, towers, an extensive library, a receiving station, an ice palace, a temple of wisdom, a temple of records, and specific buildings where aid is given to the newly arrived from the earth plane. The city's residents are busy going about their lives, but have been known to stop and aid a lost newcomer. This sparkling city is said to be the place for rest and the contemplation of one's soul journey.

Near-death experiencer and author **Dannion Brinkley** died and returned to life, recounting his experience in his best-selling book *Saved by the Light*. During his visit to the unseen spiritual world, Brinkley saw this beautiful city. He writes, "As wingless birds we shot into a city of cathedrals. These cathedrals were entirely made of a crystal-like substance that glowed with a bright light from within. I was awestruck. This place had a power that seemed to pulsate through the air. I knew that I was in a place of learning. I wasn't there to witness my life or to see what value it had had, I was there to be instructed."

In her book *Within Heaven's Gates*, author Rebecca Springer spoke of a mighty city that she had seen after her journey to heaven: "I caught my breath, then stopped abruptly and covered my face with my hands to shield my eyes from the glorified scene. I looked upon it as one but half awakened. Before us spread a lake as smooth as glass, but flooded with golden glory caught from the very heavens that made it look like a sea of molten gold. The blossom and fruit-bearing trees grew to its very border. Far, far away across its shining waters arose the domes and spires of what seemed to be a mighty city."

In the **Apocalypse of Zephaniah** (a book from the **Old Testament** Pseudepigrapha), Zephaniah visits the spiritual realm. He too witnesses a great spiritual city. He gives this description: "I went with the angel of the Lord, and I looked in front of me and I saw gates. Then when I approached them I discovered that they were bronze gates. The angel touched them and they opened before him. I entered with him and found its whole square like a beautiful city, and I walked in its midst."

## Clairalience

Another word for clairscent.

## Clairaudience

The ability to receive messages in auditory form from people in the unseen spiritual world. The psychic skill of clairaudience has been reported for more than three thousand years. Prophets such as Abraham, Moses, **Ezekiel**, Jeremiah, and **Muhamma**d all heard an unseen inner voice that guided them. In medieval times, there were several Catholic women who heard a voice from heaven instructing them to record the marvels they heard. After the Spanish Inquisition in 1492, a number of Jewish mystics settled in the northern Palestinian town of Safed. All heard *maggidem* (inner voices) and transcribed the lessons they learned about the Torah, the Kabbalah, and hidden mysteries of the Divine. Some well-known books on the subject of clairaudience by people that have experienced the phenomenon include Alice Bailey's *Tibetan,* Benjamin Crème's *Master,* **Ruth Montgomery**'s *Guides,* Mary Margaret Moore's *Bartholomew,* Pat Rodegast's *Emmanuel,* **Helen Schucman**'s *Voice,* David Spangler's *John,* Meredith Young's *Mentor,* J. Z. Knight's *Ramtha,* and Stevan Thayer's *Ariel.*

## Clairgustance
Another term for clairscent.

## Clairscent
The smelling of a scent from the unseen spiritual world. This phenomenon occurs as a result of a person on the other side attempting to communicate with a loved one in order to let them know they still exist after death. There have been reports of fragrances belonging to a deceased person lingering in the air, or the smell of a favorite flower of someone deceased mysteriously occurring. Clairscent, a term that literally means "clear smelling," can be defined also as the smell of something that is not in one's immediate surroundings. Other terms for clairscent are *clairalience* and *clairgustance.*

## Clairvoyance
The ability to see spiritual people, objects, and even animals that are on the other side. The term is also used for those with the ability to see past or future events, as well as present happenings elsewhere from a different location. The images are transmitted from the unseen spiritual world to the conscious mind.

## Clark Sharp, Kimberly

Co-founder of the Seattle-based International Association for Near-Death Studies (IANDS). Author of the extraordinary book *After the Light: What I Discovered on the Other Side of Life That Can Change Your World*. She was named as one of the forty most influential people in the Pacific Northwest for her work with death and dying.

## Clinical Death

The cessation of breathing and blood circulation. It occurs when the heart stops beating. Years ago, to most people there was not an in-between stage of life and death. There was no gray area as to whether someone was alive or dead. As a result, people were sometimes buried alive (as evidenced by scratches in coffins later opened) or awakened to find themselves in a morgue. Now, in the modern era, we are aware that there is a stage of death that can indeed be considered a gray area. Now, if a person is clinically dead, they can be revived with CPR. In fact, as medical resuscitation tech-

niques are being improved, more and more people are being brought back from clinical death. Many times, after a clinical death where the person has been resuscitated, a near-death experience has occurred. In near-death experiences, the person crosses over into the spiritual world and, after being revived in the physical realm, returns to tell of their experience on the other side. See **Near-Death Experience.**

## Clothing

Traditionally people in the afterlife, as well as angels, have been portrayed as wearing long white or light-colored robes. In her best-selling book *Embraced by the Light,* in which she relays her now-famous near-death experience, author **Betty J. Eadie** wrote of seeing "ancient-looking looms," on which material was spun to clothe the new arrivals coming in from the earth. Eadie says, when speaking of the cloth, "Its appearance was like a mixture of spun sugar. As I moved the cloth back and forth, it shimmered and sparkled, almost as though it were alive. The material was opaque on one side, but when I turned it over I was able to see through it." In her book *Between Life and Death*, **Dolores Cannon** interviews one of her subjects that is under hypnosis and regressed back to a memory of their life in the spirit world. She asks the individual how the people look and if they have clothes. The subject answers, "Here they wear robes, but not always. Whatever type of clothing they want to project as wearing, they'll do it as being part of the type of image they want to project at that particular time." Yet in another experience, the same person mentioned being dressed in a long white flowing gown, and its whiteness was different than that of any cloth she had seen before. She said there was a depth and iridescence to it, and she called it "alive white." Mystic and visionary Pére Lamy once wrote of the clothing of angels, "Their garments are white, but with an unearthly whiteness. I cannot describe it, because it cannot be compared to earthly whiteness; it is much softer to the eye."

## Coincidence(s)

In order to remain anonymous, yet assist still-living individuals, beings on the other side (e.g., our deceased loved ones, spirit guides, angels) sometimes manipulate circumstances so that the circumstances will appear as a coincidence. For example, they may arrange the meeting of two strangers: one that is in need of help, and the other who is able to give assistance. On occasions, spiritual beings come to the earth to give aid, taking on the appearance of a good samaritan who happens along at just the right moment. There have been a number of reports, given in angel books, of good Samaritans who have come to the aid of people and then mysteriously disappeared.

## Colburn, Nettie

A trance medium (1841–1892) that was famous for her connection to **Abraham Lincoln** and his wife **Mary Todd Lincoln**. Colburn conducted séances for Mary. President Lincoln sat in on at least two of those sessions. Colburn worked closely with her spirit guide, named Dr. Bamford, in the séances. Colburn was unexpectedly introduced to the Lincolns. Their initial meeting was arranged by a friend, Cranstoun Laurie, who was a high-ranking post office official who knew Mary. Colburn had gone with Laurie to his home after she had failed to receive an army furlough for her ailing brother. Laurie apparently did not provide her the details of the meeting in which she found herself. She was very surprised to be introduced to Mary, who was anxious to see Colburn's mediumship skills because she had heard so much about them. Upon witnessing Colburn in trance and making contact with the spiritual world, Mary arranged for Colburn and her brother to remain in Washington by obtaining a furlough for the brother.

Mary afterward informed her husband of Colburn's talents and, wanting to see them for himself, the president sat in on the next "circle." Colburn went into trance and someone spoke through her to the president, imploring him to move forward with the signing of the Emancipation Proclamation into law. After the séance was over, another person present asked Lincoln if he had noticed the way in which the address was given, meaning the tone and characteristics of the person speaking through Colburn. Lincoln apparently glanced towards a portrait on the wall, commenting, "Yes,

and it is very singular. Very!" The portrait was a full-length picture of Daniel Webster (1782–1852), a leading American statesman during the Antebellum period.

## Collective Apparition
An apparition that is seen by several people at the same time or seen in multiple locations at the same moment in time. Approximately one third of apparitions that are seen are collective apparitions. They are also referred to as collective vision. See also **Apparitions.**

## Collective Vision
See **Collective Apparition.**

## Comas
A profound state of unconsciousness. The affected individual is alive, but is not able to react or respond to life around him or her. A coma may occur as an expected progression or complication of an underlying illness, or as a result of an event such as head trauma. There are reports of people waking from a coma and recounting a classic near-death experience. Because of these experiences, some

believe that those in a coma state are actually out of the body and traveling within the astral world.

## Communicating Guide

An advanced, highly evolved spiritual being that guides and communicates information to people in a number of different ways. See **Guides.**

## Communication

See **After-Death Communication.**

## Communication with the Other Side

See **After-Death Communication; Greece; Medium(s).**

## Conductor of Souls

See **Escorts.**

## Consciousness, Continuation After Death

An alert cognitive state in which one is aware of oneself and his or her situation. Once the spiritual body has left the physical body and transitioned into the unseen spiritual world, it is believed by many that there is a continuation of consciousness.

## Contract

See **Soul Contract.**

## Control

An advanced spirit (also called a spirit guide) on the other side, who acts as a guide and guardian for a medium who is contacting those who have passed on. It is the job of the control to protect the medium from unwanted spirit entities and to prevent these entities from getting through to the physical world from the other side. This entity is also referred to as a protector.

## Cooke, Grace

Spirit medium and meditation teacher (1892–1978). Cooke channeled information from **Sir Arthur Conan Doyle** from the spiritual realm. Through Cooke, Conan Doyle dictated *The Book of the Beyond* and *The Return of Arthur Conan Doyle*.

## Corelli, Marie

Popular Victorian novelist (born Mary Mackay, 1855–1924). Her books have been hailed as imaginative, philosophical, and mystical. Through her writing, Corelli made it her life's mission to help cure the world of its social ills. In her mystical, spiritual, and metaphysical ideas, Corelli was ahead of her time. Her first book, titled *A Romance of Two Worlds*, is taken by some to be largely autobiographical. The story resembles an account of a near-death experience. The book itself included radical ideas not accepted in Corelli's day. In the story, the young heroine drinks a magical elixir that propels her into the spiritual world. The following passage is an excerpt:

*A dense darkness now grew thickly around me—I lost all power over my limbs—I felt myself being lifted up forcibly and rapidly, up, up, into some illimitable, terrible space of blackness and nothingness. I could not think, move, or cry out—I could only feel that I was rising, rising, steadily, swiftly, breathlessly. . . . A flashing opal brilliancy shot across the light in which I rested, and I beheld an Angel, grand, lofty, majestic. "I am thy guardian," it said. "I have been with thee always. I can never leave thee so long as thy soul seeks spiritual things."*

Other books by Corelli include *Thelma* (1887), *Wormwood* (1890), *Barabbas* (1893), *The Sorrows of Satan* (1895), *The Master Christian* (1900), *Temporal Power* (1902), *The Life Everlasting* (1911), and *The Secret Power* (1921).

## Council of Elders

Highly advanced emissaries of **God** that exist in the unseen world. They are essentially God's spokespeople. In the spiritual world the Council of Elders help individuals to adjust to their return to spirit. These beings aid in their spiritual growth, showing them which lessons they need to work on if and when the soul decides to return to earth. In addition, they help people decide how they are to progress further into the spirit realms. The Council of Elders is instrumental in the advancement of all souls entering life on earth and in the advancement of those individual's spiritual, eternal life.

A review with the Council of Elders is one of the last acts a soul performs before being sent into life on earth.

**Michael Newton** in his book *Journey of Souls*, says this explicitly: "One of the last requirements before embarkation for many souls is to go before the Council of Elders for the second time. The spirit world is an environment personified by order and the Elders want to reinforce the significance of a soul's goals for the next life. The Elders reinforce the significance of our goals for life. Once we were ready for entering the physical realm, we were like battle-hardened veterans girding ourselves for combat. This was our last chance for us to enjoy the omniscience of knowing just who we are before we adapt to a physical body."

World-famous medium **Sylvia Browne** also speaks of the Council of Elders in her book *Life on the Other Side: A Psychics Tour of the Afterlife:* "The Council, also known as the Elders or the Master Teachers, is its own phylum of eighteen highly advanced male and female beings who essentially act as God's spokespersons on The Other side. . . . The Council presides in a vast white marble room in the Hall of Justice, at a gleaming white marble U-shaped table."

## Counselors
See **Council of Elders.**

## Crisis Apparition
A phenomenon in which a person from the other world appears to a living loved one at a critical time. Examples of crises moments would include a life-threatening circumstance. The visit is normally made just before the crisis occurs.

## Crookall, Robert
One of the great pioneers in the clinical study of near-death experiences (1890–1981). Educated at Westminster College, London, and Briston University. Later, he joined the staff of the Geological Survey of Great Britain, specializing in coal-forming plants. He was awarded a doctorate in Science in 1930. But Crookall resigned from his geological work in 1952 in order to devote the rest of his life to psychological studies. Crookall was a member of the Churches' Fellowship for Psychical Study. The church was formed as an outlet for those who had psychic and spiritual experiences. It allowed individuals to tell what happened to

them and to examine their experiences in light of established church teachings on the afterlife. Crookall meticulously undertook a systematic study, complied from a wide variety of sources, including hundreds of communications from the spiritual world and personal testimonies of the experience of death and survival. He published his findings in his book, *The Supreme Adventure* (1961). Crookall found consistencies in communications from around the world. He also found consistencies in the accounts of near-death experiences, the evidence provided by high-level mediums, and accounts of those involved in out-of-body experiences.

Crookall theorized that the astral body (also known as the etheric body or the soul) is normally "enmeshed in" the physical body. As a result, most people are not even aware that it's there until they have a near-death experience or out-of-body experience, and in most cases not until they physically die. Crookall believed that the soul body consists of extremely subtle matter. He believed that during out-of-body and near-death experiences, this soul body separates from the physical body and becomes a temporary tool of consciousness. He described this soul body as "superphysical." Today, his work remains important in the field of psychical research.

## Crookes, Sir William

Highly distinguished English chemist and physicist (1832–1919). William Crookes was born on June 17, 1832, in London. He was educated at the Royal College of Chemistry and later developed into a prominent scientist, leading the world in the fields of chemistry and physics. His accomplishments include discovering the element thallium, inventing the radiometer, developing the Crookes tube, inventing the cathode-ray tube, pioneering research into radiation effects, and contributing to the fields of photography, wireless telegraphy, electricity, and spectroscopy.

As a man of science, Crookes believed it to be his responsibility to prove or disprove the claims of spiritualists and mediums claiming to be in contact with people in the unseen spiritual world. He began his research as a skeptic. He explained the reasons for his investigations, saying, "I consider it the duty of scientific men who have learnt exact modes of working to examine phenomena which attract the attention of the public, in order to confirm their genuineness or to explain, if possible, the delusions of the dishonest and to expose the tricks of deceivers." His first subject of study was the famous medium **Daniel Douglas Home.** However, it wasn't long before Crookes saw that Home's claims were legitimate. Crookes was meticulous about his experiments with Home and others. In one case Crookes purchased an accordion that he placed inside of a wire cage. Home simply put his hand on the cage, and the accordion began playing. Those who had been waiting for Crookes to expose mediums as tricksters and deceivers were stunned to find that Crookes had become a believer.

The experiments that really put Crookes on the record for providing proof of communication with those in spirit were those he did with medium Florence Cook. Through Florence's mediumship, a spirit who called itself **Katie King** would materialize. Over nearly three years, Crookes took forty-four photographs of Katie. However, when Crookes reported his work to the scientific community, he found a large amount of opposition. In an 1898 address to the British Association, he said, "Thirty years have passed since I published an account of experiments tending to show that outside our scientific knowledge there exists a Force exercised by intelligence differing from the ordinary intelligence common to mortals. I have nothing to retract. I adhere to my already published statements. Indeed, I might add much thereto." Crookes described his experiences in his books, entitled *Researches into the Phenomena of Spiritualism* (1874) and *The Spiritualist* (1873).

## Cross Correspondences

The receipt of interconnected messages from a person on the other side by several mediums at different locations. Once the various pieces of information are collected, only then can the entire message be deciphered. One of the most famous cases of cross correspondences involved **Frederic Myers,** who after his death contacted individual mediums at various loca-

tions. He gave them bits and pieces of information and told them where to take the communications. Once the communications were pieced together, the messages made sense. Through this process, Myers achieved his original goal in proving his existence after death.

## Cross References

Another term for **Cross Correspondences.**

## Crossing Over

A term denoting the transition from life in the physical world to life in the spiritual world. See **Death.**

## Crown Center

Located at the top of the head, this is the seventh chakra and the focal point for channeled information from a guide.

## Cummins, Geraldine Dorothy

Medium, automatic writer, and spiritual author (1890–1969). Cummins was born January 24, 1890, in Cork, Ireland. She was the daughter of Professor Ashley Cummins. She was best known for her work with automatic writing, which she recorded at great speed. During her automatic-writing career, she received channelings from a number of sources, including Cleophas, Phillip the Evangelist, and **Frederic Myers.**

Her first three books were interconnected and are extensions of the **New Testament** books the Acts of the Apostles and the Letters of Paul. Her first book, *The Scripts of Cleophas,* picks up after the death of **Jesus** and continues to the apostle Paul's leaving Berea for Athens. Her next channeled work was entitled *Paul in Athens.* This book is an extension of the first. Cummins's third book, *The Great Days of Ephesus,* is a continuation of the first two. These works were shown to be legitimate, as their composition was witnessed by prominent theologians and other authorities.

Cummins's fourth book was channeled from the esteemed Frederic Myers (a brilliant scholar, psychic investigator, and one of the founders of the Society for Psychical Research). The book, titled *The Road to Immortality,* looked into the development of the human soul. In *The Fate of Colonel Fawcett*, another amazing book of channeled communications, Cummins wrote from information channeled from Fawcett, who disappeared into the Brazilian jungle years before, as he searched for pieces of a the lost Atlantean civilization.

In 1951 Cummins's autobiography was published. It was appropriately titled *Unseen Adventure: An Autobiography Covering Thirty-four Years of Work in Psychical Research*. Other works by Cummins include *Swan on a Black Sea, A Study in Automatic Writing,* and *The Cummins-Willett Scripts.*

# D

## *Davis, Andrew Jackson*

Nineteenth-century clairvoyant and prophet (1826–1910). Davis was born on August 11, 1826, in Blooming Grove, New York. He is said to have been one of the most incredible predictors of the future. Davis believed that he was put on earth to assist people spiritually, and he made doing this his life's work. Not shy of metaphysical phenomena and events surrounding his life, Davis had a number of psychic abilities and talents that he used for the benefit of humankind. One of his main clairvoyant skills was being able to transcend normal consciousness and enter into a higher consciousness, which he referred to as a "superior state." Once in this higher state, Davis could access advanced information about the universe, humankind's future, and the future state of earth's sciences, including astronomy, physics, chemistry, medicine, and psychology.

Many of his scientific predictions have recently come true. In addition, entering this superior state allowed him to diagnose and prescribe treatments for individuals without having any prior information about them. Another of Davis's amazing talents was his ability to observe, at the death of an individual, the soul exiting the body and taking on the spiritual form. Davis was also capable of entering and exiting the unseen spiritual world at will. Because of this ability, he was able to relay information on life after death.

## *Death*

The process of liberation of the spirit from the material body. At the moment of physical death, the soul returns to the unseen spiritual world. This occurs when the silver cord (also known as the astral cord) breaks. The silver cord can be likened to an umbilical cord that connects the physical body to the spirit body. Once this cord is broken, it is impossible for the soul to return to the physical body. After death, the spirit preserves its individuality, personality, and characteristics. According to the numerous accounts of near-death experiences, there are certain elements of death that most people experience. There is first the leaving of the physical body. The person may either find themselves up high overlooking the body and the goings on surrounding it, or they may be standing alongside of it. They may see a brilliantly lit tunnel or find themselves traveling up and away from the earth.

If the soul is older and has had experience from many previous lives, then at the moment of death, it knows immediately that it has been set free and is going home. These advanced souls need no guide to greet them, because they remember the way to the other side. However, there are guides to meet most souls. A young soul or the soul of a child who has died may be a little disoriented until such a guide comes for them. At the end of the journey, they often find relatives, a being of light, or a religious figure that they recognize, and this guide helps them with the crossing over.

In near-death accounts, the soul is sent back, often under protest because of the pure love it found on the other side. Many souls do not want to return to physical life.

Those not returning find themselves in a place with people that are very much like themselves in temperament, energy, and vibration. The state of mind a person is in during the time of death may require the soul to take a rest to become rejuvenated. Souls dwell in the spiritual world according to their level of spirituality. The more advanced a soul is spiritually, the higher and more beautiful the realm it will ascend to. Death is an interchange station between the two worlds. After our physical death, we continue on to different realms of existence.

## Deathbed Apparition

Another name for a deathbed vision.

## Deathbed Conversions

The adoption of a religion or faith just before death. People make deathbed conversions for a number of reasons. The primary reasons are to be forgiven by **God,** and or to be able to go to heaven or paradise and participate in the benefits therein.

According to **Silver Birch,** the great spiritual teacher from the other side, there are no deathbed conversions. Birch, who is considered to be very credible and whose communications from the unseen spiritual world have been a source of study for years, commented on deathbed conversions in a book titled *Silver Birch Companion,* saying:

*We are concerned with deeds, with actions and with the life that every individual lives. We teach the supreme law of cause and effect, that none thwarts the Great Power, that none cheats the law, that man is his own savior and his own redeemer, that man pays the penalty for every wrong doing, and that man reaps the reward for every kindness that he performs. We say that the laws of the Great Power are mechanical, automatic in their action that kindness, tolerance, sympathy, service automatically make you the better because you have practiced them, and that selfishness, wrong-doing and intolerance automatically make you worse. You cannot alter the inflexible law. There is no cheap reprieve; there are no easy pardons. Divine justice rules the whole universe. A spiritual dwarf cannot pretend to be a spiritual giant. There are no death-bed conversions.*

## Deathbed Vision(s) (DVBs)

A dying person's awareness of the presence of dead relatives or friends. For thousands of years, many individuals have received personal proof of after-death survival by observing their fellow humans at the moment of death. Deathbed visions are said to be powerful, yet comforting, experiences for persons that are close to death. These visions have been found to be similar across nationalities, religions, and cultures throughout history. Common characteristics of a deathbed vision include brilliant lights, scenes of great beauty, angels or beings of light, and a sense of calmness and peace. Many deathbed visions involve seeing loved ones that have already crossed over into the spiritual world; these loved ones can appear to a living person moments, hours, days, and even weeks before their death. Deathbed visions are sometimes referred to as departing visions.

Deathbed visions often lessen the fear of dying for the individual, making the impending death easier and often more comfortable for all involved. Deathbed visions were widely reported in the nineteenth century. During that period, most people died at home, near their loved ones. Often, those close to death spoke of other-worldly scenes and deceased relatives visiting them.

In the early 1900s **Sir William Barrett,** a professor of Physics at the Royal College of Science in Dublin, published a small book on deathbed visions. He was one of the first people to examine this subject. His book, titled *Death Bed Visions,* summarized his findings. He noted that as people were close to death, they sometimes saw other worlds and saw and spoke to relatives and friends that had previously passed on. There were reports of music playing, and in some cases attendants witnessed the spirit leaving the body at death.

## Deathbed Visitation
Another name for a deathbed vision.

## Death Premonition
A forewarning of a death for oneself or someone else. Death premonitions have been known to come in the forms of a vision, a dream, or a feeling. Death premonitions occur from people in all walks of life. One of the most famous is that of President **Abraham Lincoln.** Lincoln had a dream foretelling his death and funeral. He told both his wife and his bodyguard about it just hours before his assassination. Nostradamus also prophesied his own death and was even able to give the date when his tomb would be opened. In ancient history, the wife of Julius Caesar, Calpurnia, dreamed the night before he was killed that he would be stabbed by someone he was familiar with. Death premonitions can be found today in our popular culture as well. For example, in ABC's series *Lost,* the character Desmond Hume foresees the death of another character, Charlie Pace. In the movie *Premonition*, Sandra Bullock's character, Linda Hanson, has dreams of her husband's death, only to see it played out before her eyes as she tries to save him.

## Defending Your Life
A 1991 film about a man named Daniel who had everything—a great job, good friends, and a brand-new BMW—that is, until he wrecks his car, killing himself. He wakes up in the af-

terlife in a place called Judgment City. He soon realizes that he is there to be judged. In Judgment City, the newly dead have five days to defend the way they lived their lives in order to be able to move forward instead of incarnating back on earth in yet another life. While reviewing his less-than-assertive life, he meets Julia, the woman of his dreams. If he can't prove that his life wasn't controlled by fear, Daniel will have to go back to earth, while it is clear that Julia will move forward. In the meantime, Daniel enjoys the perks of the city, such as eating all the food he can without gaining weight. The film, written, directed, and starring Albert Brooks, also stars Meryl Streep, Rip Torn, and Lee Grant. Shirley MacLaine makes a cameo appearance as herself, acting as the holographic host of the "Past Lives Pavilion"—a reference to her own personal belief in reincarnation. The movie was filmed in and around Los Angeles, California.

## Dead Again

A 1991 thriller film directed by Kenneth Branagh and starring Branagh and his then-wife Emma Thompson. Andy Garcia, Derek Jacobi, and Robin Williams are also featured. The film explores the themes of reincarnation, destiny, and justice through parallel narratives of a society murder in the Hollywood of the 1940s and a modern-day search for the identity of a woman with amnesia. Thompson and Branagh play the key roles in both stories.

## Deeds

The works done by a person while in physical life. One's works or acts on the earth plane are believed to affect one's life after the person has crossed over into the unseen spiritual world. This is the law of karma, the belief that eventually one's deeds will come back upon him or her either in this life, the next, or the afterlife. In the afterlife, bad deeds or works can affect which level or realm one returns to after death. If someone has performed very bad deeds in this life, on the other side they will find themselves with others who have also done bad deeds. And in the next life, a person may have what they sowed in the previous incarnation returned to them.

In addition, people receive a life review immediately upon entering the afterlife. It is a review of one's entire physical life. It shows the good deeds and the bad. According to many people that have crossed over and had a life review in a near-death experience, every thought, action, word, and deed we had or did while we are alive on earth is recorded and kept. Therefore, everyone is held accountable for their actions.

### Demiurge, The

The creator of the universe in ancient Gnostic beliefs. The same term can be found in ancient Judaic lore, which also names the demiurge as creator of the universe. **Plato** said the demiurge was the deity who fashions the material world. According to lore, the demiurge, or maker-god, created the world in the shape of a revolving sphere. This sphere, made of soul matter, was fashioned from the harmonious fusion of the four elements: earth, water, fire, and air. After the creation of the world, the remnants of soul matter were made into human souls.

### Dennis, Lynnclaire

Author of the book *The Pattern*. Dennis had a near-death experience in 1987 while hot-air ballooning in the Swiss Alps. She recounts the information that was given to her during her time in spirit. In The Pattern she tells both the process and the implications of the geometrical marvel called a mandala from both a scientific view and a metaphysical perspective.

### Departing Vision

See **Deathbed visions.**

### Descartes, Rene

French philosopher sometimes referred to as the father of modern philosophy (1596–1650). Descartes supported the belief in life after death. In his work *Discourse on Method,* he writes, "Next to the error of those who deny **God** . . . there is none which is more effectual in leading feeble minds from the straight path of virtue than to imagine that . . . after this life we have nothing to fear or to hope for, any more than the flies or the ants."

### Devachan

An after-death state of being in Theosophical beliefs. It is a temporary place where the soul exists between incarnations. It is said to be similar to and sometimes mistaken for heaven. In Devachan people are blissful, surrounded by friends and loved ones in a perfect environment. It is the place where most people that have lived good lives go. There, unfulfilled goals can be accomplished. However, it is not the end of one's spiritual journey. It is a stopover before entering yet another incarnation for one's spiritual growth.

## Deva(s)

The word *deva* means "shining one." Devas seem to have two roles in ancient legend and present metaphysical thought. Devas are generally considered to be a type of nature spirit and are said to carry the blueprints of nature. In Buddhist beliefs, they are higher spiritual beings believed to be invisible to humans, with superior skills and powers. In ancient Persia and India, the Devas were considered gods.

## Devil, The

In Christian beliefs, the devil, also known as Satan, is **God**'s adversary. The word *devil* comes from the

Greek word *diabolos,* which means "slanderer." Some believe that the word *devil* is derived from the Indo-European *devi* ("goddess"). It is also said to come from the Persian *daeva*, which means "evil spirit." Some facets of **Christianity** believe that the devil is behind all of the wickedness in the world. It was the devil, according to Judeo-Christian lore, who caused the fall of man, severing man's 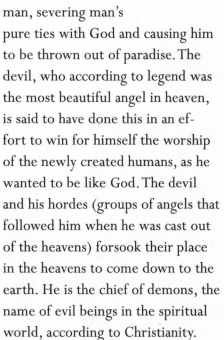 pure ties with God and causing him to be thrown out of paradise. The devil, who according to legend was the most beautiful angel in heaven, is said to have done this in an effort to win for himself the worship of the newly created humans, as he wanted to be like God. The devil and his hordes (groups of angels that followed him when he was cast out of the heavens) forsook their place in the heavens to come down to the earth. He is the chief of demons, the name of evil beings in the spiritual world, according to Christianity.

# D

## Dharmata
See **Tibetan Book of the Dead.**

## Dilum
The name of the afterlife in ancient Mesopotamian beliefs. It means "place of sunrise." It reflects humankind's earliest known belief in life after death and an unseen spiritual world. The name *Dilum* can be found in the *Epic of Gilgamesh,* a narrative poem from ancient Mesopotamia, written approximately 2500 BC. To believers, Dilum was a vast, bountiful, paradise garden that only the good were able to ascend to and partake of.

## Dimension(s)
A level of existence. Within the unseen spiritual world, there are many dimensions. Terms denoting the word *dimension* are realm and plane. The dimension to which a soul travels after death consists of two separate areas. The first is said to be beautiful, resembling Earth. It is this area that most people travel to after death. It is a place of rest, contemplation, and enlightenment. The second place has been likened to a dark empty space. It has been described as a deep dark void. Those that have lived selfish, unloving lives are believed to exist there in loneliness and confusion. According to some beliefs, the life one lives on Earth determines which of these areas one's soul will exist in after death. According to some individuals that have traveled to this dimension in their out-of-body experiences, the area we will exist in after death will depend upon the amount of love and service we gave to others while on Earth.

Dimensions higher than this are said to be for the more advanced souls. From these dimensions, humankind receives inspiration, guidance, and knowledge for spiritual growth on Earth. In addition, great spiritual teachers may descend to Earth from these realms to benefit the people of Earth. The higher dimensions remain a mystery to humankind as those that have professed to having out-of-body experiences are not permitted into those realms. It is thought that eventually, everyone will progress into the higher dimensions, though it may take eons. See also **Afterlife.**

## Direct-voice Communication (also Direct-voice Phenomena or DVP)

The term for when someone in the unseen spiritual world speaks in the physical in his or her own voice (not through the voice of a medium or by other channels). The voice may come in a whisper or normal volume. The deceased are generally heard in the voice from their last incarnation on earth. Although these cases are said to be rare, there are individuals who have heard the voice of a loved one that has crossed-over call out to them without any medium involvement. Other terms for direct-voice communication are *direct-voice phenomena* and *direct-voice mediumship*.

## Direct-voice Medium(s)

See **Direct-voice Communication; Medium(s).**

## Direct-voice Phenomena

See **Direct-voice Communication.**

## Direct Writing

A way in which those from the unseen spiritual world can communicate with those in the physical world. Direct writing involves the appearance of writing on a surface. The writing may appear gradually, letter by letter, or suddenly as a complete word or sentence. This form of communication from the unseen world reaches very far back in history and can even be found in the **Bible.** In the **Old Testament** book of Daniel (5:5), it says, "At that moment the fingers of a man's hand came forth and were writing in front of the lamp stand upon the plaster of the wall of the palace of the king."

## Disabilities

The term *disability* refers to any condition that impedes the completion of daily tasks using traditional methods. In the unseen spiritual world, there are no disabilities, sickness, blindness, or any other maladies. Once a person returns to the spiritual plane, any physical disability or ailment they previously experienced during their life on earth disappears. One thing mediums often say about those living on the other side is that the deceased can now "breathe" or "see," or that the deceased are no longer "ill." There have been cases where the deceased individual had been bed-ridden or blind in their physical life, and they made it a point to tell their still-living loved ones that on the other side, that is no longer the case. See **Prebirth.**

## Discarnate
Lacking physical form. A spirit or ghost, for example, is referred to as 'a discarnate entity.'

## Discarnate Materialization
Another name for an apparition.

## Disembodied Spirit
A spirit without a material body. A term used when referring to a ghost.

## Divination
The original purpose and definition of *divination* is to learn the will of the gods or to portend the future. It was used heavily in mankind's ancient history, by kings and noblemen. To the same extent, divination is used today by everyday people simply wanting to know their future. People also use divination as a means of communicating with higher beings, such as angels, spirit guides, and in some cases, people that have crossed over from this life to the next.

## Dominations
See **Angels.**

## Double
The word *double*, as associated with the unseen spiritual world, has two meanings: (1) the etheric counterpart of the physical body; (2) a soul viewing the physical body it has just vacated.

## Dougherty, Ned
Author of *Fast Lane to Heaven: A Life After Death Journey*. In his book, Dougherty relays his experience of nearly dying at the age of thirty-seven and having a near-death experience. At the time, Dougherty had been living the high life. He owned the popular Club Marakesh, located in the Hamptons, and a second nightclub in West Palm Beach, where he lived a decadent lifestyle

complete with limos and celebrities. His life changed drastically in 1984 after he collapsed, triggering a near-death experience. During his experience, Dougherty felt that he was floating and suspended in a dark bottomless pit. While still suspended, he witnessed his life review. Afterward, he traveled to a second realm where he saw loved ones that had previously passed on. This realm exuded the light of **God**. He also encountered a lady in the light who spoke to him about earth's future. And he was given prophetic information that included details about the September 11, 2001, terrorist attacks on New York City and Washington, D.C. After returning to the physical realm, he was able to bring back prophetic information. Today, drawing from his initial experience with the afterlife, Dougherty continues to give revelations about future events.

## Doyle, Sir Arthur Conan

Scottish novelist, short-story writer and psychic researcher, best known for his stories about the detective Sherlock Holmes (1859–1930). A zealous spiritualist, Sir Arthur Doyle was able to make contact with people from the afterlife. His research led him to write *The History of Spiritualism* (two volumes). In addition, he wrote *The Wandering of a Spiritualist*. In his novel *The Land of Mist* (1926), a spiritualist rescue circle, guided by the medium John Terbane and a long-dead Chinese philosopher named Mr. Chang, helps the newly dead find their way in the land beyond the grave. Amazingly, after his death, Doyle dictated through medium **Grace Cooke** *The Book of the Beyond* and *The Return of Arthur Conan Doyle*.

## Dragonfly

A 2002 movie starring Kevin Costner and Susanna Thompson; directed by Tom Shadyac. Movie tagline: "When someone you love dies . . . are they gone forever?" Doctor Joe Darrow (Kevin Costner), a respected expert in trauma and triage, suddenly finds himself alone after his wife, Doctor Emily Darrow (Susanna Thompson), is killed in an accident while on a medial mercy mission in a remote area of Venezuela. Through the near-death experiences of his patients, Joe soon realizes that his late wife is trying to reach him from the other side.

## Dream Incubation

A method by which a person acquires information from a spirit via a dream. It is believed that by sleeping in a specific location that has some spiritual significance to the spirit or subject at hand, a person can, in a dream, obtain the information sought.

## Dream Vision

Messages from the spiritual world are often communicated to a person while they are sleeping. The messages often come when the person is falling asleep or just waking up, a relaxed state when people are more receptive to communications from those in the spiritual world. Often, after a someone has crossed over, they will appear to their loved ones in a dream either to reassure the loved one that they survived death and are well on the other side, or to bring a message from the other side (such as information about a murder or some unfinished business). Usually, the person who has the dream is certain that the contact was made and is able to rest easier in their grief and worry over the individual. The dreams are often experienced as real events, as if the person were there with the deceased. See also **After-Death Communication.**

## Druids

Priests in Celtic society. The Druids were religious leaders, educators, judges, doctors, and astronomers. They believed in a purified and elevated earth that was the dwelling place of the gods and the souls of the dead. They taught the doctrine of transmigration of souls (the rebirth of a soul into a new body after death) and discussed the nature and power of the gods. They believed that only a thin, invisible barrier separated the spiritual dimension from the physical dimension and therefore, it was thought that the living could speak with the dead. They also believed that it was possible, through the mediation of a god, for living humans to be invited into the Otherworld.

## Drythelm
See **Bede.**

## DuBois, Allison
World-renowned medium and profiler (1972–). She is the author of the *New York Times* bestsellers *Don't Kiss them Good-Bye* and *We Are Their Heaven: Why the Dead Never Leave Us.* The popular television series *Medium* is based on her life. Born in Phoenix, Arizona, DuBois was aware of her psychic abilities as early as the tender age of six. In 1990, she graduated from Corona del Sol High School in Tempe. During college, she worked as an intern at the district attorney's office in Phoenix. She received a BA in political science with a minor in history from Arizona State University. DuBois uses her psychic abilities to aid law enforcement agencies across the United States solve crimes. In addition, she also works as a jury consultant and has helped put a number of murderers on death row.

"the life we begin with a scream
we end with a whisper"
—Bucky Sinister, "The House that Punk Built,"
*All Blacked Out & Nowhere to Go*

# E

## Eadie, Betty J.

Author of the *New York Times* best-selling book *Embraced by the Light* (1942–). Eadie was born in Nebraska to a Native American mother (Sioux) and a Scottish-Irish father. During her early years, she lived on the Rosebud Indian Reservation in South Dakota. In November of 1973, at the age of thirty-one, Eadie, a mother of eight, died following surgery. Next, Eadie journeyed to the unseen spiritual world, where she met **Jesus**. There she was given a message to share with others when she returned to the physical world. In *Embraced by the Light*, Eadie shares this message and chronicles her near-death experience, which has been hailed as one of "the most profound and detailed near-death experience ever recorded." By sharing her message of **God**'s love and the wonder of what she saw and experienced in the spiritual world, Eadie helps others to overcome their fear of death. Eadie is also the author of *The Awakening Heart* and *The Ripple Effect*. Her website, *Embraced by the Light: The Official Bettie J. Eadie Website,* can be found at *www.embracedbythelight.com*.

## Earth

The third outward planet from the sun. It is the largest of the solar system's terrestrial planets, formed around 4.57 billion years ago. All souls are said to have helped in the creation of the universe and of earth. According to some psychics and near-death experiencers, earth is a replica of the unseen spiritual world. This is because everything in the universe was first created in spirit and then recreated in the physical. The geography of the two worlds is said to be similar except for the seismology factor and the shifts of the land bodies on the earth. (**Betty J. Eadie** has addressed this idea of earth being a replica of the spiritual world in her book *Embraced by the Light*, as has medium and author **Sylvia Browne** in her books.) Not only was the earth modeled after the spiritual world, but also the theories, philosophies, and discoveries of humans often originate in the spiritual world.

On the other side, the earth is viewed as a kind of school where souls go to learn and to grow spiritually. The earth exists in a dimension where free will is practiced. Because of this, souls from the spirit world come to earth to learn important lessons of love, thus bringing themselves closer to **God.**

In the spiritual world, earth is considered a "dark planet." People in spirit are said to grieve when someone incarnates to the earth plane because they know how difficult their life on earth will be. The person traveling from the spirit world leaves a world of perfection and beauty to come to a world of war and pain. However, it is believed that incarnating to the earth is necessary for a soul's spiritual growth and its long journey back to God, where it will once again become one with the creator. The next shift for planet earth and the surrounding universe is into the fifth dimension: the dimension of unconditional love and total oneness with All That Is.

## Earthbound

See **Earthbound Realm; Earthbound Spirits.**

## Earthbound Realm

A name for an area located in the spiritual dimension between the earth realm and the higher realms. It is a dark realm where those that have crossed over and are still connected to the earth because of an addiction, strong obsession, or something negative dwell. How long a soul will remain there is up to the individual, because they must find a way to disconnect themselves from the attachment that keeps them connected to the physical. Some have likened this realm to hell.

## Earthbound Soul

Another name for an earthbound spirit. See also **Ghosts.**

## Earthbound Spirit(s)

A term used for those who have died, but not left the vicinity of the physical plane. These individuals are often tied to the earth for a reason and do not move into the spiritual world. The reasons can vary. For example, some, it is believed, do not realize they are dead, which sometimes cause them to impose themselves on those still dwelling in the material world. Often, the result of this imposition is a haunting. Others remain because they find it difficult to leave their grieving family. Some are connected to the materialism of this world, and some are attached to addictions. Others want to try and get a message to their loved ones or stay to right a wrong (such as identifying their own murderer). They can dwell on the earth plane for a short time or for many years, even decades, before either realizing they are dead or moving on fully into the spiritual world. All spirits, it is said, eventually make their way to the other side. Another term for an earthbound spirit is *earthbound soul.*

## Ectoplasm
A white material that has been known to emanate from certain trance mediums while they are communicating with the spiritual world. It has also been known to show up in areas where an earthbound spirit dwells and is attempting to make contact.

## Edison, Thomas Alva
American inventor and businessman, hailed as one of the greatest inventors who ever lived (1847–1931). He pat-

ented the light bulb, the phonograph, the motion-picture projector, and many more devices. One invention that Edison was working on just before his death was a machine that would allow people to communicate with those in the spiritual world. A believer in life after death, Edison wrote an article in *Scientific American* (1921) that said:

*If our personality survives, then it is strictly logical or scientific to assume that it retains memory, intellect, other faculties and knowledge that we acquire on this Earth. Therefore, if personality exists after what we call death, it is reasonable to conclude that those who leave the Earth would like to communicate with those they have left here. I am inclined to believe that our personality hereafter will be able to affect matter. If this reasoning be correct, then, if we can evolve an instrument so delicate as to be affected by our personality as it survives in the next life, such an instrument, when made available, ought to record something.*

Edison is thought to have been working on a prototype for this machine right up until he passed in 1931. The whereabouts of the plans or prototype for this machine are unknown.

## Edward, John

American medium, author, and lecturer (1969–). Edwards has helped thousands of people communicate with loved ones that have crossed over. He has written several books on the subject, including *After Life: Answers from the Other Side; Crossing Over: The Stories Behind the Stories; Final Beginnings;* and *One Last Time: A Psychic Medium Speaks to Those We Have Loved and Lost.* In addition to his books, Edward has also used television to bring closure to grieving people that have lost loved ones to death. His show, titled *Crossing Over with John Edward,* premiered July 10, 2000, and ran to May 1, 2004. Edward is known for his easygoing nature and the accuracy of his readings. He has been credited with convincing people around the world that there is indeed a life after death.

## Egypt (Ancient)

A civilization located in eastern North Africa. Ancient Egypt began around 3050 BC, when the first pharaoh, Menes, united the kingdoms of Lower Egypt and Upper Egypt. The ancient Egyptians strongly believed in a spiritual world. In fact, it was their hope to extend life beyond the grave and into an afterlife. The afterlife was expected to be an idealized version of their earthly lives. This idea steamed from the knowledge that in the afterlife one was free of the limitations of the physical body.

The Egyptians were concerned with three main aspects of life after death: the ka, the ba, and the akh. The ka was considered to be a duplicate of one's self—not a part of the personality, but a separate part of the self. The ba was loosely considered the soul of a person, and it was sometimes represented in art as a bird. The akh was the principal aspect of the soul of a human being or of a god. Nearly all of the ancient Egyptians' funerary customs were dedicated to one purpose: ensuring that the ba and ka were reunited with one another on the other side.

Much of Egyptian belief in the afterlife centered on the pharaoh, who represented the gods. Proper entombment of the pharaoh would secure his followers a position in a pleasurable afterlife. The shape of the pyramids was an image of the cosmic mountain or the heavenly ladder by which the pharaoh ascended to the sky after death. Inscribed on the walls within the pyramids were instructions, incantations, and prayers whose aim was to guide the pharaoh into the company of the sun or to identify him with **Osiris,** the dying-and-rising god who became the lord of the dead.

The ancient Egyptians buried the **Egyptian Book of the Dead** with the deceased. The book contained precise directions on appropriate behavior after death—so much so that the book was recited to the body while it was being prepared for entombment. It was thought that if the soul of the person failed to follow these instructions, then a union with Osiris (god of the underworld) would be unattainable. The corpse went through a complex mummification procedure to ensure that the soul would have a resting place once it crossed over into the spiritual world. In addition, many bodies were entombed with personal items that the deceased had treasured in life, so that the person could have them in the next life.

A part of the transition into the afterlife, and what was said to be the final step in crossing over, was the judgment in the Hall of Maat (the god of justice) by Horus (the god of the sky) and Thoth (scribe of the dead). The ceremony, called the Weighing of the Heart, was performed by comparing the *ab* (the conscience) and a feather. Only those whose hearts were lighter than a feather would make it to the next life; those whose hearts were weighted down with their bad acts were devoured by the god Ammut. A creature with a crocodile head, who was called the Devourer of Souls, swallowed heavy hearts. The souls of the good were led to the Happy Fields, also known as the **Fields of Reeds** and Field of Peace, where they joined Osiris. Many spells and rituals were created to ensure the soul received a judgment of approval in the spiritual world. These spells and rituals were recorded in the **Egyptian Book of the Dead.** This way, once on the other side, a soul could enjoy a life much better than it had on earth.

**Near-Death Experiences.** In ancient Egypt, if one wanted to become a part of certain mystical cults, he or she was required to have a near-death experience in order to become a member. Bringing the initiate close to death often brought on near-death experiences. By having this experience, the person would know what to expect when it was their time to die. It is believed that these induced near-death experiences are what prompted and formed the information found in the Egyptian Book of the Dead. See also Egyptian Book of the Dead.

## Egyptian Book of the Dead
A collection of ancient funeral texts of the ancient Egyptians. The texts are meant to help the soul when, at death, it crosses over into the unseen spiritual world. The book contains

prayers, spells, and hymns to be used by the soul for guidance on its journey to the next life. A copy of the text was usually buried with the deceased. The original name of the text was *The Book of Coming Forth By Day.* The name *Book of the Dead* was given to the writings by Karl Richard Lepsius, an German Egyptologist who published a section of the text in 1842. The book gives guidelines about what souls can expect after death and the journey through the afterlife, as well as how to maneuver around the hurdles that might prevent their transitioning and reaching the **Field of Reeds,** which was their primary objective in the afterlife.

## Elect
*Elect* is a Christian term that refers to **God**'s choice of people who will go to heaven—or in some Christian terminology, "will be saved." In other words, the elect are those called by God to salvation. These elect are selected not by their actions (e.g., morality, charity, kindness), but simply because God chooses them. This selection is be-

lieved to have occurred before the creation of the world, making the elect predestined to go to heaven. This view of election was especially held by Calvinists who believed that the elect could be identified by their wealth, indicating God's favor and blessings toward them. According to Mormon doctrine, the elect of God are those men and women who have demonstrated great faithfulness to the teachings of **Jesus**. Mormons believe that they will be elevated to godhood in the afterlife. Jehovah's Witnesses teach that there are 144,000 individuals chosen (or elected) by God to go to heaven.

## Electronic Manipulation

See **After-Death Communication; Electronic Voice Phenomena (EVP).**

## Electronic Voice Phenomena (EVP)

The recording of voices of those that have passed on and exist in the spiritual realm. See **American Association of Electronic Voice Phenomena (AA-EVP); Estep, Sarah;** and **Jürgenson, Friedrich.**

## Elder

A highly evolved and extremely wise entity. *Elder* is also a term used when referring to members of the **Council of Elders.**

## Elemental(s)

A type of nature spirit. An elemental is a spiritual being that is attuned with one of the four earth elements: air, earth, fire, and water. They are the spiritual essence of that element. Elementals are living beings that are similar in appearance to humans, but dwell in a different realm. They have never existed in a physical incarnation, although they have the ability to manifest a physical body. They are thought to be made of an etheric substance that is distinctive to their specific element. They are also referred to as nature spirits.

## Elk, Black

A famous *wichasha wakan* ("medicine man" or "holy man") of the Oglala Lakota, or Sioux (1863–1950). Born to a medicine man who followed Crazy Horse, Black Elk witnessed the Battle of Little Bighorn in 1876. In *Black Elk Speaks*, he describes his childhood and early adult life and the spiritual life of the Sioux. He also speaks of an experience of visiting the spiritual world. His experience is considered to be one of the best-known modern records of a visionary journey to the spiritual world. At the tender age of nine, he had his first visionary experience. It came to him when he was struck down by an unexplained paralysis. While he lay apparently dead, he was called out of his body by two thunder beings, who escorted him to a tipi in the clouds. There the six grandfathers, as the great powers of the sky, the earth, and the four quarters were known, gave Black Elk the talents of healing and spiritual insight. After this experience, Black Elk could no longer live the life of a normal child. He returned from his near-death experience changed, with newfound powers and a special mission in the world. Black Elk is also said to have had several visions in which he met the spirit that guides the universe.

## Elysian Fields
See **Elysium.**

## Elysium
A paradise in the underworld in Greek mythology. It was the final resting place of those souls that lived righteous, virtuous, and heroic lives while still on earth. Also called the **Elysian Fields** or **Field of Reeds.**

## "Emanations"
Title of an episode from the *Star Trek Voyager* television series. First aired in March 1995, it dealt with the afterlife beliefs of an alien race called the Vhnori. While investigating an uncharted asteroid inside an asteroid belt containing a new element, Commander Chakotay, Ensign Harry Kim, and B'Elanna Torres stumble upon the burial ground of the Vhnori. After Chakotay and B'Elanna are beamed aboard *Voyager,* Kim is pulled into a "subspace vacuole" and switched with a dead body. He finds himself on an alien world, the same one from which the bodies in the burial ground originated, and the body, which is now on *Voyager,* is revived. The crew learns from the person whose body mistakenly ended up on *Voyager* that the asteroid belt is where an alien society transports its dead in the belief

that they evolve into a higher state of consciousness after death. Kim's appearance on the Vhnori home world begins to raise questions, doubt, and uncertainty about what really happens after a person dies. Some even begin to examine the validly of believing in an afterlife.

## Embodied Spirit

Another name for an incarnate spirit.

## Enlightenment

A higher state of consciousness in which a person becomes aware of their connection with **God** and realizes that they are a part of the Divine, a part of God.

## Endor, Witch of

The witch of Endor is a medium found in the **Bible.** In the first book of Samuel, the witch of Endor used a talisman to call up the spirit of the dead prophet Samuel for Israel's King Saul.

## Energy Body

Another name for the astral body or etheric body. This spiritual body carries the nonphysical human principles.

## Enoch

A biblical character who was the seventh descendent of Adam and Eve. He was the son of Jared and father of Methuselah. In Islamic beliefs he is called Idris and considered a prophet. He is characterized in the **Bible** as being a righteous man who was devoted to **God.** Some biblical translations refer to him as a "man who walked with God." Because of this devotion and unique relationship with God, tradition holds that he never experienced dying. The Bible (Genesis 5:22–24) states that when Enoch was 365 years old, God "took him." (During the time of Enoch, 365 years was considered a short lifespan. His son Methuselah lived to be 969.) It is thought that God took Enoch because he was too good of a person to continue to dwell on the earth and that not experiencing actual death was Enoch's reward. Legend holds that upon his arrival in heaven, God transformed him into a glorious spiritual being. The apocryphal **Books of Enoch** record Enoch's travels in the spiritual realm.

## Entity

Another term for beings. Entities can be found within the physical worlds, as well as the spiritual realms.

## Escorts

Spiritual beings that assist souls at death as they cross over to the next life. They are also known as greeters. It is their job to provide safe passage to the afterlife realms. The idea of otherworldly beings (often gods or angels) escorting the souls of the dead is not uncommon. In fact, the belief in after-death escorts into the spiritual world can be found in many spiritual, religious, and mythological beliefs. The **Bible**'s book of Luke (16:22) speaks of angels carrying the soul of a dead man to heaven. In Greek mythology, the god Hermes was the escort for the dead, helping them find their way to the underworld (the afterlife realm according to Greek mythology). In Zoroastrianism, Mithras conducted the souls of the righteous to paradise. According to Aztec and Toltec beliefs, Xolotl (god of the underworld) helped those that had died to reach Mictlan (the afterlife). During the Middle Ages, the archangel **Michael** was considered to be the conductor of souls. Other names for escorts are *celestial escorts, conductors of souls,* and *psychopomps.*

## Estep, Sarah

Pioneer in the research of electronic voice phenomena (EVP) in the United States, and the author of *Voices of Eternity* (an introduction to EVP) and *Roads to Eternity* (1925–2008). The subject of life after death had fascinated Estep from a young age. During that time, she enjoyed reading material centering on the paranormal. She was very much interested in discovering whether or not a person was completely gone at the death of the physical body or if they lived on somehow. It was while reading a book entitled *Handbook of PSI Discoveries* that she first became fascinated with electronic voice phenomena. In 1976 Estep began experimenting with an analog recorder, in an attempt to communicate with those residing in the spiritual world. She followed the suggestions laid out in the book, which included asking questions. A week passed with no answers from the other side, and Estep decided to change her questions. She asked, "Please tell me what your world is like?" and received a one-word answer: "beauty." After that, she was hooked and continued to research the subject of electronic voice phenomena. Today, her collection of EVP recordings is said to be around 20,000, and the voices come from different dimensions and from people that have crossed over.

In 1982, Estep founded the **American Association of Electronic Voice Phenomena (AA-EVP)** and was its director for eighteen years. Her reason for creating this organization was, in her words, to "provide objective evidence that we survive death in an individual conscious state." To record messages, Estep generally used an audiotape recorder and external sound source. She also had success recording in the field with a regular hand-held cassette recorder. Her ability to acquire spirit voices on tape gave extremely important evidence of the existence of the afterlife. See also **Jürgenson, Friedrich.**

## Extract from Captain Stormfield's Visit to Heaven

A satire on the afterlife, written by American humorist, satirist, lecturer, and writer Mark Twain. The story was inspired by a dream of an acquaintance of Twain's, named Captain Edgar Wakeman. Twain had met Wakeman on a trip aboard a steamship *America* traveling from San Francisco to New York. In *Extract from Captain Stormfield's Visit to Heaven,* Twain merges science fiction with a satiric look at conventional views of the spiritual world. It is an amusing story, where the main character, who died thirty years prior, whizzes around outer space at "a million miles a minute." He notices "a tremendous long row of blinking lights away on the horizon ahead." These are heaven's entryways. Stormfield enters heaven, and his wacky escapades commence. The story draws sharp contrasts between Stormfield's notions of what heaven is like and the truth of what really happens when one crosses over. One of the interesting realities Stormfield faces is one that has been described by certain modern-day mediums: the spiritual world does not just hold the souls of human's crossing over, but also the souls of beings from other worlds as well. Another lesson Stormfield learns is that earth is not the main planet of heaven's sights. After thirty years of traveling in the afterlife, Stormfield finds he can no longer even locate earth on a map.

## Extraterrestrials

A sentient soul who is not originally from earth. According to Swedish mystic **Emanuel Swedenborg,** in his phenomenal book *Life on Other Planets*, "Spirits of the deceased from every inhabited planet congregate around that planet and serve the sentient beings that live there." Swedenborg said that the spiritual world is made up of more than just the spirits of people that have crossed over from it, but it also includes the spirits of human beings from other worlds as well. In addition, there are some near-death experiencers, such

as a number of **Raymond Moody**'s subjects, who have returned to earth to report that while in the spiritual world, they had become aware of souls from different worlds.

## Ezekiel

A major prophet of the **Bible**'s **Old Testament.** During the exile of the Jews in Babylon, **God** used Ezekiel, whose name means "God strengthens," to bring comfort and hope to the people. His biblical book includes many references to the spiritual world and out-of-body experiences. For example, Ezekiel 3:12 says, "Then the spirit lifted me up, and I heard behind me the noise of the Lord rumbling as the Glory of the Lord rose from its place." It appears that Ezekiel's soul is leaving his physical body and is hearing the vibratory rushing sound that is so often reported by out-of-body and near-death experiencers.

## Facilitated Apparition

A vision of a person in the spiritual world seen psychically through items such as mirrors, cauldrons, water, ink, or fire.

## Fairies

See **Nature Spirit(s).** See also **Deva(s); Elemental(s).**

## Feeling a Presence

The feeling that one is not alone. Many people report feeling that a loved one that has passed on is present or around them, although the loved one cannot be seen, heard, or felt physically. See **After-Death Communication.**

## Fenimore, Angie

Near-death experiencer and author. Her book *Beyond the Darkness: My Near-Death Journey to the Edge of Hell and Back* offers a rare look of a near-death experience during a suicide attempt. The book details Fenimore's experience of committing suicide, journeying to the spiritual world, and what happens after she arrives there. In her experience, Fenimore showed that her suicide did not free her from her troubles, nor did she find herself in the light, but instead in a place of darkness and desolation. Fenimore was later brought back to life and returned to recount her experience and assist others in learning about life after death and the spiritual world.

## Fenwick, Peter

Neuropsychiatrist and a fellow of the Royal College of Psychiatrists (1935–). Fenwick is a highly regarded expert and researcher on the subject of near-death experiences, having examined over three hundred experiences. Fenwick has co-authored three popular books with his wife, Elizabeth, including *The Truth in the Light: An Investigation of Over 300 Near-Death Experiences; Past Lives: An Investigation into Reincarnation Memories;* and *The Hidden Door: Understanding and Controlling Dreams.*

## Ferryman of the Dead
See **Greece** and **Charon.**

## Field of Reeds
Another name for **Elysium** or the **Elysian Fields.**

## Fifth Dimension
A higher plane of existence. The fifth dimension is a place where there is complete love and harmony with the Divine. It is the plane where most people go when they leave physical life on earth. (Other areas that people gravitate to when they pass on are lower overtones of the fourth dimension or an in-between area to consider their spiritual life and the possibility of incarnating once more.) It is said that the next shift for earth and our universe will be into the fifth dimension. See also **Dimensions.**

## Findlay, Arthur
A great psychic historian and afterlife researcher (1883–1964). Major works include *The Curse of Ignorance (Volume 1* and *Volume 2)* and *The Psychic Steam.* Finlay started out as a stockbroker and agnostic. He became convinced there was a spiritual world after sitting at one of direct-voice medium **John Sloan**'s séances and hearing the voice of his father, who was deceased, and a family friend, who relayed information to him not known to any other living person. He became a regular sitter at Sloan's séances and worked closely with Sloan to conduct experiments. He published his findings in two books, *An Investigation of Psychic Phenomena,* which contained a preface by **Sir William Barrett** (one of the founders of the American and British Society for Psychical Research) and *On the Edge of the Etheric.* In this second, larger volume, Findlay graded his cases A1 and A2 according to the quality of the evidence they presented. In examining three of the 180 A1 communications, Findlay said, "An eminent mathematician, on calculating the chances of correctly guessing all the facts recorded, answers that to have reached such accuracy represented the equivalent of 1 to 5,000,000,000,000. In other words, the odds were 5,000,000,000,000 to 1 against chance being the explanation."

**The Arthur Findlay College.** In 1964, Findlay gave his home, Stansted Hall, built in 1871 and located in

Essex, England, to the Spiritualists' National Union to become a college for studies involving psychic science. There, in a supportive atmosphere, students are able to study the psychic sciences, including such topics as spiritualist philosophy, practice, healing, and more. Students from all over the world have attended this phenomenal place of learning to improve and enhance their spiritual skills. You can contact the college at *www.arthurfindlaycollege.org*.

## Flight 401
See **Ghosts of Flight 401.**

## Flint, Leslie
A highly respected and gifted direct-voice medium (1911-1994). In his autobiography, *Voices in the Dark*, Flint speaks of his rare gift known as the independent direct voice. With this skill, Flint could hear voices, originating from a voice box on the other side of the ectoplasm, in the air around him. He described the voices of the dead as speaking directly to their friends or relatives from a space located "a little above" his head and "slightly to one side" of himself. Flint relayed that the voices are objective and that sitters could record them on their own tape recorders to play later in private. Flint gave sittings in hotels, homes of strangers, churches, and theaters—all with the same successful result.

**Recordings.** There are over 120 recordings of those from the spiritual world speaking during the Flint's sessions. To hear some of Flint's voice sessions on the Internet, go to *The Leslie Flint Educational Trust* website at *www.leslieflint.com* or the website *Paranormal Voices* at *www.xs4all .nl/~wichm/death_ra.html*.

## Forces of Darkness
Entities in the spiritual world that choose dark conduct over that of love and light. Their focus is to disseminate negativity and thus prevent others from growing spiritually and becoming enlightened.

## Forces of Light
Entities in the spiritual world that choose light and love over dark conduct. The forces of light work on the side of the Divine to assist others in spiritual growth and spreading the light of the Divine into the universe.

F

## Ford, Arthur Augustus

American trance medium who was also clairaudient (1896–1971). He was the founder of the International General Assembly of Spiritualists. Ford was born in 1896, in Titusville, Florida. As a youth, he was a truth seeker, which led him to various denominations of **Christianity.** It was not until World War I, while serving in the army, that Ford realized he was clairaudient. He would hear voices saying the names of people he had worked with—people who later turned out to be deceased. This realization prompted him later to seek information on psychic phenomena. Afterward, he began his association with spiritualists and established himself as a trance medium. His control, named Fletcher, first introduced himself to Ford in 1924 while Ford was in trance. It was Ford, along with Fletcher, who broke the Houdini code (a secret code that **Harry Houdini,** along with his wife, Beatrice, had conceived to prove life after death). This discovery brought Ford attention. Ford suffered a setback in 1931 after he and his sister were in a car accident in which his sister died. Ford himself was severely injured and relied on alcohol and morphine to ease his pain, eventually becoming addicted to both. For the next twenty years he struggled to gain control of himself and fight this addiction. However, Ford continued his psychic work during this period. On January 4, 1971, Ford died. From the spiritual world, he made contact with his friend, psychic **Ruth Montgomery.** Montgomery published the information that she received from Ford in her book *A World Beyond.*

## Fortunate Isles

The spiritual world and afterlife of Pythagoras, Cicero, and **Plato.** In Greek mythology and Celtic folklore, it was the idyllic place where preferential people and heroes were greeted by the gods and where all of their dreams were fulfilled. It was also known as the **Isles of the Blessed,** Islands of the Blest, and the White Isle. The islands were believed to be located in the western ocean near the encircling River Oceanus. The Madeira islands, the Canary Islands, and Cape Verde have been thought to be these islands. In order to travel there safely, moving against dark forces along the way, souls must purge themselves of all that's left within them of their association with life on earth and overcome the dark forces, which attempt to destroy them. One means of conquering these negative energies, it was thought, was to perform special sacred ceremonies while still in physical life.

## Fortune, Dion

British medium and author (born Violet Mary Firth, 1890–1946). She was also founder of the Society of Inner Light (a mystery school within the Western esoteric tradition). Fortune was a powerful psychic and a key persona in twentieth-century esoteric thought. She began her life as Violet Mary Firth, born in the village of Bryn-y-Bia, in Llandudno, Wales, on December 6, 1890. Her father worked as a solicitor, and her mother was a Christian Science healer. In fact, Christian Science was rigorously practiced in her home. As a young girl, Fortune displayed strong psychic and mediumship abilities. She reportedly had visions of Atlantis as early as four years of age and believed herself to have been a temple priestess in a previous incarnation.

As an adult, Fortune took up a strong interest in the occult. She also became a member of the Theosophical Society. In addition, she undertook lessons in psychology and psychoanalysis at the University of London, and she became a lay psychotherapist at the Medico-Psychological Clinic in Brunswick Square. She was a believer of Christian mysticism, pantheism, and magic, and was associated with the hermetic Order of the Golden Dawn and the Fraternity of the Inner Light.

In her channelings, Fortune received information from an intelligence that she said was located in a higher plane of existence. She insisted that she was not contacting those that had passed on. She was very sensitive to disturbing people that had crossed over and vehemently did not wish to bother them. In fact, on the subject of the afterlife, Fortune made her own contribution in writing with her book *Dion*

*Fortune's Book of the Dead* (originally published as *Through the Gates of Death* in 1930), a metaphysical guide to understanding the changes that come with the death of the physical body. It explains how to assist an individual on their after-death odyssey and how to avoid impeding the soul's progress after death. It also discusses why it is inappropriate to try and contact the dead (under most conditions).

An incredibly prolific writer, Fortune's list of esoteric and metaphysical books also include *Psychic Self-Defense, The Mystical Qabalah, The Training and Work of an Initiate, The Sea Priestess, Moon Magic, Cosmic Doctrine, Applied Magic, Glastonbury: Avalon of the

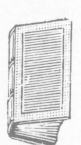

Heart, The Esoteric Philosophy of Love and Marriage, The Goat Foot God, Esoteric Orders and Their Work, Aspects of Occultism, The Winged Bull, The Demon Lover, Sane Occultism, Dion Fortune's The Secrets of Dr. Taverner, Spiritualism and Occultism,* and *The Light of Occult Science.*

## Fox, Oliver

British astral travel pioneer and author (1885–1949). Because he began experiencing out-of-body episodes from an early age, Fox experimented to find a way to gain control over his astral projection ability. He succeeded and wrote an enlightening book on the subject, entitled *Astral Projection: A Record of Out-of-the-Body Experiences* (1939), which details how to have astral experiences.

## Fox Sisters
See **Spiritualism.**

## Free Will
The ability to choose a course of action or make a decision without being subject to restraints. It is said that the greatest gift of **God** to humans is free will, which allows humans to move through their spiritual evolution at their own pace. Free will also applies to their life in the spiritual world as well as their physical incarnations. It is believed that, while in the spiritual realm, human souls use their free will to choose their parents and other forthcoming life circumstances; thus, human lives

on earth follow a plan. Metaphysicians believe that once humans are born into this lifetime, they must stick with that plan, so free will then becomes limited as the soul lives out the path it charted for itself.

Italian humanist philosopher Pico Della Mirandola spoke on the subject of free will, saying, "God placed man in the middle of the world without a secure place, without a distinctive identity, without a special function, while all these things were granted to the rest of his creatures. Man is created neither earthly nor heavenly; he can degenerate into a beast, he can ascend to heaven; everything depends solely and entirely on his will. It is granted to man to possess what he wished, to be what he wants." In **Christianity,** the concept of free will explains the existence of evil: God did not create evil, but gave his human creations free will so that they could freely choose whether to follow him or not; those that choose to turn away from him bring those things that are evil—things not of God—into the world.

**Free Will and Other Beings.** Humans, however, are not the only beings in God's creation who are believed to have free will. The angels dwelling in the spiritual realm are also thought to have this free choice of action. Origen of Alexandria maintained that God created a number of spiritual beings that were equal and free. Some, through their free will, chose to leave their positions in the spiritual world and slowly drifted away from God; some drifted so far away that they became dark spirits. In the metaphysical arena, it is believed that some spirits living in the spiritual world chose through free will to come to the earth to perfect their souls.

## French, Emily S.

American direct-voice medium from Buffalo, New York (1830–1912). Famous for her medium work, as well as for her integrity, French was said to have never charged money for her services. She had a Native American spirit control by the name of Red Jacket. Many experiments and investigations were conducted to prove that her mediumship skills were not fraudulent. She voluntarily helped with "rescue circles," in which earthbound spirits were assisted in crossing over.

"All we can touch, swallow, or say
aids in our crossing to God
and helps unveil the
soul."
—Saint Theresa of Ávila, "I Loved What I Could Love"

# G

## Gabriel

A great archangel in the spiritual world. Gabriel, whose name means **"God** is my strength,"** is one of the two highest-ranking angels in **Judaism, Christianity,** and **Islam.** He is best known for bringing important announcements to humankind. He is first encountered in the **Bible's Old Testament,** when he appears to the prophet Daniel (8:16) to explain a vision. He later appears to Daniel a second time to announce the coming of the Messiah. In the **New Testament** he announces the birth of John the Baptist to John's father Zechariah (Luke 1:11–22), and the birth of **Jesus** to his mother Mary (Luke 1:26–33). During the Middle Ages, Christians believed him to be the angel of light. In Islam the translation of the name *Gabriel* is *Jibril.* It was Jibril who revealed the **Koran** to **Muhammad**. For this reason, Jibril is also referred to as *Faithful Spirit, Faithful Servant,* and the *Bringer of Good News.* He is also the guardian angel of Muhammad. In Essene beliefs he was the angel of life. In ancient Judaic lore, Gabriel was thought to be female—the only female to be listed in the archangel class. Variations of the name *Gabriel* are *Gavriel* and *Gabriella.*

## Gan Eden

A term from ancient Jewish tradition, meaning "paradise," "Garden of Eden," and "World to Come." It comes from the descriptions of the afterlife found in the Talmud (a collection of traditional oral Jewish tales and teachings). It was believed that all souls would ascend above Gan Eden and become one with **God,** who existed in the highest plane.

## Gandhi, Mahatma

Indian nationalist leader, who, appalled by the treatment of Indians, established his country's freedom through a nonviolent revolution (1869–1948). Even though Gandhi grew up Hindu and lived his life according to those beliefs, he remained open minded about other religions, believing that they all lead to the truth of **God.** He said, "I consider myself a Hindu, Christian, Muslim, Jew, Buddhist, and Confucian." He believed that Truth is God and so in seeking to know Truth, humans seek to know God. He felt that all people were brothers and sisters because all came from the same God and each individual carries God within them. Gandhi looked forward to life after death, where he would exist in a spiritual world. He once said, "What I have been striving and pining to achieve these thirty years is to see God face to face."

## Garrett, Eileen Jeanette Vancho Lyttle

Renowned trance medium, author, publisher, entrepreneur, and one of the most important people of the parapsychological world (1892–1970). She made considerable contributions to the investigation and understanding of mediumship and related phenomena. A natural sensitive (she was very much aware of people's emotions and feelings), Garrett was considered one of the most respected trance mediums of the twentieth century.

Born in 1892, in Beauparc, County Meath, Ireland, as Emily Jane Savage (later she became known variously as Jane Savage and Jean Lyttle or Little in her writing), Garrett recognized at a very early age that she was different. As a child she had spiritual playmates, which she called "the children." In addition to people, she would see animals and various energy light forms, which she called "surrounds." Later (between 1924 and 1928), Garrett's psychic talents were further developed by James Hewat McKenzie, the founder of the British College of Psychic Science.

As a medium, Garrett was superb. One of the most amazing mediumship experiences, and one that also brought her international attention, happened when she received a message from Flight Lieutenant H. Carmichael Irwin, the deceased captain of the dirigible *R101* (an airship developed for commercial use by the British), which went down in Beauvais, France, on October 5, 1930, killing forty-eight of its fifty-four passengers. During a séance at the National Laboratory of Psychical Research, where Garrett had been trying to contact spiritualist

**Sir Arthur Conan Doyle** (author of *Sherlock Holmes)*, Irwin unexpectedly—and before the news of the airship's crash was made public—relayed the frightening details of what happened leading up to the crash and what ensued just moments before the airship went down. His description of what happened consisted of a large amount of mechanical information, which was later confirmed by an official investigation.

Garrett was also a psychic researcher. She recognized the need for scientific, unbiased studies of psychic phenomena. For this, she enlisted the aid of scientists and psychic investigators. In 1931, Garrett received an invitation from the American Society for Psychical Research to visit the United States. She worked with Duke University, under the direction of prominent psychologist William McDougall and Joseph Banks Rhine (founder of the parapsychology lab at Duke University). In her paranormal research work, Garrett also worked with other well-known investigators of the paranormal, including Nandor Fodor (psychoanalyst and psychical researcher) and Hereward Carrington (British psychical investigator). Garret also experimented with telepathy, extrasensory perception (ESP), and other related areas.

It was Garrett's utmost desire to educate others about her experiences with the spiritual world through her writing and lecturing. In the 1940s, Garrett began a monthly magazine titled *Tomorrow*. It was hailed as one of the most intelligent periodicals on paranormal subjects during that period. She also started two publishing companies, Creative Age Press and Helix Press. Her greatest achievement, however, was the founding of the Parapsychology Foundation in 1951, in New York. The foundation published the *International Journal of Parapsychology* and held its first global symposium at the University of Utrecht, Holland, on July 29, 1953. Today the Parapsychology Foundation is one of the most highly regarded organizations of its kind. It continues to turn out enlightening information in its periodicals and reports.

Garrett authored a number of books, including *Telepathy: In Search of a Lost Faculty; Awareness: Ancient Answers to the Secret of Personal Fulfillment; The Sense and Nonsense of Prophecy; Life Is the Healer; Many Voices;* and *My Life as a Search for the Meaning of Mediumship.*

In the preface of her autobiography, *Adventures in the Supernormal*, she writes: "I have a gift, a capacity—a delusion, if you will—which is called 'psychic.' I do not care what it may be called, for living with and utilizing this psychic capacity long ago inured me to a variety of epithets—ranging from expressions almost of reverence, through doubt and pity, to open vituperation. In short, I have been called many things, from a charlatan to a miracle woman. I am, at least, neither of these." Garrett passed into the spiritual world on September 15, 1970. She was buried in Marseilles, France.

## Genetic Recall

A term for memories that are passed down within a person's genes. The genes hold the accounts of one's ancestors and of past-life experiences.

## Ghost(s)

A person that has passed on but chooses to stay in the physical world even though he or she is in spirit form. In her book *Proud Spirit,* famed medium **Rosemary Altea** says, "The term ghost is used to describe the apparition of a dead person or animal." Ghosts are real, and they do share space with us in this life, although they are in a different realm of existence.

They are usually the spirits of people who have become trapped in our dimension, hovering somewhere between the earth realm and the afterlife. Often these spirits are earthbound, held here by their own desires or because they haven't yet accepted that they are physically deceased. Some remain here for many years before fully accepting their fate and crossing over into the spiritual world. Often, spiritual beings, such as guides and angels, are sent from the other side to talk the person over. Therefore, it is believed that eventually all ghosts will go home to the spiritual world.

Ghosts have been seen by every culture in the world and reported since the beginning of human history. Ghosts, whether malevolent, benevolent, or simply sad, appear in the legends and folktales of many cultures. The word *ghost* is derived from the German word *geist,* which means "spirit," or the Old English word *gast,* which means "soul" or "spirit."

Manifestations of a person that has crossed over into the spiritual world often occur when the death of the person is recent and the spirit is still close to the physical world (usually within the first three months of their transition). Ghosts have also been known to manifest years later, during a time of crisis or just before a tragedy or death. They may appear when a still-living loved one is in great need. The sighting and length of appearances vary, and the recipients of such unexpected visits are usually upset by them.

Ghosts, when manifested, can be seen in a variety of ways. They may appear in their most recent human form, sometimes fully materialized, sometimes in a semitransparent state. They have also been seen as silvery, shadowy, or

fog-like. Those that do not materialize use other phenomena, such as moving an object or manipulating electronic media, to be noticed. Earthbound ghosts show themselves more often and appear in a semitransparent state, sort of half in and half out of the physical, although they have been known to also appear solid. It seems that the longer the person has been deceased, the more transparent their spiritual form is. Spirits of people that have crossed over successfully usually go about undetected in our world unless they choose to make themselves known.

In the West, ghosts are often perceived as restless spirits. Restless ghosts are believed to have unfinished business in the physical plane. For example, they may be seeking justice or revenge after being the victim of a murder or violent death, or they may have not completed their will or may have an inheritance concern. In some cases, loved ones cannot locate a will or estate papers, or the person passed without conveying the secret location of an important document. There may be many other reasons why a person may linger on the physical plane. For instance, criminals are believed to sometimes linger on the earth plane to avoid punishment on the other side.

In many Asian cultures, most of the populace believes in reincarnation. They believe that ghosts are people in the spiritual world that have not reincarnated due to some unfinished work or business they still have in the physical plane. People in both the East and the West believe that ghosts wander about places that they knew and were familiar with when alive and, in some cases, places where they died.

## Ghost

A 1990 movie starring Patrick Swayze as Sam Wheat, Demi Moore as Molly Jensen, Whoopi Goldberg as Oda Mae Brown, and Tony Goldwyn as Carl Bruner. It was written by Bruce Joel Rubin and directed by Jerry Zucker. *Ghost* is part romantic comedy, part fantasy with an afterlife theme. It is a story of two lovers whose lives are turned upside down when one is killed by a rival. Finding himself in the spiritual world, unable to be seen or heard by the living, Sam stumbles upon a medium (Oda Mae) that is able to hear him. With her assistance, he communicates with

his beloved (Molly) and is able to resolve his murder. The end of the story shows Sam moving into the spiritual world. The movie itself has several underlying spiritual themes, including life after death, the spiritual world, and of course, ghosts.

## Ghost and Mrs. Muir, The (Movie)

*The Ghost and Mrs. Muir* was a 1945 novel by R. A. Dick. In 1947, a movie was made based on the book. It starred Gene Tierney as Mrs. Muir and Rex Harrison as the ghost. From 1968 to 1970, there was a television series (a situation comedy) produced based on the film. In that version of the story, Hope Lange played Mrs. Muir and Edward Mulhare played the ghost.

The movie centers on a cottage on the seaside of England, around 1900. A young widow and her daughter move into the cottage to find it haunted by the former owner, Daniel Gregg, who was once a sea captain. The captain appears only to Mrs. Muir. When Mrs. Muir runs into financial problems, Gregg attempts to assist her in saving the cottage by dictating his memoirs. The book is published and becomes a bestseller. Mrs. Muir and her daughter and maid are able to continue living in the house. During this period, the ghost and Mrs. Muir fall in love. Knowing that they cannot exist in two different worlds and be together, the captain encourages her to find a live man and disappears from her life. While she is sleep, he convinces Mrs. Muir that her experience with him was all a dream.

Later, daughter Anna returns to the cottage and informs her mother that she, as a child, had spoken with Captain Gregg, triggering her mother's memories. Mrs. Muir lives out her life at the cottage and eventually dies. At the moment of death, the sea captain shows himself to her and reaches out to her. Her spirit is lifted from her body, and the two of them walk together happily into the spiritual world.

## Ghost Dad

A 1990 movie comedy starring Bill Cosby as a workaholic father who is never home. His life changes when he is picked up in a taxi and the driver runs off the bridge, causing Cosby's death and his transition to a ghost. He is then at the mercy of his children, who help with darkening his office, so he can be seen. As time goes on, Cosby's character grows closer to his children even though he is in spirit form.

## Ghost Dance

A ritual spiritual dance that originated among the Paiute Native Americans in Nevada around 1888. Its founder was a young Native American named Wovoka (1856–1932), who was a Paiute mystic and medicine man. In 1888 Wovoka (also known as Jack Wilson) contracted a dangerous fever. At that same time, there was a solar eclipse. Wovoka, during his fever, had an out-of-body experience in which he visited the spiritual world and met **God.** On the other side, he received a divine vision. In the vision, Wovoka saw the resurrection of the Paiute dead. He witnessed the removal of the white race, and all they had done, from North America. As a result of that vision, many Native Americans believed that they would again take their rightful place in the world and one day be reunited with their departed loved ones. He believed that in order for this vision to become a reality, Native Americans must live honorable lives and perform a traditional round dance, known as the Ghost Dance. Wovoka supplied them with the necessary songs and dances to perform the dance ceremony. Other Native American tribes also embraced this revelation and the dance. The Ghost Dance, also known as the Spirit Dance, consisted of men and women together, holding hands, moving slowly around in a circle—all the while facing the center. The songs and dances were performed without any musical instruments.

## Ghost Whisperer

American television drama series. *Ghost Whisperer* premiered on CBS on September 23, 2005. It was created by writer-director-producer John Gray. The show stars Jennifer Love Hewitt as Melinda Gordon, a gifted psychic who has the ability to communicate with people that have died, but are earthbound and in need of her help. Melinda assists them by relaying important information and messages to those still alive on the earth plane. She is often met with skepticism by the friends and relatives of the deceased individual. However, when she is able to help both sides, those that have passed on and those still alive on earth, she recognizes that her ability is truly a gift and not a liability.

## Ghosts of Flight 401

A book by American investigative writer John G. Fuller. In the book, Fuller documents one of the most amazing and true ghost stories ever told. On December 29, 1972, an Eastern Airlines TriStar jetliner, flight 401, crashed into a Florida swamp, killing 101 people. Among the crash victims were the pilot, Captain Bob Loft, and the engineer, Don Repo. Following the tragedy, crews of Eastern Airlines' other TriStars, dubbed the Whisperliners by the airline, began to report seeing the ghosts of Loft and Repo on board their aircraft. They were seen on other airliners from which pieces from the downed jetliner were used. In total, there were twenty sightings of the two men, who took it upon themselves from the spiritual world to make certain this tragedy did not repeat itself.

## Gimli

Heaven or paradise in Norse mythology. Legend has it that Odin, the chief divinity and creator god, existed before time. He is said to have created the heavens and the earth and all the creatures to mirror his glory. The creation of the earth and humans was his definitive work. He created humans with an eternal soul that could reside with him forever. As a result, at death, the good go to reside forever with Odin in his glorious paradise, called Gimli. There they find lush meadows, as well as banquet and ballrooms where great celebrations are held. The unfavored souls, due to their wicked acts on earth, were destined to spend eternity being tormented in the palace of **Hel**.

## Gnomes

A type of elemental (or nature spirit) representing earth. According to legend, gnomes dwell in forests. They manifest in the form of elderly dwarfs. They are the guardians and healers of the animals of the forests and protectors of earth's treasures. They are also called trolls.

## Gnosticism

A movement in Greek philosophy that stresses the secret knowledge of **God** as an escape from the material world. Gnosticism also emphasizes a return to the spiritual world by the souls of individuals through a process of mystical knowledge (gnosis) and a belief in reincarnation.

Gnosticism thrived during the second and third centuries AD. The word is taken from the Greek *gnosis,* meaning "revealed knowledge." The word *Gnosticism* is a general term for any number of philosophies and religions that existed during the time immediately before and after the birth of Christ. It was a system of belief blending ideas taken from Greek philosophy, astrology, reincarnation, Oriental mysticism, and **Christianity,** and it emphasized salvation through gnosis. Gnostics believed in two gods: one who created the spiritual world (the **Logos),** the other who created the world of matter (the **Demiurge).**

Gnostics placed special emphasis upon a contrast between the material and spiritual realms. They believed in a spiritual world, which was good, and a material world that was evil. Gnostics believed that flickers of God fell from the spiritual world into the material world and were captured in the bodies of humans. The flickers from God that dwell within humans were said to have been sent by God to save humankind. These flickers imparted a mysterious knowledge of the divine realm and God. By being reawakened by this knowledge, this godly aspect of humankind could go back to its rightful position within the spiritual realm.

According to Gnostic lore, from the original mysterious God, lesser gods were produced. The last of these was Sophia. Sophia longed for the forbidden, which was to be knowledgeable about God, who was mysterious and unknowable. From her longing, the Demiurge, an evil entity, was formed and is said to have fashioned the cosmos and the world within.

In Gnostic beliefs there are a number of other spiritual entities. The highest beings are called **Aeons** and Archons. The Aeons are superior angels said to be the first beings created by **God.** The **Archons** stand guard over the nations of the material world. The Pistis-Sophia is the mother of the Aeons, and the Schechinah is the queen of angels.

The Gnostics believed that God gave the angels free will. He recognized that if they were to exercise their free will, he would have to remove himself, so that they could pursue their own destinies. He then decided to withdraw, leaving the angels on their own.

## God

The divine source of all there is, known by many titles, including Supreme Being, Creator, and Ruler of the Universe. In general terms, God is a being envisioned as the perfect, omnipotent, omniscient creator of the universe and the primary object of worship in religious practices, particularly in monotheistic beliefs. Some religions believe God is one, others that God is dual, and still others that God is a trinity. Some believe that God is positioned high above in the spiritual world, looking down on planet earth and its inhabitants. Others assert that God is everywhere.

It has been said by many who have had near-death experiences that God's presence is felt everywhere in the spiritual world. The spiritual realms are made of different dimensions with different vibrational energy. God, who is made up of pure energy, is believed to exist in the highest dimension, or realm. Few if any, it is believed, actually see God. This is because few can raise their energies enough in this life to make it to the highest realm. It takes much love, a light vibrational energy, and a strong belief to actually see God.

In addition, whether or not one sees God or any of the archetypes (e.g., **Jesus, Muhammad,** the archangels) is said to depend on one's spiritual and afterlife beliefs. In general, most people, when entering the spiritual world after death, are met by their loved ones and friends that have crossed over previously. However, the higher one's vibration, the more light they carry in their soul, the higher they will go in the spiritual realms. The higher one ascends, the more chance there is of seeing God.

In early Christian beliefs, the joy of seeing God face to face, once one has ascended to the upper realms, is called the beatific vision. *The Catholic Encyclopedia* defines the beatific vision this way: "The immediate knowledge of God which the angelic spirits and the souls of the just enjoy in Heaven." Although **Christianity** does not teach the idea of ascending to the highest dimension, it does teach that upon one's death one sees God. In some religious beliefs, reaching the point where a person can actually see God is a time when the soul is united (and in some beliefs reunited) with God. This belief is held by many faiths, including Judaism, **Christianity, Islam,** and some Asian religions. Christians believe that in the afterlife, seeing and being with God is the reward for living out lives on earth. Some facets of Christianity believe that all righteous souls will dwell with God in heaven after their death. In some metaphysical thinking, souls resided with God before incarnating on earth and will return to dwell with God after completing their journey, eventually graduating, so to speak, to the highest realm, returning to God.

**Visions of God.** According to some of the world's great religions, there have been prophets who have literally seen God in a vision, an out-of-body experience, or in some cases, during a journey to heaven. In most cases, these circumstances are simply referred to as visions of God. In Judeo-Christian beliefs, **Ezekiel** was granted a vision of the throne of God. He says that when witnessing the likeness of God, "I fell upon my face." The prophet Isaiah, again from Judeo-Christian beliefs, saw God enthroned in his temple, attended by the seraphim (the highest order of angels), who were singing, "Holy, holy, holy." Stephen, whose martyrdom is recorded in the **New Testament,** had a vision of God moments before he died (Acts 7:55–56). The apostle John also had a vision of God, as well as an out-of-body experience. He witnessed God on the heavenly throne, surrounded by angels and elders (Revelation 4:1–6). The prophet Muhammad of Islam witnessed the overwhelming brilliance of God. Muhammad's vision of God is described in the **Koran** as "something too stupendous for the tongue to tell of or the imagination to picture."

**Throne of God.** According to ancient Judaic lore, the throne of God is where God sits while the court of heaven convenes. There, as God is seated upon the throne, the deeds of men are weighed, and judgment is served. The seven archangels stand at the throne of God. There are twenty-four elders who also stand near God's throne. The angels called seraphim, cherubim, and thrones encircle the throne of God. When the court convenes to judge the deeds of humankind, the angels of mercy stand to God's right, the angels of peace stand to his left, while the angels of punishment stand in front of him, waiting to do his bidding.

**Body of God.** It is commonly believed that God is a spirit, bodiless and formless. However, there were some cases in various religious books and scriptures where the prophets saw God embodied in their visions. This embodiment arguably was a form that the human mind could easily comprehend. For example, in the biblical book of Daniel (7:9–10) it states, "I kept on beholding until there were thrones placed and the Ancient of Days [God] sat down. His clothing was white just like snow, and the hair of his head was like clean wool." In another passage from the pseudepigraphic book of 1 Enoch (8–25), the prophet **Enoch** is describing a vision:

*And behold I saw the clouds: And they were calling me in a vision, and in the vision, the winds were causing me to fly and rushing me high up into heaven. And I observed and saw inside it a lofty throne— its appearance was like crystal and its wheels like the shining sun. And the Great Glory [God] was sitting upon it—as for his gown, which was shining more brightly than the sun, it was whiter than any snow. None of the angels was able to come in and see the face of the Excellent and the Glorious One; and no one of the flesh can see him—the flaming fire was round about him, and a great fire stood before him. No one could come near unto him from among those that surrounded the tens of millions that stood before him.*

**God and Dimensions.** God is thought to exist in several dimensions at once. The idea is that God could not have created the universe if he were in it. Therefore, he must have existed in another dimension during the creation of the universe. According to particle physics and relativity, at the time that the universe came to be, there were at least ten dimensions of space already in existence. It is believed that God must have been able to operate in all of those dimensions and more in order to have created the universe.

### Greece

The ancient Greeks believed in an afterlife and unseen worlds similar to heaven and hell. In Greek beliefs, the god Hermes conducted the dead to the underworld, which was ruled by the god **Hades.** There they were judged. The good souls ascended to the **Elysian Fields** (also referred to as **Elysium),** a beautiful paradise. The bad were sent below to the fiery Tartarus. There they were punished eternally. Some, however, were allowed to repent. After a long penance, they were then deemed worthy of entering the Elysian Fields. Souls who were judged to be neither totally good nor totally bad were sent to Asphodel, where they would exist in an indeterminate state.

**The Ferryman of the Dead.** In Greek mythology, the way to the underworld was barred by the **River Styx,** or Acheron, a marshy river. In order to cross it, the souls had to pay **Charon**, the ferryman of the dead, a coin. Charon then carried them by boat across the river. Charon would only ferry those souls whose bodies had been buried or cremated with the appropriate rites. In addition, each soul was required to pay him an *obolus* (coin) or *danace* (ancient Persian coin) for their journey. For that reason, the bodies of the dead could be found buried with a coin under their tongues. Souls found without a coin were not accepted by Charon and were left to wander along the Styx for one hundred years.

**Communication with the Other Side.** The ancient Greeks used *psychomanteums* (rooms used for mirror gazing) to contact and consult spirits of the deceased.

**Spiritual Beings of Greece.** In Greek mythology there were gods and goddesses who performed angelic functions in the spiritual realm, sometimes moving back and forth between their plane and the physical realm. These gods and goddesses became archetypal angels of later religious systems, such as Judaism and **Christianity.** They include the horae, which were winged spiritual beings that guided and protected the Greeks; the winged god Hermes, who ran messages between the spiritual realm and earth for Zeus; the goddess Iris who was a messenger for Zeus's wife Hera; Eros, the winged god of love; and Proserpina, queen of the underworld.

See also **Sibyl; Thanatos.**

## Greeters

Spirits that guide those that are new to the spiritual world. They assist the newly arrived spirits with the transition from physical life to the spiritual.

## Group Soul

A group of souls that agreed to incarnate together in the physical plane. While still in the spiritual realm, these souls made a plan to aid each other in their spiritual development by meeting at some point in life. They may come together for a short time or for their entire lives. These souls often recognize each other on a deep level, as all of the souls in the group vibrate at the same frequency. Group soul is also referred to as the over soul, the Greater Self, and the Higher Self.

## Gregory the Great

Sixth-century pope, spiritual worker, and one of the most notable figures in ecclesiastical history (540–604 AD). In his work entitled *Dialogues,* in the fourth and final piece of the book, Gregory looks at the soul's eternal life and gives examples of near-death experiences, deathbed visions, and ghostly appearances experienced by people who lived in medieval times.

For example, he wrote of a hermit who, after dying, revived and told of his journey to hell and what he saw—namely, men in the fires of hell. The hermit explained how he was rescued from an eternity of burning by an angel, who then sent him back to life, warning him to be watchful about how he lived his life. Another man named Stephen,

a businessman, died while traveling to Constantinople. He discovered, however, he had been taken to the spiritual world in error, and he was returned to life. He discussed with Gregory how he hadn't believed in hell until his brief visit there.

In addition, Gregory's *Dialogues* tells the story of a soldier that was killed and journeyed to the other side. After reviving later, he relayed to Gregory what he had seen in the afterlife. He described a bridge over a gloomy, bad smelling river. Across the bridge was a beautiful meadow with lush grass and fragrant flowers. He saw people dressed in pure white. He witnessed a house made of gold bricks being constructed. The bridge it seemed was a test, because only just people could cross to the other side. The unjust simply slipped off the bridge and would fall into the foul river. The soldier observed one man that he had known of in life, who had died prior to his own experience, lying in the slime underneath the bridge and weighted down with an iron. That man had had a reputation for enjoying performing cruel acts of punishment on others.

The *Dialogues'* last chapter ends with the image of another man named Stephen, who had slipped and fallen from the bridge, but was still holding onto it. Horrible men from the river below came up to pull him into the water by the hips, while from above good spirits tried to pull him up and back onto the bridge. The person witnessing this was sent back to life, back into his body, and never knew what happened to Stephen. The unresolved image is forever imbedded in the reader's mind as a metaphor for the struggle between good and bad.

## Greyson, (Charles) Bruce

One of the world's leading near-death experience researchers and editor-in-chief of the *Journal for Near-Death Studies* since 1982 (1946–). He was a founding member of International Association of Near-Death Studies (IANDS) and served for many years on its board of directors, as its president, and as its director of research. His near-death research for the past three decades has focused on the aftereffects of the experience. Greyson also authored the overview of near-death experiences for the *Encyclopedia Britannica*.

## Guardian Angel(s)

Spiritual beings believed to be sent by **God** for protection. A belief in a protective spiritual being can be found around the world in many ancient and modern belief systems.

Perhaps the most well-known guardian spirits are the guardian angels of Judeo-Christian beliefs. These angels are said to often appear at a moment's notice to rescue their charges from harm. They sometimes appear in human form, sometimes in the form of an animal, and sometimes as a voice or a vision. Many people have relayed experiences of being rescued by invisible hands, or by a dream they had before the danger occurred.

Ancient Romans believed that guardian spirits called *lares* protected each family. Romans also believed in *genius,* spirits who protected men and boys, and *juno,* spirits who guarded women and girls. Pakistani and Burmese people believe in guardian spirits called *nats.* Nats are thought to dwell next to the people they were guarding. In **Islam** there are the *malaika,* known as the guardians of mankind, and the *hafazah,* who protect humans against the *jinn* (demons). The **Koran** states, "He [God] sends forth guardians who watch over you and carry away your souls without fail when death overtakes you." Guardian spirits called *genii,* are found throughout the Near East. In Zoroastrianism there are the *fravashi,* ancestral spirits who are also guardian angels. Native Americans believe in guardian spirits that are much like the guardian angels of other religious belief systems. Each clan or tribe has a guardian that is believed to remain with it forever. Personal guardian spirits are sought after by individual members of a tribe.

**Guardian Angels and Children.** It has been suggested that children have several guardian angels. This is because children are more vulnerable and in need of more protection when they are young. As they grow, they are thought to need less angelic protection as they become aware of the dangers around them. Some, but not all, of the angels leave a child as he or she matures. In Catholicism it is taught that every child has two guardian angels, one good and one bad, that sit upon each shoulder. The Guardian Angel Prayer is a prayer taught to Catholic children. It speaks of God sending angels to children for protection and guidance. It says, "Angel of God, my guardian dear, to whom His love, commits me here; Ever this day [or night] be at my side, To light and guard, to rule and guide."

**Personal Guardian Angels.** The famous German clairvoyant **Rudolph Steiner** believed that the guardian angels remain with a person through each incarnation and carry the complete history of the soul of the person. Once the individual has finished the last incarnation, the guardian angel's role is completed, and it leaves that individual.

The guardian angels of individuals, according to lore, come from the order of angels simply called "angels." They rank last in the angelic hierarchy and are the closest angels to mankind. These angels are assigned to individuals to protect and guide them from birth. They are sometimes referred to as personal angels and companion angels. Guardian angels use a variety of methods to reach individuals, including intuition, thoughts, and dreams. Sometimes they work through people and manipulate circumstances in order to relay messages. Although guardian angels do appear from time to time, most of their work is done invisibly. When they do appear, however, they may take on a variety of forms, including people, animals, and lights. When appearing as humans, they appear in forms that are in accord with the beliefs of the individual, disguising themselves in the appropriate cultural clothing. There are many reports, too, of angels appearing in full angel regalia, including halos and wings.

## Guardian Spirits
See **Guardian Angels.**

## Guide(s)
See **Spirit Guides.**

# H

## Hades

In ancient Greek mythology, Hades is the name of the god that rules the netherworld. Later, the netherworld itself, also came to be called Hades. In ancient legends, Hades was believed to be beneath the earth and was home to the dead.

The passage to Hades is mentioned several times in works by **Homer,** especially in the eleventh book of the *Odyssey,* where the roving hero, Odysseus, travels to visit the dead seer Tiresias. There Odysseus finds that those in Hades are miserable.

In apocryphal lore, the ruler of Hades was the archangel Uriel, who was believed to hold the keys to the gates of Hades. In the **Apocalypse of Zephaniah,** the angel Eremiel is listed as the overseer of Hades, and Baal-Beryth is the master of ceremonies in Hades. Judges at the entrance to Hades decided the soul's next incarnation.

## Hall of Records

A great hall said to be a prominent structure in one dimension of the spiritual world. It is said to be a place of great supernatural beauty. It has been described as being pure white and designed in ancient Grecian-style architecture. Some believe that the **Akashic Records** are located there. After a person has passed and traveled to the spiritual world and been reunited with loved ones, they are taken to the Hall of Records for their life review, according to some sources. It is mentioned by several metaphysical sources, from psychics to hypnotists and past-life regressionists. For example, the Hall of Records is mentioned in **Sylvia Browne**'s book *Life on the Other Side: A Psychic's Tour of the Afterlife*, by **Edgar Cayce** in his Reading 294-19 report file, on Kevin Williams's website, Near-Death Experiences and the Afterlife, and in **Dolores Cannon**'s book *Between Life and Death*. The Hall of Records has also been seen in many near-death experiences.

## Hamilton, T. Glen

Afterlife researcher (1877–1935). A graduate of Manitoba Medical College, Hamilton was a physician and a member of the Canadian Parliament. He became interested in afterlife communication in 1916, which led to his interest in conducting studies on mediums. His research consistently and successfully proved that survival after death is real.

Hamilton held his experiments in his laboratory under tightly secured and controlled conditions. The tests were conducted via an assortment of fourteen electronic flash cameras, which were set up to photograph apparitions simultaneously and from all angles. Witnesses of the testing included medical doctors, lawyers, and electrical and civil engineers. All of the observers attested to seeing dead persons materialize, which gave credibility to Hamilton's work.

Through his research, Hamilton made an enormous contribution to the belief in communication between those living in the physical world and those in the spiritual world and the belief that there is indeed life after death. Reports of his studies, including photographs, are on public display at the University of Manitoba in Canada.

## Hare, Robert

A respected professor of chemistry at the University of Pennsylvania (1781–1858). Hare was born in Philadelphia on January 17, 1781. His father was a state senator. He was well known for his scientific discoveries, including the oxy-hydrogen blowpipe, for which he became famous. He was also a staunch advocate against spiritualism. Hare considered it his duty as a scientist to speak out against such ideas in the interest of reason and science. He eventually became so frustrated with the speed at which these beliefs were evolving that he set out to disprove spiritualism, as well as mediumship. So at age seventy-two, he began studying the phenomena to disprove its validity. He created several devices that, to his surprise, proved without a doubt that there was an unseen power and intelligence in control. As a result, Hare became a staunch believer in not only life after death, but also in the idea of publicizing his findings so that all could be privy to the knowledge of what happens once a person was deceased and the hope that knowledge provides. The university in which Hare worked denounced him and his findings, and Hare eventually stepped down from his position. Later, Hare himself became a medium. By that time, his scientific reputation was diminished. In 1855, Hare's book *Experimental Investigation of the Spirit Manifestations* was published.

## Harrison, Minnie

A physical trance medium (1895–1958). Harrison was the youngest of eleven children, all of whom displayed mediumship abilities. She began her mediumship journey as a child. In fact, by the time she was a teenager, she recognized that she was both clairvoyant and clairaudient. Minnie held a mediumship circle that met regularly from 1946 to the mid-1950s. Many amazing things occurred within that circle, including apports appearing as gifts for those present and voices of the dead being heard. Perhaps the most amazing

were the materializations of entities from the spiritual world. Harrison's son, Tom Harrison, kept a detailed journal of all that he saw while sitting in on the circles. He has written a book entitled *Visits by Our Friends from the Other Side*.

## Haunting(s)

The regular reappearance of an apparition in the same location or to the same individual (or both). It is also known as a recurring apparition or haunting apparition. Residual hauntings, also known as energy implants, are when earthbound spirits linger because they do not know they are deceased or have unfinished business. See **Apparition(s); Ghost(s)**.

## Hearing a Voice

See **After-Death Communication**.

## Heart and Souls

A 1993 movie with an afterlife theme. The film stars Robert Downey Jr., Charles Grodin, Alfre Woodard, Kyra Sedgwick, Tom Sizemore, David Paymer, and Elisabeth Shue. The story revolves around the characters

Harrison, Penny, Julia, and Milo. The four find themselves together aboard a city bus that crashes, putting an end to their physical life on earth. At the same time, their spirits become attached to the consciousness of a still-living man named Thomas (played by Downey Jr.). They remain earthbound and tied to Thomas, due to unfinished business from their physical lives on earth. These four spirit friends were known only to him when he was a child, which eventually led to his parents having him see a psychiatrist, thinking that there was something wrong with their son. At that point, not wanting to disrupt his young life any further, the four spirits decided to disappear from Thomas's view until later. When he nears the age of thirty, they suddenly contact him again. Thomas is at first shocked and upset over seeing them again, as he quickly realizes that his childhood friends were real and that they had left him. However, they inform him of their unfinished business on earth and ask for his help. Until their business is finished, they cannot go to the spiritual world. The adult Thomas becomes the medium for the four. Because they

are now souls without physical bodies, they must use Thomas's body to live out their last dreams on earth. Afterward, one at a time, they each leave happily for the spiritual world.

## Heaven

The name of one plane of existence in the spiritual world. According to ancient Judeo-Christian beliefs, there are thought to be seven smaller levels of existence within the heavenly plane.

The term *heaven* is one that most people are familiar with and is commonly used in Judeo-Christian beliefs. It is generally used as a catchall word for what is a very vast spiritual universe. However, it is also used to refer to the plane that the majority of people travel to upon death—a plane found in most of the world's beliefs. Because it is also a place thought to be visited during astral travel, it is usually described the same way in most of the world's religious beliefs. It is believed to be a place of immense beauty and happiness, where souls rest after their lives on earth. In some religious beliefs, it is also the abode of **God** and the angels.

An area located just above our own physical dimension, yet beyond our perception, heaven is believed by many to be the purest and most sacred dimension. It is, however, just one of many realms and dimensions found within the unseen world. Heaven is actually a large part (but not all) of what many refer to as the afterlife.

**Qualifications for Entering Heaven.** Many religions that believe in heaven have different ideas as to how one qualifies to get into it. Most often, entrance into heaven is believed to be conditional. Some religions purport that those who go to heaven get there because of their faith and belief in a particular deity. Some believe that only the good, the just, and the righteous will enter heaven. Others, such as some facets of **Christianity** (such as in Calvinists and Jehovah's Witnesses), believe that only those predestined and chosen by God will be allowed in. Still others, like Universalists, believe that everyone goes to heaven regardless of whether or not they lived a "good life."

According to many near-death experiencers, prophets, mystics, and holy men, and some psychics, entrance to heaven is not based upon judgment or favoritism from God; instead, it is based on the level of one's spirituality. The majority of people go to what we know as the "heavenly realm." One's character, one's good deeds in life, and how much love one showed, it is said, are what will cause a person to move into the heavenly realm after death.

**Traveling to Heaven.** Although it is possible for a living person's spirit to leave its body and travel through the spiritual world, spirits seldom travel to heaven unless the body has died. However, in this modern age and due to the latest technology, there have been many cases of the spirits of "clinically dead" people leaving their bodies, traveling to the spirit world, and then returning to tell about it. In most cases, the spirit proceeds through a tunnel to the place many refer to as heaven. Most people's spirits leave their bodies in their sleep, and travel to and often throughout different realms of the spiritual world, but they do not necessarily go to heaven.

**Streets of Heaven.** There has been much said about the streets of heaven. They are said to be paved with gold. People that have traveled there in near-death or out-of-body experiences have given various descriptions of these streets. Apparently, the streets are made not only of gold, but also gems and jewels. Says Rebecca Springer, in her popular book *Within Heaven's Gates,* "Passing up a slight upward slope, we found ourselves in a broad street that led into the center of the city. The streets I found were all very broad and smooth, and paved with marble and precious stones of every kind."

## Heaven and Hell
See **Emanuel Swedenborg.**

## Heaven Can Wait
A 1978 movie starring Warren Beatty as Joe Pendleton, a quarterback who has an accident and meets with an untimely death. Joe teams up with two angels who help him to search for a suitable earthly replacement for Joe's spirit. The film also stars Julie Christie, Jack Warden, Dyan Cannon, Charles Grodin, James Mason, Buck Henry, and Vincent Gardenia. It was directed by Warren Beatty and Buck Henry.

## Heavenly Archives
See **Akashic Records; Archives; Book of Life.**

## Heavenly Books
See **Akashic Records; Archives; Book of Life.**

## Heavenly City
See **City of Light.**

## Hel
See **Norsemen.**

## Hell
A place of punishment and torment, as taught by many of the world's mainstream religions. There are many beliefs surrounding the idea of a hell. It is said to be a fiery place ruled by a devil, and the condemned souls in hell are in this devil's possession, forever deprived of seeing **God.** Some believe that hell exists beneath the earth. Others say that it is a spiritual realm separated from heaven. Some

people believe the fire of hell to be literal, some metaphorical. To the ancient Jews, Sheol was a hell where souls wander about woefully. Ancient Greeks believed that upon dying, spirits of the dead went to an underworld called **Hades** (Hades was also the name of the ruler of the netherworld). In some facets of **Christianity,** it is thought that there exist in hell all sorts of hideous demons who were once angels in heaven, but who rebelled, sinned, or fell away from God's laws. Some religions argue that hell is not real and that a god of love would not torment people forever.

Evidence shows that the idea of a hell was born in early Christian beliefs as an opposition to the perfect state of heaven. In fact, eternal damnation was created by clerics to control and manipulate the hearts and minds of the people and as a means of converting them. The more modern idea of hell is that it is

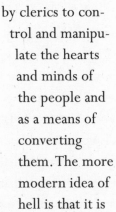

the separation from God. A person who chooses to separate himself from God is said to be in the worst possible state.

Within the spiritual world, there are, however, dark realms where some people may find themselves after death. These realms have been seen by people that practice astral projection, as well as by some who have had near-death experiences. It is rare that visits to these realms on the lower astral plane are reported; for the most part, the upper, more beautiful realms are seen. The lower realms are said to be dark, unpleasant, and cold, and some even say they are ghastly. However, they are not eternal places. They are temporary homes for dark souls until they change. It may take a long time, maybe ages; however, all souls have the opportunity for change and growth and to leave the dark realms.

**Gates of Hell.** According to ancient Jewish lore, there is a gatekeeper to the lowest realm, known in the physical world as hell. The archangel Uriel is said to be keeper of the keys to the gates of hell.

See also **Earthbound Realm; Hell Realms; Void.**

## Hell Realms

The dark realms located between earth and the spiritual realms of light are known by some as the hell realms. They are also referred to as the outer darkness. Some specifically refer to them as the earthbound realm and the void. In general, people travel past these realms quite quickly in order to reach the higher realms after death. However, those with addictions or strong earthly connections may stay behind in the earthbound realm until they free themselves of their earthly attachment. Fortunately, they are able to do so eventually, with the help of angels and higher beings that may come to their aid once they are ready. It should be noted that a spirit's arrival in one of the darker realms does not mean it is being punished; it is its spiritual state that puts it there. The more spiritual and less negative a person is, the higher he or she will travel to the higher realms of light within the unseen spiritual world.

## Hemingway, Ernest

American author of such works as *The Sun Also Rises* and *The Old Man and the Sea* (1899–1961). Hemingway had a near-death experience while serving in the trenches near Fossalta, Italy, during World War I. It was about midnight on July 8, 1918, when a mortar shell exploded near Hemingway, who was then just nineteen years old. Flying shrapnel badly wounded his legs, and at that moment, Hemingway died. But he survived the accident of war, and he later told of feeling his soul coming out of his body, describing it as, "like you'd pull a silk handkerchief out of a pocket by one corner. It flew around and then came back and went in again, and I wasn't dead any more." He convalesced in Milan. Hemingway later sent a letter to his family, saying, "Dying is a very simple thing. I've looked at death and really I know." Hemingway used his own near-death experience in *A Farewell to Arms* when he has his fictional hero, Frederic Henry, undergo a similar experience. In that novel, the protagonist is also positioned in the Italian trenches when "a blast-furnace door is swung open and a roar that started white and went red . . . in a rushing wind."

Henry feels his spirit rush out of himself and soar with the wind. He believes himself to be dead and realizes that there is an existence beyond physical death. "Then . . . instead of going on, I felt myself slide back," Henry says. "I breathed and I was back."

## Higher Self

Another term for the over soul.

## Hildegard of Bingen

German composer, abbess, mystic, and writer (1098–1179). She has been called one of the most important figures in the history of the Middle Ages and the greatest woman of her time. Born in Böckelheim, Germany, Hildegard knew at a very young age that she wanted to spend her life serving **God**. At the age of eight, she was placed by her aristocratic parents in the care of nuns at Disibodenberg, near Bingen, Germany. She later became head of the convent. There she became known as a powerful mystic, spending much of her time meditating on the mysteries of God, having visions in which she saw heaven and hell, and giving prophecies about the future. She recorded these visions in a book entitled *Scivias,* which took her ten years to complete and brought her much fame throughout Europe. She wrote of her vision of God and the spiritual world, in which she described heaven as a royal court where the saints are dressed in silk, standing about the throne of God. She envisioned the throne of God as being surrounded by nine concentric circles of angels. The most wonderful part of heaven, according to Hildegard, is beholding the face of God.

## Hinduism

A major world religion that originated from the ancient religions of India. It is a diverse religion made up of the philosophy and culture of native India. Hinduism teaches that through the laws of karma, a soul is freed from rebirth and then becomes one with Brahma (the one eternal). Souls may be reborn in the various spiritual paradises or lower undesirable realms, or they may come back as a lower life-form.

In Hindu beliefs, above the earthly plane are seven spiritual planes of existence: the Bhu plane, the Bhuvas plane, the Svar plane, the Mahas plane, the Janas plane, the Tapas plane, and the Satya plane. Below the earthly planes are six spiritual planes on the darker side, referred to as the nether planes: Atala, Vitala, Sutala, Rasaataala, Talatala, Mahaatala, and Paatala. Below these are twenty-eight different hellish dimensions. **Moksha** is the term for the spiritual destiny of all souls. Moksha is the liberation from the cycle of earth and its suffering. It is a transitioning to a higher spiritual consciousness and ultimately becoming one with the universe. Before this can be achieved, one must first reach a place in their soul journey where they will no longer need to be reincarnated. Eventually, the soul will become one with **God** (i.e., the universe).

**Spiritual Beings.** Hinduism includes a number of spiritual beings, including God. In Hinduism, God can be understood in several ways. Philosophically, God is understood as Brahma. In popular religion, many gods are worshiped for having his or her own function; however, these gods, too, are understood to be manifestations of Brahma. In this way, Hinduism stresses God's immanence.

The abundance of gods illustrates the many faces of God, the unknown, as he interacts with humankind. Other spiritual beings of Hinduism include the *apsaras,* who resemble beautiful fairies. They specialize in giving sensual pleasure to the gods. They were sometimes sent to earth from the spiritual world to prevent wicked men from doing harm by distracting the men with their beauty and sexual expertise. There are also the *shakti* and the *devi,* who are the manifestations of God in the female form. Popular devi and shakti include Durga, Kali, and Lakshmi. See also **Atman; Vedas.**

## Homer

A major ancient Greek poet and principle figure in literature. Homer is best known for his two classical epic poems, *The Iliad* and *The Odyssey*. Homer composed detailed depictions of the spiritual world. In *The Odyssey,* he explains how the hero, Odysseus, descends into the land of the dead, also known as the underworld, or **Hades,** ruled by the god of the same name. The Homeric view of the underworld shows souls that are unhappy, shadowy, formless spirits. Homer also portrayed an afterlife called **Elysium**, where the good were thought to go after death. There, the soul enjoyed a state of spiritual blissfulness. Views of the afterlife by Homer can be found in *The Odyssey,* book 11, "The Nekuia (The Book of the Dead)."

## Home, Daniel Douglas

One of the most famous physical mediums of the Victorian era (1833–1886). Born to William and Elizabeth Home in Currie, Scotland, Daniel Douglas Home was believed to have inherited his abilities from his mother, who was also psychic, as were a number of her relatives. They were specifically known to have "second sight" and were also referred to as seers. As a child, Home was considered to be fragile and overly sensitive. He was therefore sent to live with his childless aunt, Mary Cook (his mother's sister) and her husband. While still a young boy, Home displayed his ability to see events before they occurred. He predicted the death of a cousin; the death of a childhood friend (which he saw in a vision); the death of his brother, who perished at sea; and even the death of his mother. As an adult, he was best known for his unusual ability of rising high into the air (also known as levitation). Home moved to the United States with his aunt and uncle when he was a young boy. After becoming a successful medium, Home eventually took up residence in England. There he is said to have conducted numerous sittings for people hoping to contact loved ones on the other side.

## Hope, William

Spirit photographer from Britain (1863–1933). Hope has been hailed as the best-known British photographic medium of the twentieth century. Through his great skill and talent, as well as his mediumistic insights and gifts, Hope was able to photograph hundreds of people existing on the other side. He was even able to capture deceased pets on film. Careful not to be seen as a fraud, he had persons verify the pictures of their friends, relatives, and pets that he was able to capture in spirit. Famed trance medium Lilian Bailey was one who sat with Hope in an effort to have a photograph taken of her mother, who had passed away. However, Bailey received a photograph of a person she perceived to be a stranger. Eventually, it was discovered that the photograph was that of her spirit guide, William Hedley Wootton (a World War I soldier). The photograph even picked up a dark area over Wootton's temple. He had been shot and killed in that very place.

## Houdini, Harry

American magician (born Ehrich Weiss, 1874–1926). Houdini abhorred fake mediums. He went so far as to vow that if indeed there were life after death, then after his passing he would send a message back in the form of a code to his wife, Beatrice. Before his death, Houdini had created a message with Beatrice. He explained that only a real medium would be able to give her his message. Many attempted and failed. Then famous medium Arthur Ford tried

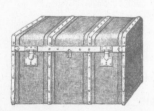

and was successful. Ford gave Beatrice the message, "Rosabelle, believe." This was done in the long, complicated code that the two Houdinis had used in the vaudeville act they had performed many years before. Ford's message delivery was witnessed by a number of people including reporters from *The Scientific American*, Beatrice, and others. Beatrice said no other person knew about the code. She even signed a formal document stating that the code had come from Houdini and was totally correct, thereby proving that the magician himself had survived bodily death.

## Hughes, Marilynn

Out-of-body experience expert, author, and founder of the Out-of-Body Travel Foundation (1965–). A former news anchor, reporter, and producer, Hughes has been researching and experiencing out-of-body travel and comparative religious mysticism since 1987. Through her work, she has helped people become enlightened about the unseen world and what lies beyond our physical senses. One popular series by Hughes is *The Mystic Knowledge Series,* in which Hughes details such subjects as out-of-body travel, ghosts, lost souls, spirit guides, guardian angels, reincarnation, karma, spiritual warfare, angels, death, the afterlife, heaven, hell, and more. In addition to her mystic knowledge series, Hughes has written books on out-of-body travel, world religions, miraculous images, and suffering. She has also written children's books. Her foundation's website is located at: *www.outofbodytravel.org.*

## Hypnagogic State

The state of being on the edge of falling asleep and still being awake. It is thought by some that in order to engage in astral projection, one needs to be in the hypnagogic state.

"Wild men who caught and sang the sun in flight
And learn, too late, they grieved it on its way,
Do not go gentle into that good night."
—Dylan Thomas, "Do not go gentle into that good night"

# I

## Ice Palace
See **City of Light.**

## Immortality of the Soul
A term denoting life without beginning or end, also referred to as eternal life. From the beginning of human history, mankind has displayed a desire to live forever. In fact, most cultures and religions believe in an eternal life that involves a soul or spirit continuing after the physical death. This belief is still held strongly in today's modern era. Today, there is evidence that the soul of a person certainly continues after death. Information gleaned from near-death experiences and some of the ancient religious teachers, mystics, psychics, scriptures, and sacred texts allude to the fact that our life on earth is just a short journey of the soul. It is the soul that lives forever and continues on in various lives and situations to gain knowledge that ultimately will aid its enlightenment as it moves along a path that will eventually lead back to **God.**

## Incarnate Spirit
A spirit with a material body, living on earth or on other worlds. It is the opposite of a disembodied spirit.

## Incarnation
The manifestation of a spiritual being into a physical body. All persons that have lived on earth existed in the unseen spiritual world before incarnating. The reasons for incarnating vary. Most spiritual beings do it in order to learn. They are using planet earth as a school for spiritual growth. A given incarnation may be a soul's first incarnation or one of several, as a soul is allowed to incarnate many times for its spiritual advancement. In the spiritual realm, these souls work closely with counselors to help chart their spiritual course. Just before they incarnate, the souls meet with these counselors, and upon returning, they meet with the counselors again to review their life on earth and evaluate what lessons they learned, what type of life they lived, what type of person they were, and the love and also the hurt they may have caused others.

When incarnating, each individual is assigned a spirit guide from the other side who will go with them and help steer them through that life. The individual's spirit guide is always with him or her, throughout all of the learning experiences and ordeals of life. They are also there at death to help the person transition to the spiritual world.

In Hindu mythology people's incarnation is based on their deeds from the previous life. A person may be born into a harsh world or a paradise upon their return to the physical plane. Those that practice good karma and *bhakti* (the practice of unselfish loyalty to a deity in order to gain salvation) throughout their lives are granted Moksha, which is the liberation from the cycle of death and rebirth.

According to research on out-of-body experiences, astral projection, and near-death experiences, as well as channeled sources from the unseen spiritual realm, earth is not the only world that souls can incarnate to.

## Incas

An ancient South American empire that was technologically advanced for its time period. The empire stretched well over three hundred miles along the Andes mountains, from present-day Ecuador to Chile and Argentina. It was the largest empire in the world at the time of its fall. The Incas were a highly intelligent and sophisticated people, excelling in art, metallurgy, jade carving, astronomy, textile making, and gold working. Even though they lacked a written language, they lived a rich life. In their cities one could find stone palaces and beautiful artwork. The ancient Incas held to a dualistic philosophy about life after death. At death, one soul was thought to return to its place of origin in heaven, while the other soul remained with the corpse. The soul that remained behind was thought to have many needs, and it was necessary for the physical body to be preserved in order for those needs to be fulfilled.

## India

See **Hinduism; Jainism; Vedas.**

## Infused Knowledge

Information that comes directly from a spirit or guide or someone in the unseen spiritual world that is trying to convey needed information to earth.

## Inner Voice

See **Clairaudience; Intuition.**

## Inspiration

It is believed by some that our creative thoughts and imaginations are sometimes possible communications from the spiritual world. This idea stems from the fact that many times the inspired get ideas that they had never thought about before or experienced. Some of the world's most phenomenal artwork, music, and medical cures are thought to be inspiration given from the spiritual world. When this inspiration is given, the recipient may experience a sudden wave of knowledge, images, or an urge to create or produce something. That urge can be so strong that the person may feel the need to immediately produce what he or she sees or feels. Some of this world's greatest minds are thought to be working with guides from the spiritual world in an effort to cure some of this world's problems. Inspiration is different from automatic drawing and writing. There is no channeling involved. The person simply creates what they feel from their inspiration and builds on the idea. Often, the foundation for whatever work is being accomplished from the information can already be found in the individual recipient.

Many great artists have claimed that angels inspired their work. These angels are sometimes referred to as the angels of inspiration. **William Blake** credited his creative genius to angels. Visionary and mystic **Emanuel Swedenborg** wrote many books that were inspired by angels, including *Heaven and Hell*, hailed as his greatest work. In Greek mythology there were nine muses who were credited with inspiring the ancient masters of history, art, science, and religion. These muses were the archetypal angels of inspiration.

## Instrumental Transcommunication (ITC)

The recording of messages from the other side. Communications can be kept on a variety of technical equipment including such items as recorders, computers, video cameras and other means. ITC allows those in the spiritual world to communicate with their friends and loved ones still in the physical. This method is similar to that of electronic voice phenomena (EVP), which records voices. For more information, see the website for World ITC, a nonprofit corporation established to encourage empirical investigations: *www. worlditc.org.*

## Interlife

The existence of the soul in the spiritual world, between incarnations. During this period, a person in spirit will work out the details of their next life, with the help of special counselors. Each person maps out exactly what it is they want to learn and work on (e.g., showing love, tolerance, patience), and how they will live their lives, even going to the point of choosing their parents, careers, and the area in which they want to live.

## Intermediate State
See **Bardo; Interlife.**

## Intuition

Intuition is a person's ability to understand or know things without conscious reasoning. Guardian angels, spirit guides, and loved ones that have passed on often work through an individual's intuition in order to assist them in making decisions, solving problems, and protecting them from dangerous situations. Intuition is sometimes referred to as the inner voice. In his book entitled *Divine Love and Wisdom*, Swedish mystic **Emanuel Swedenborg** writes about spiritual beings and intuition: "Do not believe me simply because I have discoursed with angels . . . Believe me because I tell you what your consciousness and intuitions will tell you if you listen closely to their voice."

## Inuit(s)

The indigenous natives of the Arctic regions of North America, as well as some areas of Greenland. The Inuits, or "the People," believe in a spiritual world where all virtuous souls will ascend after death. They refer to it as the Land of the Moon. There the virtuous will dwell eternally in a restful and peaceful state. Those that have not lived such a life will descend into Adlivun, which, according to legend, is located at the bottom of the ocean. The spiritual beings of this cold world are believed to live a dark and empty existence.

## Irish
See **Celts.**

## Islam
Founded in Arabia in the seventh century AD, Islam is one of the three major world religions that profess a belief in a single **God.** Islam is based upon the teachings of the prophet **Muhammad.** One who practices Islam is referred to as a Muslim. Muslims follow the revelation (the **Koran)** that was given to Muhammad by God. Muslims believe in an unseen spiritual realm as well as a host of spiritual beings.

In Islam, there is the belief in a paradise, called **Al-Janna,** where the good go after their life and physical death on earth. The wicked will suffer punishment in hell. Non-Muslims can reach paradise only after the soul goes through a period of cleansing and purification.

**Questioning of the Dead.** Islam teaches that before the soul moves forward into paradise or hell, it must first be questioned by two angels, named Munkar and Nakeer, about their good deeds and bad deeds. The person's answers determine if they will ascend to paradise or the darker realm of hell. The angels visit the tombs of those who have recently died, and ask several questions, such as, "Who is God?" ; "What is the name of God's prophet?" ; "What is the true religion?" Souls responding with such answers as "Allah is God," "Muhammad is God's prophet," and "Islam is God's true religion," are considered righteous individuals and are immediately allowed entrance into paradise. The unrighteous souls, those who did not respond correctly and did not live lives that served God, are left at the gates of hell. Muslims also believe that God (Allah) keeps detailed accounts of the deeds of all humans and therefore would not rely solely on a system of questioning to determine whether a person should go to Al-Janna or hell.

Spiritual beings figure prominently in Islam. In paradise, **God** is said to sit on his throne in the seventh heaven, surrounded by angels who minister to him. There are four archangels in Islam. The Koran lists only two: **Jibril (Gabriel),** the "faithful servant," and Mikhail **(Michael),** "who provides men with food and knowledge." The other two are Azrael, the angel of death, and Israfel, the angel of music who praises God in many languages. It was Jibril who revealed the Koran to Muhammad. He also took Muhammad on a tour of the seven heavens. The archangels in Islam are believed to record the good and bad deeds of humankind.

There are also the *huri,* a group of female spiritual beings who inhabit paradise; the *jinn,* which are demons; nineteen guardians of hell; and the *el-karubiyan*, or cherubim. According to early Muslim lore, the el-karubiyan were created from the tears of Mikhail when he cried over the sins of the faithful. In addition to recording men's deeds, the *malaika* are protectors of humankind; they are neither male nor female, but are thought to be androgynous. Other angels include Harut and Marut, who gave into sexual temptation; Malik, the ruler of hell; Isa **(Jesus),** who is a semiangelic character; and Iblis (Satan). In Islam, angels are said to sit in the mosques, listening to and recording the prayers of men. See also the **Koran**.

*Isles of the Blessed*
See **Fortunate Isles.**

# J

## Jacob

Hebrew patriarch. He was the younger of the twin sons of Isaac and the grandson of Abraham. According to biblical lore, Jacob had a number of experiences with spiritual beings. In one instance, in a dream, Jacob had a vision into the spiritual world in which he saw angels ascending and descending a ladder as they went about their work between heaven and earth (Genesis 28:11–12). Jacob was also met by angels on his return home to Canaan from Haran. He named the place where he met the angels Maha-naim (Genesis 32: 1–2). In one biblical account, Jacob wrestled with an angel. At Genesis 32: 24-26 it states, "Then a man came and wrestled with him until just before day break. When the man saw that he was not winning the struggle, he hit Jacob on the hip, and it was thrown out of joint. The man said, 'Let me go; daylight is coming.' 'I won't, unless you bless me,' Jacob answered." There have been a number of theories as to which angel Jacob actually wrestled with. Camael, Uriel and even **God**

have been named. This angel is also called "the dark angel." Jacob named the spot where he wrestled with the angel Peniel. Genesis 32:30 states: "So Jacob called the place Peniel, saying, 'It is because I saw God face to face, and yet my life was spared.'"The archangel Raphael reportedly healed his thigh joint. The story of Jacob wrestling with an angel later became a popular artistic subject. Three of the most popular portrayals were painted by Paul Gauguin, Gustave Doré, and Eugene Delacroix.

## Jainism

An ascetic religion of **India** that was founded in the sixth century BC. It emphasizes reverence for all living things and nonviolence. It teaches the immortality and transmigration of the soul and denies the existence of a perfect or supreme being. In Jainism, the soul is reborn until it reaches enlightenment and is freed. Through the laws of karma, the soul can be reborn in the spiritual realm or in hell, or it can return to earth as a lower form of life. Once the soul becomes liberated, it then becomes an all-knowing, all-powerful god.

## Jesus

Jewish prophet and teacher (c. 4 BC–c. 30 AD). The life and teachings of Jesus are the inspiration for the Christian religion. In Judaism he is a prophet. In **Christianity** he is the son of **God**. In **Islam** he is called Isa and is also a prophet. The name *Jesus* is the Greek version of the name *Joshua (Y'shua),* meaning "savior." The title *Christ* is derived from the Greek *Christos,* a translation of the Hebrew word *mashiakh,* meaning "anointed one" or "messiah." Jesus preached and taught in Palestine almost two thousand years ago. According to biblical lore, even before Jesus was born, his life was connected to the spiritual world and filled with angelic, spiritual beings. His birth was announced by the archangel **Gabriel** to his mother, Mary (Luke 1:26–33). When he was born, angels appeared to shepherds in a field, announcing his birth (Luke 2:9–15).

As a man, Jesus was tempted by the dark forces. Once, when he was feeling distressed, an angel came and strengthened him (Luke 22:43). He once revealed that he could call on several armies of angels to give him aid (Matthew 26:53).

Jesus tried fervently to convey to his followers that the death of the body was not the end of life, that they had something to look forward to in the spiritual world beyond. He spoke on the subject, saying, "He who hears my word . . . has eternal life; he does not come into judgment, but has passed from death to life' (John 5:24). After his death, Jesus purposely appeared to his followers to show them that he was alive and well in the spiritual world. He reappeared on earth in spirit form between six and ten times after he ascended. For example, Paul's first letter to the Corinthians, chapter 15, versus 3–8, reads, "Christ died . . . . He was buried, He was raised on the third day . . . and that he appeared to Cephas, then to the twelve. Then He appeared to more than five hundred brethren at one time. . . . Then He appeared to James, then to all the apostles. . . .

He appeared also to me." In addition, there are a number of references in the **Bible** to Jesus' materializations, including Luke 24:15, 16, 29–31 and John 20:12, 14, 19, 26.

**The Resurrection of Jesus.** The **New Testament** says that Jesus came back to life in his body three days after his crucifixion and entombment. Most Christians believe that Jesus' resurrection proves that one day they and/or all people will also physically rise from the dead and be restored to their bodies.

The gospels of Matthew (28:1–7) says that three days after the crucifixion of Jesus, Mary Magdalene and another woman, also named Mary, went to visit his tomb. Suddenly there was a fierce earthquake. The women watched as an angel of God descended from heaven. He rolled away the stone of the tomb and then sat down upon it. His appearance was like lightening. His clothing was "as white as snow." At the sight of him, the guards at the tomb fainted. The angel told the two women not to be afraid. He told them that Jesus had been resurrected and to go and tell his disciples. In the account of

Luke (24:1–10), Mary Magdalene, a woman named Joanna, and another Mary (identified as the mother of James), went to the tomb of Jesus and found it empty. There, two angels appeared to them, wearing "bright shining clothes." The angels reminded them of Jesus' words, that he would be resurrected in three days.

## Jibril

A powerful spiritual being in **Islam.** *Jibril* is the Islamic name for the archangel **Gabriel.** Legend has it that he has sixteen hundred wings and hair the color of saffron. Daily he enters the ocean, and when he comes out, a million drops of water fall from his wings and become angels who sing praises to **God.** He is called the Faithful Spirit and also the Faithful Servant. It was Jibril who dictated the **Koran** to **Muhammad.** He first appeared to Muhammad when the prophet was meditating on a mountain near Mecca. Stunned, Muhammad turned away. However, everywhere he turned, Jibril's face appeared. On the Night of Glory, when Jibril dictated the Koran to Muhammad, his wings were outstretched, his face illuminated, and between his eyes was written, "There is no God, but God, and Muhammad is the prophet of God." On another occasion, Jibril appeared and ordered Muhammad to call men to **God.** One night, angels appeared to Muhammad to prepare him for a journey through paradise. Jibril awakened Muhammad and removed his heart. After washing and purifying the heart, Jibril put it back into Muhammad's body. Muhammad was then filled with wisdom and faith. Jibril is also the guardian angel of Muhammad. Variations of the name Jibril are *Djibril, Jibreel,* and *Jabrail.*

## Jinn

In **Islam** jinn are considered demons. But according to Arabic legend, jinn are spiritual beings that act in a capacity similar to that of guardian angels. They have supernatural powers that are used to grant wishes and protect their charges. They were popular in Near Eastern literature and were portrayed in art both with and without wings, which indicated their relation to the divine and their movements between the invisible and visible.

Classic stories that include jinn are *The Arabian Nights,* also known as *The Thousand and One Nights.* The television show *I Dream of Jeannie* featured a jinni in its story line. *Jinni* is the singular form of jinn. Variations of the name jinni are *jinee, genii,* and *genie.*

## Joan of Arc

A national heroine of France, who was canonized a saint in 1920 (1412–1431). She was born in Domremy, a little town of Champagne, which sat on the banks of the Meuse. Her neighbors were later witnesses of her pious conduct and her love of **God,** church, and prayer. Often referred to as the "maid of Orleans," Joan (or *Jeanne* in French) began to hear the voices of angels at the age of fourteen. In the beginning, she heard only one voice, which was sometimes accompanied by a brilliant light. Later, as she began to hear more voices, she began to see the beings behind the voices, which turned out to be the archangel **Michael**, Saint Catherine, and Saint Margaret. Joan reported that the beings visited her many times during the week. She said that she could see, hear, and touch them, and that she felt such love and peace when she was with them that she used to cry when they left and wished that they would take her with them. When she was sixteen, the voices admonished her to go and help the dauphin of France to rescue their country from English control. The Catholic Church claimed her hearing and seeing spiritual beings as evidence of witchcraft and heresy and sentenced her to death. She was burned at the stake on May 30, 1431.

## Julian of Norwich

Medieval mystic and writer (c. 1342–c. 1429). She has the distinction of being the first woman to write a book in English. In May 1373, at thirty years old, Julian of Norwich became gravely ill and on the point of death. Then after days, the medical crisis passed, and she had a series of fifteen visions—or "showings," as she referred to them—believed to have come from the unseen world.

The visions brought her great joy and peace. She made a swift recovery and wrote down her experiences in a short book. Soon afterward she became an anchoress (recluse) living in a small room attached to St. Julian's Church, prompting her to take the name of Julian. (Her real name is now unknown.) She dedicated the rest of her life to prayer, studying, and contemplation. She eventually wrote the main book based on her experience, *The Revelations of Divine Love*, which has become regarded as a spiritual classic. People who knew her went to her for strong spiritual insight and guidance. Since her death, she is still giving insight through her writings. Her book is a gentle meditation on **God**'s eternal and all-encompassing love. In *The Revelations of Divine Love*, Julian writes: "God is kind in his Being. That is to say, the Goodness which is Kind, is God. He is the Ground: he is the Substance: he is the very thing called Kindness. And he is the very Father and the very Mother of kinds."

## Jung, Carl

Swiss psychiatrist and founder of the school of analytical psychology

(1875–1961). Jung's most famous concept, the collective unconscious, has had a deep influence not only on psychology, but also on philosophy and the arts. Jung introduced the concepts of the collective unconscious, the archetype, and the introvert and extrovert. In addition, he wrote at length about his dreams and visions. In his book *Memories, Dreams, Reflections*, Jung describes a near-death experience he had in the beginning of 1944. He had broken his foot, and after that a heart attack ensued, followed by an astonishing near-death experience. Jung writes:

> *It seemed to me that I was high up in space. Far below I saw the globe of the earth, bathed in a gloriously blue light. I saw the deep blue sea and the continents. Far below my feet lay Ceylon and in the distance ahead of the subcontinent of India. My field of vision did not include the whole earth, but its global shape was plainly distinguishable and its outlines shone with a silvery gleam through what wonderful blue light. In many places the globe seemed colored, or spotted dark green like*

*oxidized silver. Far away to the left lay a broad expanse the reddish-yellow desert of Arabia; it was as though the silver of the earth had there assumed a reddish-gold hue.*

He continued, "Later I discovered how high in space one would have to be to have so extensive a view of approximately a thousand miles! The sight of the earth from this height was the most glorious thing I have ever seen."

## Jürgenson, Friedrich

Electronic voice researcher (1903–1987). Friedrich Jürgenson was born on February 8, 1903, in Odessa to a Swedish mother and a Danish father, who was a physician. Jürgenson was a man of many interests and talents. He spent the early part of his life as a singer and musician. In addition, he was also a realist painter specializing in portraits, still lifes, and landscapes. He also spent some time chronicling archaeological works that were buried beneath the Vatican. Jürgenson was fascinated with the subject of electronic voice phenomena. On June 12, 1959, he and his wife went to their vacation home, hoping to enjoy the summer there. He was interested in recording bird songs, and during his first attempt, he realized that in addition to the birds there were also human voices on the tape, even though there had been no one around during the taping. Afterward, Jürgenson began making recordings in quiet places, and continued to find voices, including that of his mother, on his tapes. He eventually published a book on the subject, *Voices from Space* (1964). Jürgenson soon became well known for his recordings. He abandoned his painting and theater aspirations and devoted more of his time to his recordings. Later he worked closely with **Konstantin Raudive,** another pioneer in the field. He concluded that all of the mysterious voices on his recordings were those from people that had crossed over. In 1967 he published *Radio-Link with the Dead*. In October of 1987, Friedrich Jürgenson transitioned to the other side. He left hundreds of tapes that reflected his passion for this important work.

"We know nothing until we know everything."
—Saint Catherine of Siena, "This Place of Abundance"

# K

## Ka (or Koi)

A term used by the ancient Egyptians when referring to the astral body. In the **Egyptian** hieroglyph, it is depicted with uplifted arms.

## Kachina

Nature spirits whose characteristics resemble those of angels. Found in the belief system of the Pueblo peoples who reside in America's Southwestern region, they are sacred spirits that connect the physical realm with the spiritual. Kachina dolls are given to children to remind them of the invisible spiritual realm surrounding them.

## Kailasa, Mount

Also known as the paradise of Shiva, Mount Kailasa is located in Tibet. It is a place of rest for the weary soul that has just gone through the cycle of life, death, and rebirth. Upon death, the deserving enter through the Palace of Opulence and ascend to a place filled with beauty said to far surpass that of earth. There they find an abundance of luscious fruits, beautiful flowers, pure water, and more. The souls will rejuvenate there before continuing on their soul's quest for enlightenment.

## Kami

In the Far East, the word *kami* signifies the deities of heaven and the spirits of the shrines where they are worshiped.

## Kant, Immanuel

German philosopher from Konigsberg in East Prussia (now Kaliningrad, Russia; 1724–1804). He is regarded as one of the most influential thinkers of modern Europe and the last major philosopher of the Enlightenment period. Kant provided what has come to be known as the "moral argument" for the immortality of the soul. Kant acknowledged that mankind cannot demonstrate, as a matter of certainty, things like the existence of **God** and the immortality of the soul. However, in *Critique of Practical Reason*, he writes, "It is morally necessary to assume the existence of God" and that morality requires mankind to pursue a state of complete virtue, which is "only possible on the supposition of the immortality of the soul."

## Kardec, Allan

A popular French medium, known today as the systematizer of Spiritism (1804–1869). His real name was Hippolyte Leon Denizard Rivail. He apparently took the name Allan Kardec after a person on the other side, identifying himself as Zefiro, came through in a communication and revealed to Rivail that in a previous life, Rivail had a Druid name—Allan Kardec. Rivail evidently liked the name and took it as his spiritual pen name. As a medium, he was said to be adept at having people on the other side use spirit tapping in his sittings. Spirit tapping is a method in which those on the other side let the medium and sitters know they are present. In 1857 Rivail, under the pseudonym of Allan Kardec, published his first book, *The Spirit's Book*. The book contained 1,019 questions about the nature of spirits and the spiritual world. He later wrote other books, including *The Book on Mediums* and *The Gospel According to Spiritism*. He also published a journal entitled *Revue Spirite*. It was Rivail who coined the term *Spiritism*. On Rivail's tombstone it is written, "To be born, die, still to reappear and progress unceasingly, such is the law."

## Karma

The word *karma* originates in **Hinduism.** Karma is the belief that the good and bad a person does in this life will return to that person either in the present life or one in the future. It is similar to the idea of "what goes around comes around." In fact, the plan for reincarnating on earth is to repay as much karma in one lifetime as possible and in doing so avoid having to return again and again. While in a physical life, a person is in the process of clearing past-life karma or adding to future-life karma, until they reach their last physical incarnation.

## King, Katie

The famous spirit control (a spirit who relays messages through a trance medium) of Florence Cook. She claimed to be the daughter of John King. She began to manifest in the Cook's house when Cook was fifteen. King was seen almost daily, the first time in April 1872, revealing her deathlike face between curtains. Later her materializations became more perfect; after only a year of experimental work, she could walk out of a cabinet and show herself in full figure. She was said to talk a great deal. A criminal in her physical life, King said she was given the assignment of working with those in the physical world as a means of doing penance for her earthly transgressions. On her farewell appearance, after three years of constant manifestations, she said that her years of suffering were now over and that she would be ascending to a higher realm in the spiritual world. From there she could correspond with her medium only through automatic writing.

## Knowledge (in the spiritual world)

It is supposed that when one transitions from this world to the next he or she becomes omniscient about life, death, and the universe. However, according to some near-death experience accounts, this is not true. The character and personality of the individual remain intact. However, the soul still learns and grows in knowledge on the other side.

## Koran

The holy book of **Islam.** Muslims regard the Koran as a revelation communicated from **God** (called Allah) to **Muhammad,** through the angel **Jibril** (**Gabriel** in Judeo-Christian beliefs) on what is called the Night of Glory. The Koran was revealed to Muhammad in the Arabian Desert during the seventh century. Muhammad memorized the Koran and then dictated it to his companions, after which it was written down by scribes. Not one word of its 114 chapters (suras) has been changed over the centuries, so the Koran is, in every detail, the miraculous text that was given to Muhammad fourteen centuries ago. It was revealed to Muhammad over a period of 23 years and is regarded by Muslims as the word of God and his final revelation to humankind. One of the highest acts of devotion to God for Muslims is to memorize the entire Koran and then be able to recite it. One who has mastered the sacred text is called a *hafiz.*

The Koran speaks a great deal of spiritual beings. There are one hundred and four references to angels in the Koran. Angels of the Koran include Jibril and Mikhail **(Michael).** There are also the *hamalatal-'arsh,* the four throne bearers of God, symbolized by a man, a bull, an eagle, and a lion. God is praised by many angels, which are created from his breath to glorify and exalt him. He is also praised by Israfel, the angel of music, in many different languages. There are the *hafazah,* which are guardian angels, and the *malaika,* angels who record mankind's deeds. Other angels include Harut and Marut, angels who gave into sexual temptation; Malik, the ruler of hell; and the al-zabaniya, 19 guardians of hell, also known as the "violent thrusters." About angels the Koran says, "You shall see the angels circling around the Throne, giving glory to their Lord."

See also **Guardian Angels.**

## Kübler-Ross, Elisabeth

Thanatologist, researcher, author, and activist for the bereaved and dying (1926–2004). She was one of the leading experts on the subject of death and dying in the United States. In the late 1970s the popular acceptance of the work of Kübler-Ross brought sharp scientific focus on the question of what happens to humans after the experience of physical death. After listening to the remarkable accounts of her dying patients, Kübler-Ross wrote in her book *Death, the Final Stages of Growth,* "Beyond a shadow of a doubt, there is life after death." She surmised that after people die, they are not alone, but helpers in the form of angels, relatives, and spirit guides or beings of light are there to help those in the dying process to cross over. Kübler-Ross's discoveries and the publication of her books *On Death and Dying* and *On Life After Death* broke the taboo people have of talking about death.

# L

## Land of the Dead

Another name for the underworld in ancient Greek beliefs. See **Greece.**

## Land of the Moon

See **Inuits.**

## Lare(s)

In ancient Roman beliefs, lares were the guardian spirits of ancestors, who watch over homes and cities. Each household was believed to have a lare watching over the family. The lare was believed to be the spirit of the family's founder. It was traditional to thank the lare during meals (much like the Christians give thanks to **God** during meals). Some households even set a place for the lare at the table. The lare was credited as the source of the family's inspiration and creativity, and was considered a part of their everyday life.

## Leland, Kurt

Award-winning poet, composer, clarinetist, and channeler (1958–). Leland has personal experience with the unseen spiritual world. He is the author of such otherworldly books as *Otherwhere: A Field Guide to Nonphysical Reality for the Out-Of-Body Travel* and *The Unanswered Question: Death, Near-Death and The Afterlife*. His books detailing his adventures are popular and have aided in the understanding of what happens when a person is able to leave their body and travel in the spiritual realm and other places. In *The Unanswered Question*, Leland examines what happens after one's physical death. He also looks at what life is like in the spiritual realm. His research consists of near-death experience accounts, ancient books and writings, and his personal out-of-body experiences. Since 1984, Leland has maintained a consulting practice, called Spiritual Orienteering, in the Boston area. Its purpose is to help people develop and maintain a soul-based approach to the challenges and opportunities of life. In 1996 he was featured in a list of the top one hundred psychics in America.

## Leonard, Gladys Osborne

English medium (1882–1968). Born to Isabel and William Osborne,

Gladys was the eldest of four children. As a small child, she witnessed beautiful visions of the spiritual world. She described the visions having "lovely trees and banks covered with flowers" and "people who looked radiantly happy." In her first known encounter with the unseen world on December 18, 1906, she awakened to a vision of her mother surrounded by light. She noted that her mother appeared considerably younger than when Gladys had seen her before going to bed. She awakened the next morning to learn that her mother had died in the early hours of the morning.

Years later, Gladys began her life's work, that of communicating with those in the spiritual world. She later discovered that she had a spirit guide named Feda, a Hindu girl that had been married to Gladys's great-great-grandfather, William Hamilton. Feda informed her that she had been looking after Gladys from birth and waiting for Gladys to develop her psychic abilities, so that Feda could work with her.

Gladys was the medium **Sir Oliver Lodge** visited soon after the death of his son. After putting Gladys through a series of tests, Lodge concluded that his son, Raymond, had indeed survived death and that the information coming through Gladys was from him. Because of Gladys and Feda, Lodge was able to pen the very insightful book, *Raymond, or Life and Death*.

## Library (in the spiritual world)

According to several sources, there exists in the spiritual world a building that is a great library. The library houses the spiritual records that contain the history of earth, humanity, and the universe from creation to the present day. Amazingly, it is said to hold the experiences of every person in the universe. It is a spiritual library of knowledge. Some people have traveled to this library either during an out-of-body experience or a near-death experience and returned to tell of what they saw. Psychics who have been able to tap into unseen records and retrieve information also call this great repository a library. The records they accessed are called the **Akashic Records.** This library is also called the **Hall of Records.**

## Life After Death
See **Afterlife.**

## Life Review

The life review is a record of a person's entire life history. According to near-death experiencers, once a person passes from physical life into the spiritual world, they are shown their life review. (The term *life review* has become popular in the past few years as more and more accounts of near-death experiences have become available to the general population.) The review has been described as a vivid, full-color, three-dimensional, panoramic review of every single act and thought a person did in life, including the good and the bad.

Near-death experiencers have witnessed the life review in different ways. Some say that it is presented on a large screen or imaging machine. Others have seen it as images swirling around them. And, unlike many religious beliefs in which **God** judges the review, each individual essentially judges him- or herself. After witnessing the life review and judging its actions and behavior in the most recent life, the soul decides whether it will ascend in the spiritual world or return to another incarnation on earth.

Each life lived has a life review. It has been suggested by some, such as the theosophists, that when recalling past-life experiences, people are actually recalling an end-of-life review.

## Light, The

We see it portrayed often in religious pictures and in metaphysical books with people journeying towards it, and we've heard of it many times in near-death, religious, and mystical accounts. This very brilliant light, emanating love and warmth, permeates the spiritual world. This light is one of attraction, and those that have experienced it say that once they entered it, they never wanted to leave. Anyone who has traveled into this light and lived to tell about it has relayed the feeling of warmth and love they felt while being engulfed in it. This light is described in various accounts as blinding and either white or golden. It is often associated with the tunnel that the soul passes through after death. As the soul journeys through the tunnel, it sees at the end a luminous white light and is automatically drawn toward it. This light grows ever brighter as souls travel up through the spiritual realms, and it also radiates downward through the heavenly spiritual dimensions.

This light is believed to be the light of the divine source, the light of **God.** Many who have experienced it express the feeling that they knew they were in God's presence and in God's love. Ancient Jewish lore says that God's light radiated through the heavens and downward to the earth. The farther away from God, the dimmer the light was. This light, the ancient Jews believed, was also representative of God's love, which was also said to radiate downward. In some religions the white light is symbolic of eternal peace. White and light are associated in many cultures with goodness. The white light is, therefore, interpreted by some to mean "eternal good."

Spirits are said to be surrounded by this bright light. People that have seen loved ones visiting from the spiritual world sometimes speak of a special glow or light surrounding these spirits. Those that have had glimpses of the spiritual world in near-death and astral-travel experiences say that the more spiritually developed a person, the brighter the light they radiate. The less spiritually developed someone is, the dimmer their light is said to be. If someone has lived a particularly heinous life on earth, in the afterlife the soul of that individual may find itself completed surrounded by darkness, devoid of all light. This darkness has been described as particularly stifling, scary, lonely, and vast.

It is said that humans each carry this light within them, even while on earth during a physical incarnation. When it is time for a person to pass on, their inner light begins to blink, and loved ones on the other side know it's the person's time to cross over. Hospital nurses have reportedly seen a white glow or light that left the body at the moment of some patients' deaths.

Beings of light in the spiritual world are said to be so luminous that it is difficult to see a form of the spirit within the light. Beings of light, angels, enlightened beings and ascended masters dwelling in the various spiritual realms are often described as "white as snow," "like lightening," and "shining ones." Catholic priest and mystic Pére Lamy once wrote, "These bright Angels are enveloped in a light so different from ours that by comparison everything seems dark." In his *Divine Comedy*, **Dante** wrote, "They had their faces all of living flame, And wings of gold and all the rest so white that never snow has known such purity."

## Light Body

Another name for the soul.

## Lincoln, Abraham

The sixteenth president of the United States (1809–1865). Lincoln had an interest in spiritual phenomena and was an avid believer of spiritualist concepts. It is known that Lincoln attended séances, both at the White House and other locations. Evidence supports that he used spiritualism during the Civil War to obtain military information, and spiritualism also may have played a role in his issuing the Emancipation Proclamation.

Interestingly, Lincoln had a strange dream about his death several days before he was assassinated. He relayed his dream to his friend Will Lamon:

*There seemed to be a death-like stillness about me. Then I heard subdued sobs, as if a number of people were weeping. I thought I left my bed and wandered downstairs. I went from room to room . . . the same mournful sounds of distress met me as I passed along . . . I kept on until I arrived at the East Room, which I entered. There I met with a sickening surprise. Before me was a catafalque, on which rested a corpse . . . "Who is dead in the White House?" I demanded of one of the soldiers. "The President," was the answer, "he was killed by an assassin." Then there came a loud burst of grief from the crowd, which awoke me from my dream. I slept no more that night; and although it was only a dream, I have been strangely annoyed by it ever since.*

The book *The Reincarnation of Abraham Lincoln* by Richard Salva is said to be a fascinating look at the possibility that Lincoln returned to this life to complete his life's lessons and life's work. See also **Colburn, Nettie; Webster, Daniel.**

## Lincoln, Mary Todd
See **Colburn, Nettie.**

## Lily Dale Spiritualist Community

Founded in 1879 and located in Chautauqua County, New York, Lily Dale is a spiritualist community of the modern spiritualist movement. It was created as a retreat and home for spiritualists, psychics, and mediums. Today it is a great spiritual center, known for spreading enlightenment. In fact, it is the world's largest center for spiritual development and the practice of the Spiritualist religion (a religion in which people believe they can communicate with those that have passed on).

In the early days, it was a place filled with mystery and excitement, and people embraced the idea of communicating with loved ones lost to the other side. Many had their hopes of talking to their loved ones again fulfilled there. Amazingly, there were trumpet mediums, who used lo-fi megaphones to "communicate" with visitors' friends and relatives that had crossed over. Some witnessed messages from the other side appear-ing on chalkboards. "Message services," as they were termed, were available at the "Inspiration Stump." There, mediums called out predictions and communications from those in the next life that wanted to make contact. The scene there was much like those we see today on the modern, televised medium and psychic shows.

Today, participants travel yearly to Lily Dale during the summer months to take advantage of the popular classes, lectures, workshops, and other activities. These events feature best-selling authors, powerful medi-ums, healers, and leading authorities in the spiritual field. A sampling of summer offerings include clairvoy-ant demonstrations, healing services, and development circles. Lily Dale is also the home of several mediums and spiritual consultants. In order to work at Lily Dale as a registered psychic or medium, a person must pass three thirty-minute test readings, which are assessed by the members of the Lily Dale Assembly.

## Lifetime
The period of time in which a being exists in the physical realm. In order

to come into life on earth, a spiritual being, through the birth process, takes on the persona of a physical being for a period of time. This period of time is their lifetime. It is temporary and sometimes short. Spirit beings that take on this process come into life knowing that it is not forever. There is no time, no growth, no age, and no death for spiritual beings on the other side. However, as physical beings, they grow, change, and experience their life, learning lessons as they progress. In addition, during a lifetime, all lives lived previously are forgotten. The spirits' memory of the spiritual realm from which they originated is also gone. This amnesia is considered a necessity, so that the individual will not long for the blissful world from which they came. They can instead focus on their reason for coming into life, the lessons they are to learn, and the mission they are to uphold and achieve.

## Lodge, Sir Oliver

World famous British physicist (1851–1940). Lodge has been hailed as one of the greatest scientists of his time and a fearless champion of after-death survival. It is said that Lodge never missed an opportunity to talk about his beliefs that death is not the end, that there are higher spiritual beings, and that communication between the spiritual world and physical world is possible. In fact, he was able to make contact with his own deceased son, Raymond. This experience aided him in writing about the afterlife.

Lodge's first experiences in psychic research occurred in 1883 and 1884, when he joined Malcolm Guthrie on his investigations of thought-transference in Liverpool. Lodge made notable observations of afterlife phenomena as he observed medium Eusapia Palladino conduct four séances. Lodge reported on the séances in the *Journal of the SPR,* in which he wrote: "I am constrained to admit; there is no further room in my mind for doubt." In 1908, Lodge said that he believed that he had genuinely spoken with friends in the afterlife and that the boundary between the two worlds was wearing thin in places.

Lodge's most famous work on his belief in life after death came in the form of a book about his son, *Raymond, or Life and Death*, published in 1916. It was the story of the return of his son, who had died in action in World War I.

## Logos

A term from **Gnosticism.** Logos was a god and creator of the spiritual world.

## Lommel, Pim van

Dutch cardiologist and researcher/lecturer on near-death experiences (1943–). He is the author of the best-selling book *Endless Consciousness*. Van Lommel conducted research on 344 Dutch patients, all of whom had suffered from cardiac arrest in the hospital. Sixty-two of them had a near-death experience. In 2001, Van Lommel published his findings in the renowned medical journal *The Lancet*, and his article made headlines around the world. Lommel concluded that when a person's physical body dies, their consciousness continues on in another dimension—one that is invisible to the human senses.

## Lost Souls

A term sometimes used (albeit incorrectly) to mean a person that has died physically, but has not transitioned completely into the spiritual world. There are no lost souls in the literal sense. All souls have a choice to move into the spiritual world or not. Staying is done of their own volition.

Souls sometimes do not transition fully into the spiritual world for a number of reasons. One of the reasons given in "lost soul" accounts is that the person's death occurred so suddenly that they were left confused and did not understand that they had died. In the cases of some murders, a person's spirit may remain behind to help give clues to solve it, so that the family may find peace and closure. Unresolved business is another reason a person's spirit may not immediately cross over; for example, the person may have died without having left instructions for their estate or telling someone the location of their will. A person may be so attached to something on the earth plane (e.g., material possessions, a career) that they are unwilling to move on. Or the individual may have died in a tragedy of some sort and would like to prevent a similar occurrence (see **Ghosts of Flight 401**).

Individuals who do not immediately cross over are also referred to as wandering spirits. The spirit may wander indefinitely without a body, stuck between two worlds, feeling part of neither. Spirit guides are dispatched after these souls to try and retrieve them and assist them in their return to the spiritual world.

## Love

Those who have had near-death experiences say love permeates the spiritual world. **God**'s unconditional love is said to be felt everywhere. It has been explained to some near-death experiencers, as they visited the other side, that it is showing love and being of service to others that enables us to ascend into the higher, more beautiful realms. The main aspect of the spiritual world is love. It is through the life review that some, who returned to tell their experience, learned about love and could see firsthand how much love they had showed to their fellow humans. In addition, they could see how much more work was needed in order for them to obtain a level of love so high that they would never have to return to the physical realm again. Love dominates the afterlife. This love emanates from God and spreads down and throughout the cosmos. Those who have found themselves in the light after death and have returned to tell about it relay a feeling of love emanating from the light. They often express that it is more love than they have ever felt before—so much that they don't want to leave it. Many who have experienced this love in the light say that love is the reason for our existence, the reason we came into being, the reason we are alive. It is thought that the higher we go in the heavenly or spiritual realms, the more love we feel.

## Loved One(s)

Individuals who are new to the afterlife, usually within three to six months of passing, often make contact with those on the physical plane. This means that through dreams, apparitions, visions, and other means, they attempt to make contact with friends and relatives in order to give proof that they still exist. In some instances they go through mediums and strangers in order to get a message through. It is thought that when someone is about to die in the physical world, the loved ones of that individual on the other side are informed so that they can welcome their loved one into the spirit world. This makes the transition easier for the newcomer. People in the physical world have this to look forward to when their time is finished on earth. In addition, loved ones on the other side have more of an advantage than those of us remaining behind. Those that have crossed over can still see and hear those dwelling on earth, and they can work at helping and communicating with the living. Some travel back and forth to check on them.

Unfortunately, those in the physical plane cannot (in most instances) perceive those in the spiritual one. Most people are not aware of the fact that their loved ones visit them and keep track of the events and happenings in their lives. Those on the other side often try fervently to let their loved ones over here know that they are alive and well in the afterlife realms. In some cases they are able to manifest in a way that their loved ones can see (although this manifestation is temporary and often for only a very short period). Other innovative ways that loved ones let the living know that they "survived death" include bedside visions, moving objects, and manipulating electrical equipment.

## Lower Realms
See **Hell Realms; Outer Darkness.**

# M

## Maclean, Dorothy

Spiritual writer and educator (1920–). She was one of the founders of the Findhorn Foundation in northeast Scotland. She is also the author of the popular book entitled *To Hear the Angels Sing,* which discusses her experiences with angels within the devic kingdom—the realm of spiritual beings that dwell alongside humans, but are invisible on the physical plane. From her telepathic communications with the angels, she developed the Findhorn Garden (a beautiful garden that grew from sand and in adverse conditions) and the Findhorn Community.

## MacDougall, Duncan

An early twentieth-century physician of Haverhill, Massachusetts (c. 1866–1920). In 1907, MacDougall sought to measure the weight that was lost by the human body when the soul vacated it at death. His aim was to prove that a person's soul was material and therefore had mass, making it measurable. He believed that there would be an immediate, measurable drop in the weight of the individual at the moment the soul vacated the body. With this in mind, MacDougall created a special bed, arranged on a light framework and built upon very delicately balanced platform beam scales sensitive to two-tenths of an ounce. MacDougall weighed six terminally ill patients in succession before they died, so that after the soul left the body he could then determine the soul's mass. He observed the patients before, during, and after the process of death, and measured any corresponding changes in weight. He did the same with fifteen dogs and reportedly found no change in the animals' mass. In the end, MacDougall determined that the soul weighed twenty-one grams. As a result, this number has become identified with the measure of a soul's mass. In March of 1907, accounts of MacDougall's experiments were published in the *New York Times* and the medical journal *American Medicine.*

## Macy, Mark

Instrumental transcommunication (ITC) researcher and pioneer (1949–). He was able to communicate for thirteen minutes with the deceased scientist **Konstantine Raudive** through ITC. Macy is the founder of Continuing Life Research and World ITC *(www.worlditc.org),* a nonprofit corporation established to encourage empirical investigations.

## Materialization

Name given to the psychic phenomenon produced by certain mediums. During materialization, a spirit acquires an artificial body and makes itself materially visible.

## Mayans

American Indian people. The Mayans had a large interest in the spiritual world. They believed that there were several spirit creatures and gods and goddesses to see them through life in the physical world. The sun god, the maize god, the planet Venus, and numerous death gods were among the deities that watched over the Mayan world from the spiritual plane. The Mayans believed in an afterlife consisting of a paradise where pleasure and delights were in abundance. They also believed in a lower realm similar to hell, to which evildoers would go and suffer such unpleasant conditions as freezing, starvation, and grief.

## Medium

An American television series (drama) that is based on the life of medium **Allison DuBois,** author of the best-selling books *Don't Kiss them Good-Bye* and *We Are Their Heaven: Why the Dead Never Leave Us.* The show (which premiered on NBC, January 3, 2005), revolves around a medium, played by Patricia Arquette, who works for an Arizona district attorney's office. The show was created by Glenn Gordon Caron and produced by Picturemaker Productions and Grammnet Productions in association with CBS Paramount Television.

## Medium(s)

A medium is an intermediary for communication between the material and spiritual worlds. Those in the unseen world use this person to send messages to the living. Mediums connect the physical world with the spiritual realm. They are gifted with the ability to receive messages from the deceased.

These messages can arrive in a variety of ways. There are, therefore, a number of different types of mediumship. Some mediums are clairvoyant—they can see people from the other side or receive visions from people in spirit. There are also mediums that are clairaudient, or able to hear voices from those in spirit. Some mediums are gifted with both abilities.

**Materialization Mediums.** A medium that is able to assist a spirit being in manifesting itself in the physical plane. Ecotoplasm plays an important role in this type of mediumship, which is rarely used today. During the 19th century, humanity was just learning and accepting the idea of life after death and the eternal existence of the soul (even though it had been taught for centuries in most religions). In the modern era, there is more acceptance of this reality, and proof like that which is given through materialization mediumship is not necessary. This is a benefit, because materialization mediumship is energetically draining for the medium.

**Photographic Mediums.** A form of mediumship in which one is able to capture the images of spirits on film during a séance. This type of mediumship is no longer popular, as modern photographic equipment is able to capture spirits on film without the help of a medium.

**Trance Mediums.** A type of mediumship that allows the medium to go into a temporary state of suspended awareness, thus allowing a disincarnate spirit to inhabit the body and speak through it. Trance mediumship first came into prominence in the early 19th century. It is still practiced by some mediums today.

**Physical Trance Medium.** Another term for trance medium.

**Direct-voice Mediums.** Direct-voice mediums have the unique ability to enable people living in the afterlife to speak audibly, so sitters in a séance can hear the deceased's voices and the voices can be recorded on a tape recorder. (See **Direct-voice Communication.**) One of the most famous direct-voice mediums is **Leslie Flint.** On cassettes of his séances, recorded by Betty Green and George Woods, deceased people talk about their deaths and crossing over into the next life.

In most cases, these speakers are people who lived ordinary lives while on earth. However, voices of notables such as Frederic Chopin, **Mahatma Gandhi,** Rabindranath Tagore, George Bernard Shaw, Valentino, and Oscar Wilde can be found on the cassettes.

**Mediums via Guides.** Mediums via guides is a term that applies to mediums who do not communicate directly with the dead, but who work through a guide. A guide is a spirit who has passed on, but remains close to the earthly plane in order to assist humanity. When working with a medium, the guide communicates with departed spirits and then acts as a go-between, getting messages from that spirit to the medium.

**Mental Mediums.** A medium that uses telepathy to bring messages from those dwelling in the spiritual world is called a mental medium. This particular form of mediumship allows the person to mentally hear, see, and even feel messages from spirits on the other side. The mental medium is different than a nonmental medium in that they produce physical phenomena, such as voices, lights, levitation,

or in some cases, the manifestation of ectoplasmic figures.

When a medium is giving a reading for an individual, that individual is known as a "sitter."

See also **Altea, Rosemary; Bailey, Lilian; Barbanell, Maurice; Borgia, Anthony; Browne, Rosemary; Browne, Sylvia; Channeling; Colburn, Nettie; Cooke, Grace; Crookes, Sir William; Direct-voice Mediumship; Doyle, Sir Arthur Conan; DuBois, Allison; Edward, John; Flint, Leslie; Findlay, Arthur; Ford, Arthur; French, Emily S.; Garrett, Eileen; Piper, Leonore; Sloan, John; Terry, Dame Ellen; Van Praagh, James.**

## Meek, George W.

An American inventor, designer, and manufacturer of devices for air conditioning. He established the Metascience Foundation in Franklin, North Carolina, which sponsored the famous Spiricom research. The Spiricom research demonstrated extended, two-way instrumental communication between people alive here on earth and people living in the spiritual world. Meek authored a number of books, including his famous *After We Die, What Then?* Meek's wife, Jeanette, transmitted accurate information from the other side after she had passed and Meek was still on the earth plane.

## Meetings
Shortly after a person has crossed over to the other side, they will likely see someone they know. More often than not, it is a very close relative or personal friend, trying to ease the person into their new existence or, in the case of a near-death experience, informing the person that they must return to physical life because it is not time for them to cross over. Meetings of this nature usually have an unforgettable impact on the individual returning to life and helps lessen their fear of dying.

## Melanesia
Melanesia is a region of the South Pacific Ocean made up of Fiji, New Caledonia, the Solomon Islands, and Vanuatu. The spiritual life of the Melanesians, the indigenous people of the islands, was filled with a diverse group of gods and spirits. Various

spiritual beings were associated with creation, sustaining the cosmos, fruitfulness, wars, and prosperity. To the Melanesians, those that had passed on were still near, although in spirit, and they continued to be a part of the community. The Melanesians also believed in ghosts and were careful to not hurt the feelings of those that had died. In fact, ghosts were often distinguished from the settled dead. The Melanesians worried about those that had died in war, believing that these restless souls needed to be placated. Some believed that if a family member was killed unexpectedly, they would cause problems for the living.

Melanesian dead were believed to go to Adiri, the Melanesian land of the dead. Some thought Adiri to be an island; others though it was a mountain located in the west beyond the sunset. It was a place free of sorrow and pain, where its spiritual inhabitants were young forever. It was believed that immediately after death, the soul passed through hazardous circumstances before reaching its destination of Adiri. Those souls that were unable to complete the journey faded out of existence forever. They also disappeared for eternity if relatives and loved ones on earth forgot them.

**Tum.** Another afterlife belief found in the ancient Melanesian culture is that of Tum. It was believed that when an individual passes on, the spirit of the person journeys to Tum, a beautiful paradise full of material delights. It was believed that one could only reach Tum by riding on the back of a large serpent. In addition, only those with a special mystical birthmark or tattoo could enter. Once a resident of Tum, an individual could enjoy the sumptuous foods, joy, and peaceful existence it offered.

## Mental Medium
See **Medium(s).**

## Meru, Mount
A sacred mountain in Buddhism, **Hinduism,** and **Jainism.** It was believed to be the center of both the physical and spiritual universes. It was also thought to be home to Brahma, Indra, and a number of other gods.

## Messenger(s)
The idea of spiritual messengers that travel back and forth between the physical and spiritual worlds can be traced back to ancient history. Such messengers can be found in ancient Sumerian drawings, Babylonian legends, Greek and Roman mythology, as well as Judeo-Christian and Muslim writings. The Babylonians had the *sukalli,* which translates into "angelic messengers." The Greeks had Hermes, the winged messenger of Zeus (supreme being in Greek mythology). The Greeks also had Iris, who was messenger for Hera (Zeus's wife). In **Rome,** there was Mercury, the messenger of Jupiter. These ancient gods became the archetypes for the angelic messengers of the monotheistic religions. Dionysius stated that angels are "messengers which carry Divine Decrees." In Judaic lore, the messengers were angels who brought messages to the prophets such as Abraham and Daniel. The Christians had **Gabriel**, the angel of revelation, who delivered messages regarding important births such as those of John the Baptist and **Jesus.** The **Koran** states, "**God** sends forth the angels as His messengers, with two, three, or four pairs of wings." In **Islam, Jibril** (Gabriel) brought **Muhammad** a revelation from God.

## Methetherial

A term coined by **Frederic Myers** meaning beyond the ether, the transcendental world in which the spirit exists.

## Metempsychosis

An ancient Greek philosophical term for reincarnation. In Eastern beliefs it refers to the doctrine of transmigration of the soul, which is the belief that at death, the soul of the person passes into another body. The body can be human, animal, or inanimate.

## Michael

A prominent, powerful spiritual being, according to Judeo-Christian lore. Michael, whose name means "who is as **God**," is one of the mighty seven archangels. He is still called upon today for help and protection. According to religious lore and angelology, Michael is God's warrior who leads the celestial army and is the ruler of the seventh heaven. In art he is depicted as muscular, youthful, and handsome, wearing the breastplate of righteousness and the shield of faith. The **Bible** states that it was Michael and his army who defeated Satan and his hordes in the war in heaven, throwing them out of heaven and down to the earth: "And war broke out in heaven: Michael and his angels battled with the dragon, and the dragon and its angels battled, but did not prevail, neither was a place found for them any longer in heaven. So down the great dragon was hurled, the original serpent, the one called Devil and Satan, who is misleading the entire inhabited earth; he was hurled down to the earth, and his angels were hurled down with him" (Revelation 12:7–9). Michael is also said to be the angel that Revelation 20:1–3 says will descend from heaven with the key to the abyss and will lock Satan away for a thousand years. According to ancient Judaic lore, it was Michael who prevented Abraham from sacrificing his son Isaac. Legend has it that it was also Michael who appeared to Moses in the famous burning-bush story. He has been credited with freeing the apostle Peter from prison and rescuing Daniel from the lion's den (Acts 5:19; Daniel 6:22).

In **Islam** Michael is named Mikhail. The **Koran** says the cherubim are created from the tears of Mikhail. During the Middle Ages, the church portrayed Michael as a psychopomp (an escort of souls to the spiritual world) in order to attract non-Christians into the church. The Dead Sea Scrolls calls Michael the prince of light and says he battles against the sons of darkness. He leads the good angels against the fallen angels, which are led by Belial. **Joan of Arc** named him as one of the angels who encouraged her to help the French dauphin fight the English. In 1950, Pope Pius XII declared Michael "protector of police officers." In the Book of Raziel (a compilation of spiritual, cosmological, and mystical Hebrew works), he is listed as an amulet angel who is summoned by women in childbirth to ensure their babies have a safe delivery.

## Middle Ages

During the Middle Ages (476–1453 AD), beliefs in spiritual beings were a part of people's day-to-day thinking, philosophy, and Christian theology, especially amongst the Europeans. A belief in the presence of both good and bad supernatural spiritual beings predominated. These beings, it was thought, had a number of functions related directly to the physical world. It was believed that spiritual beings or angels were in charge of the four seasons, the planets, the twelve months of the year, the seven days of the week, and even the hours of the day and night. As a result, representations of spiritual beings flourished in art, including poetry, paintings, sculpture, and architecture, and many such beings took on a feminine appearance.

However, the belief in a spiritual world filled with enlightened beings helping to run the universe was equally balanced with a belief in dark spirits or demons. Christians of the period regarded dark spirits as powerful and considered them to be present everywhere in the physical world. This belief is seen in the great gothic cathedrals from the period, which have carvings of demons, as well as gargoyles, on and around the rooftops.

Theologians of the period spent time discussing and debating spiritual beings. They sought to be enlightened on the nature of these beings and determine whether or not they were omnipresent, as **God** is. They wondered if these beings could be in two places at once and what their relationship was to the space-time continuum. The famous question of how many angels can stand on the point of a needle came from theologians of this period.

In the Middle Ages, access to the spirits of the dead was obtained through the art of necromancy (a form of divination in which spirits from the afterlife are called upon).

See also **Alighieri, Dante.**

## Mills, Roy
See **Prebirth.**

## Ministering Angels
See **Angels.**

## Mohammad
See **Muhammad.**

## Moksha
See **Hinduism.**

## Monroe, Robert
A successful businessman and noted pioneer/researcher in the investigation of human consciousness and astral projection (1915–1995). He is the author of *Journeys Out of the Body, Far Journeys,* and *Ultimate Journey.* In addition, he invented Hemi-Sync (a patented technology) and founded the Monroe Institute, a worldwide organization dedicated to expanding human potential. Monroe began to astral travel, to his surprise, in 1958. His out-of-body experiences started without warning. At first, afraid of what people might think, he told only a few close friends about what was happening. However, as time passed, and he could not find any books to help him understand the phenomenon, he decided to write his own. He also began experimenting with sound waves as a way of aiding astral travel.

## Mons
The site of a famous apparition involving a band of spiritual beings from the unseen world, believed by some to be angels. In August of 1914, German troops claimed that while fighting British soldiers in World War I at Mons, Belgium, they saw spectral riders, armed with bows, arrows, and swords, battling in the sky, hampering their attack on the British.

## Montgomery, Ruth

Renowned journalist turned psychic channeler (1913–2001). A former foreign correspondent, syndicated columnist, and president of the Women's National Press Club, Montgomery stunned her peers by stepping out of a lucrative career in journalism and into a world of psychic phenomena, channeling, and ultimately making contact with the other side. At the encouragement of her friend, famed medium **Arthur Ford,** Montgomery made contact with her spirit guides from the other side, who would channel through her via pen and paper. She soon began to channel startling answers to questions about life after death, the spiritual world, what happens after a person dies, where souls go, and what life is like on the other side. The author of some fifteen books, Montgomery wrote extensively about the spiritual world, life after death, near-death experiences, extraterrestrials, walk-ins, earth changes, prophecies, and more.

## Moody Jr., Raymond A.

World-renowned near-death researcher, lecturer, and the best-selling author of eleven books, including the classic *Life After Life,* which has sold over 13 million copies worldwide (1944–).

Moody is known as the father of near-death experience research and has interviewed over a thousand people that have had near-death experiences. In fact, it was Moody who coined the term *near-death experience.* He has studied and chronicled many of these experiences in several books.

Moody's fascination with the phenomenon began in 1965 after he heard of **George Ritchie**'s near-death experience. As Moody trained to become a physician, he came across several patients that had been clinically dead before being revived. In 1975, after he had become a doctor, Moody published *Life After Life,* which contained 150 experiences of people that had died, or almost died, and then recovered. Since that time Moody has continued his work in near-death experiences and authored a number of other books, including *Reflections on Life After Life, The Light Beyond, Reunions,*

*Life After Loss, Coming Back,* and *The Last Laugh.* Moody is currently the head of the Consciousness Studies program at the University of Las Vegas.

Moody's findings showed nine common occurrences in the near-death experience: (1) hearing a strange sound, (2) experiencing peace and painlessness, (3) having an out-of-body experience, (4) entering a tunnel, (5) ascending quickly into the heavens, (6) meeting friends or relatives that have previously crossed over, (7) meeting a being of light, (8) receiving a life review, and (9) having a reluctance to return.

## Mormonism

In Mormon beliefs, the soul or spirit immediately goes to the spiritual world. The fate of the soul is based upon whether or not the person was good and righteous in life. If it was, the soul will live in a state of paradisiacal joy. The Mormon spiritual paradise is said to be a combination of natural beauty and include gold houses and jeweled streets. The souls of unbelievers (those who do not practice the Mormon faith) and wicked people will exist in a sort of spiritual prison where they will exist in unhappiness. This state, however, is only temporary—if the imprisoned souls take the opportunity to repent. There is a final judgment and resurrection in which the majority of souls will move into one of three heavenly kingdoms. Only the worst of the worst will spend eternity in suffering and darkness.

Mormons also believe in life before birth. This belief helps them to understand who they are, where they originally came from, and their purpose for coming into physical form. In order for a couple on earth to remain married after they pass on, they go through a ceremony that will seal their marriage in the afterlife. Only those who adhere to Mormon standards can be sealed in this way through marriage, as it is through a special Mormon ceremony that this eternal joining takes place.

## Mors

The god of death in Roman mythology and the equivalent of the Greek god **Thanatos.** Mors carried the souls of humans to the underworld after they died. He was the archetypal angel of death.

## Morse, Melvin

American pediatrician, neuroscientist, best-selling author, and near-death experience researcher and expert. Morse's first experience with the subject of near-death experiences occurred in 1982, when he revived a nine-year-old girl who had drowned in a swimming pool. The girl, Katherine, told Morse that during the time she was dead she met what she thought was her guardian angel. Morse was so taken with the experience that he delved into researching the subject of life after death. He first set out to find details of Katherine's out-of-body experience that would prove that she really had seen the other side. He realized that while she had been dead, she made observations about what was happening in the physical world. Her descriptions of what was occurring during the time when she supposedly had no awareness of the physical world proved to Morse that she had indeed left her body and, from the spiritual world, was observing what was transpiring as she lay dead.

According to Morse, when people experience death, they become fully conscious. Senses are more keen and aware of the world around them. In addition, there is a wisdom about them that they hadn't possessed during their life on earth. Morse believes that human beings are not using their brain to the fullest extent. He contends that the unused portion of our brain is the area responsible for our intuition and psychic gifts. As a young physician, Morse continued to research the near-death experiences of children. In time, his research lead him to the locating of our God Spot, which is our natural connection to the universe.

Morse is also the author of *Closer to the Light*, *Transformed by the Light* (with Paul Perry), *Parting Visions,* and *Where God Lives* (with Paul Perry). For further information on Melvin Morse's research, see his website: *www.melvinmorse.com.*

## Muhammad

The founder of **Islam** (570–632 AD). Muhammad is of key importance to Muslims as a living example of the "ideal Muslim," the model for all to learn from and copy. Muhammad was born in Mecca, a commercial, cultural, and religious center in Arabia, in the year 570. After the death of his mother (his father died before his birth), he was raised by an uncle from the tribe of Quraysh. Growing up, he became known for his sincerity, honesty, and generosity. Historians describe him as calm and meditative, a man of a deeply religious nature who had long detested the decadence of his society. It became his habit to meditate from time to time in the Cave of Hira, near the summit of Jabal al-Nur, the "Mountain of Light," near Mecca.

One day, at the age of forty, while meditating, he heard a voice that commanded him, "Recite!" Muhammad, stunned and confused, wondered if he was hearing voices and worried that there was something wrong with him. Frightened and bewildered, he responded that he had nothing to recite. Again the voice commanded him to recite. Finally, the words came to him: "Recite in the name of your Lord who has created man out of a germ-cell. Recite for your Lord is the Most Gracious One Who has taught by the pen, Taught man what he did not know!" Afterward (around the year 610), Muhammad began to receive a series of revelations through the angel **Jibril.** Like the biblical prophets, Muhammad spent many years communicating the messages he received from **God**, calling upon people to repent their sinful ways and to return to the worship of the one true God. Over the next twenty-three years, Muhammad wrote under divine dictation a book so beautiful that people are said to have wept upon hearing it. The **Koran** affected the lives of all the Arab tribes in his region and, in only a few generations, spread across all of North Africa and as far east as **India.** Muhammed continued receiving divine revelations until shortly before his death at the age of sixty-two.

In addition to the visions and revelations he received, Muhammad underwent a journey in which he ascended to the higher realms and saw many great things. This journey secured his fate as God's messenger in Muslim beliefs and established the model for later Islamic literature on the path of souls at death. On another occasion, angels washed and purified his heart and filled him with wisdom and faith. They then took Muhammad on a tour of paradise.

## Muldoon, Sylvan Muldoon

American pioneer on the subject of astral projection, or out-of-body experiences (1903–1969). Muldoon was born on February 28, 1903. He grew up in the small country town of Darlington, Wisconsin. From a very early age, Muldoon was able to leave his body and travel within the astral world. Muldoon first had an out-of-body experience when he was just twelve years old. He awakened in the middle of the night to find himself conscious, but not knowing where he was. He realized that he was floating in the room above his bed. He could see his physical body lying asleep on the bed below. He saw, between himself and his body, a cord connecting the two. The cord ran from the back of the head of his spirit body to a spot between the eyes of his physical body. Muldoon attempted to walk to another room to wake someone. To his shock, he walked right through the door and through the bodies of other sleepers, too. Not knowing or understanding what was

happening, he was scared. He continued to walk around the house, unsure of what to do, when he began to feel the pull of the cord and was pulled back into his body.

Muldoon went on to experience hundreds more projections. As a result, he unwittingly became an authority on the subject of astral travel. His books on the subject were written during a time when people were not as open-minded to the possibility of the spirit body separating from the physical, and few had heard of the phenomenon. That didn't deter Muldoon, who, seeking answers, continued on his quest of discovery. Today, his books are considered classics in their field. They include *The Projection of the Astral Body,* which is mainly an account of Muldoon's experiences. His second book, *The Phenomena of Astral Projection,* includes over a hundred astral projection cases and details about the subjects relating to them, such as the different types of astral projection, the astral cable, the hypnagogic state, flying and falling dreams, dream control, cosmic energy, telekinesis, consciousness, methods of projection, and the nature of the ghostly form.

## Multidimensional Travel
Another term for astral projection.

## Multilocation
See **Bilocation.**

## Muslims
See **Islam.**

## Myers, Frederic
A scholar, psychic investigator, and one of the founders of the Society for Psychical Research (1843–1901). In addition to the psychical research he did during his life on earth, after his death, Myers initiated a series of cross-correspondences, complex messages designed in and sent back from the spiritual world to different mediums in various parts of the world. Alone, the messages Myers sent meant nothing. But when put together, they made sense.

To many, the cross-correspondences were the most persuasive evidence for the existence of a spiritual world and the existence of an afterlife. In addition, Myers's method of communication proved that mediumship had nothing to do with the medium reading the minds of the sitters. My-ers, however, did say it was extremely difficult to transmit his messages from the spiritual world to the mediums. He described it as "standing behind a sheet of frosted glass which blurs sight and deadens sound."

## Mysteries of Heaven
A term used in the **Books of Enoch** when referring to knowledge that is known only by higher beings in the spiritual world. In the Books of Enoch, **God** informs **Enoch** that the "mysteries of heaven" were no longer accessible to a particular group of angels because of their relations with the women of the earth. God accused these angels of telling the women the mysteries of heaven and said that the people of earth would use this knowledge to perform evil deeds. These mysteries are also referred to in the chronicles of Enoch as "eternal secrets."

## Mystics
Throughout history, mystics have claimed to be in contact with the spiritual beings. Some famous mystics who had these types of experiences include Jacob Boehme, who had visions of

angels; **Emanuel Swedenborg,** who communicated directly with the enlightened spiritual beings and learned a great deal about heaven and hell; **Rudolph Steiner,** who conversed regularly with spiritual beings and learned much about the spiritual realm, as well as mankind's evolution; **William Blake,** who had visions of angels and believed that his creative genius was guided by angels; and **Teresa Palminota,** who regularly received visits from heavenly people.

# N

## Nats

The name used by **Burmese** and Pakistani people for guardian spirits. Through propitiatory ceremonies, they are called upon for protection and to give assistance when needed. Nats can be either good or evil spirits.

## Nature Spirit(s)

Angels of nature (a.k.a., fairies). From the blueprints of nature that are carried by the devas, the nature spirits take the structure of nature and "flesh it out" into physical existence. They are also responsible for overseeing the physical requirements of nature.

## Near-Death Experience(s) (NDEs)

A phenomenon in which the soul of a person whose body is clinically dead leaves the physical body and travels to the spiritual world, and then later returns to life to tell about it.

Near-death experiences have been reported throughout recorded history. They are not limited to people of a particular culture, age, or religion. Written accounts of NDEs go back more than two thousand years and have been reported the world over. They can be found in ancient scriptures and writings, including the Aztec Song of the Dead, the **Bible,** Gregory the Great's *Dialogues,* the **Egyptian Book of the Dead,** the **Tibetan Book of the Dead,** and **Plato's** *Republic*.

In the mid-1970s, the work of such noted researchers as Maurice Rawlings, **Raymond A. Moody Jr., Melvin Morse, Kenneth Ring,** and **Elisabeth Kübler-Ross** brought the subject to the attention of the general public. The term *near-death experience* was coined by Moody, who used it to describe the reports of people that had died and, after being resuscitated, told stories of having left their bodies and seeing such things as tunnels, beings of light, deceased relatives, buildings, and more. There are variations on the experiences, such as traveling above the planet, stepping into a meadow, crossing a bridge, and seeing religious figures. The experiences are now somewhat common, especially since the development of cardiac-resuscitation techniques. There are thousands of these experiences documented, and for many, they lend credence to the belief that we continue on after death.

A 1992 Gallup Poll survey estimates that thirteen million people in the United States have had at least one NDE. That equates to about a third of those adults who are resuscitated from the grips of death in a clinic or hospital environment. The figure for children, however, is over seventy-five percent, as established by Melvin Morse and his associates in a landmark study done of children's NDEs, chronicled in his first book *Closer to the Light*.

Since 1975, there have been many studies on the subject. Because of this worldwide interest, there are now several international associations and journals for the examination of NDEs.

According to Moody's studies, there are nine basic occurrences found in NDEs: (1) hearing a strange sound, (2) experiencing peace and painlessness, (3) having an out-of-body experience, (4) entering a tunnel, (5) ascending quickly into the heavens, (6) meeting friends or relatives that have previously crossed over, (7) meeting a being of light, (8) receiving a life review, and (9) having a reluctance to return.

**Frightening NDEs.** An NDE in which the person enters a dark place, often described as a void, is a frightening experience. There is generally a sense of loneliness and foreboding and the presence of an evil force. Going into this dark place is the opposite of going into a white light, seeing loving beings, and finding oneself in a beautiful and peaceful environment, as usually happens during an NDE.

One of the best-known frightening NDEs (the result of a suicide attempt) is that of **Angie Fenimore.** In her book *Beyond the Darkness: My Near-Death Journey to the Edge of Hell and Back*, Fenimore writes of finding herself in thick blackness. She tells of witnessing young people dressed in black, who looked forward with a blank gaze, paying no attention to their surroundings. As she continued on, she witnessed crowds of thousands upon thousands of other people who emanated darkness and seemed not to think or experience emotion.

Fenimore felt this world was a place where there was neither exchange nor connection with other people and that the people there lived in solitude. Fenimore saw this darkness and solitude as particularly frightening.

**Well-Known NDE Researchers and Experiencers.** Popular NDE researchers include James H. Lindley, Jeff and Jody Long, Craig R. Lundahl, **Raymond A. Moody Jr.,** Diane Morrissey, **Melvin Morse,** Kenneth Ring, Pim Van Lommel, **P. M. H. Atwater,** and Ken Vincent.

Some of the most well-known accounts of NDEs are those of **Josiane Antonette, Mellen-Thomas Benedict, Betty Bethards,** Susan Blackmore, **Dannion Brinkley,** Don Brubaker, Grace Bubulka, Nancy E. Bush, **Lynnclaire Dennis, Ned Dougherty, Betty J. Eadie,** Brian Krebs, Laurelynn Martin, Dianne Morrissey, Juliet Nightingale, **Captain David Perry,** Jan Price, **George Ritchie,** Barbara Rommer, Kimberly Clark Sharp, Jayne Smith, Tiffany Snow, Nora Spurgin, **Ian Stevenson,** Howard Storm, Evelyn Elsaesser-Valarino, RaNelle Wallace, and **Arthur E. Yensen.**

## New Testament
See **Bible.**

## Newly Arrived
Those that have recently physically died and crossed over. It is believed that usually within three months of transitioning to the other side, persons are permitted to transmit messages visually to those left behind. They can do this using dreams, apparitions, and other means to give evidence that they are still alive and are doing well in the unseen world. Many even chose to stay around and attend their own funerals. However, new arrivals to the other side have some conditioning and transitioning to undergo before they can return to their true former selves and get back to their soul's journey.

## Newton, Michael
Hypnotherapist and best-selling author of *Journey of Souls: Case Studies of Life Between Lives, Destiny of Souls: Case Studies of Life Between Lives,* and *Life Between Lives: Hypnotherapy for Spiritual Regression* (1931–). Newton is a pioneer in uncovering the mysteries about life after death through the

use of spiritual hypnotic regression. He has an international reputation as a spiritual regressionist who has mapped out much of humans' life-between-lives experience. He has appeared on numerous national radio and TV talk shows to explain what immortal life in the spirit world is like. The Newton Institute for Life Between Lives Hypnotherapy provides information, support, education, therapist training, and referral services to individuals desiring an experiential understanding of their nature as an eternal spiritual being through the process of life-between-lives spiritual regression. This hypnotic-regression method offers a means of accessing soul memories through a trance-induced, "superconscious" state of awareness that brings a deep sense of love and compassion and an understanding of one's life purpose. Information on the Newton Institute can be found at *www.spiritualregression.org.*

## Nirvana

In Buddhism, nirvana is the state of enlightenment in which the causes of rebirth are eliminated and the self becomes one with the all.

## Norsemen

The Norsemen had an extensive belief system in a spiritual world where people traveled after death. In Norse mythology, Asgard was the name of the spiritual world. The dwelling place of the gods and the home of souls that had crossed over after death, it was believed to be a multifaceted city divided into twelve realms. It has been described as having luxurious palaces, huge banquet halls, and walls covered with jewels. (The description is very similar to that of the **City of Light,** witnessed by so many of today's near-death experiencers.) Asgard was believed to be reached via a bridge, called Bifrost, that stretched between Asgard and the mortal world. Gladsheim was the highest realm of Asgard. It was also referred to as the palace of Odin, chief of the Norse gods. **Valhalla** is perhaps the most famous of the realms. It is where the Valkyries (beautiful spiritual warrior maidens) carried the souls of fallen soldiers. According to lore, Valhalla was the place where soldiers went after a heroic death on the battlefield. Legend has it that after a war, the Valkyries would search the dead for soldiers whom they considered worthy to enter paradise. They would then take the spirit of the soldier to Valhalla, where the spirit would enjoy celebrations and great revelries. In Valhalla, soldiers' spirits would enjoy lavish feasts and listen to tales of their heroic deeds. Soldiers who died unheroically were destined for the gloomy afterlife palace of the goddess **Hel,** called Sleetcold (sometimes referred to also as Hel). **Gimli,** another part of Asgard, was for warriors who died, but not in a war. All of the other Norse people went to a realm where the soul existed in a kind of a limbo state.

"Being is not what it seems, nor non-being.
The world's existence is not in the world."
—Rumi

# O

## Old Soul

See **Soul(s).** See also **Children.**

## Old Testament

See **Bible.**

## Orbs

Small spheres that sometimes appear in photographs. They are rarely seen outside of a photograph. They are generally whitish, pastel-colored, or translucent. There are several theories surrounding orbs that show up in pictures. They are believed by many to be ghosts. Some say they are angels, and still others say they are souls or spirits. The most widely accepted explanation these days is that they are the energies of deceased loved ones around the people in the photo. Theory has it that spirits' pure energy shows up on film as these balls of light, and from there spirits are able to show themselves as apparitions, if they so desire. Orbs have also been spotted during near-death experiences.

## Origen

An Egyptian Christian philosopher and scholar (185–254). Also known as Origines Adamantius. At the age of seventeen, Origen became head of the catechetical school of Alexandria, where he had studied under Clement of Alexandria. Origen taught in Alexandria, Egypt for 28 years. He became famous for his interpretation of the Christian scriptures. Origen believed in a spiritual world, writing that spiritual beings were placed over the four elements of earth, water, air, and fire, as well as over the plants and animals. He taught that every person has two angels, one good and one evil.

## Osiris

Egyptian god of the underworld and the supreme god of the ancient Egyptian pantheon. He presided over the dead, the netherworld, and the spirit world. With him came the hope of continued life after death, and that the quality of that afterlife would match the lifestyle people had

become accustomed to on earth. He was associated with the Nile, whose yearly rise brought renewed life to the earth. His cult probably came the closest to a universal religion in pre-Christian Egypt.

## Other Side

A term used when referring to the spiritual world.

## Other Where (Other world)

One of many terms that have been used to refer to the afterlife realms. Some other terms include *the other side, heaven, the other world, the astral world,* and *the spiritual world.*

## Out-of-body Experience(s) (OBEs)

An out-of-body experience generally involves a sensation of floating outside of one's body and, in some cases, perceiving one's body from a place outside it (a perception commonly referred to as autoscopy). An OBE happens when the spirit or consciousness separates itself from the confines of the body and brain, thus becoming free to experience other worlds. It has been estimated that around one in ten people have had an OBE at some point in their life. This experience is also known as astral travel, astral projection, and traveling clairvoyance. A typical OBE can last anywhere from a minute to an hour. It ranges from a simple sense of floating above oneself to more elaborate flights that can take place around the house or in another dimension. Often those that have an OBE report looking down on their body and surroundings from a height.

**Causes of OBEs.** Reasons for and causes of an OBE vary. In some cases, an OBE is spontaneous. In others, it occurs due to a mental or physical trauma or as a result of taking certain types of drugs. There are also those OBEs that are purposely induced through visualization, while a person is relaxed and in a meditative state. Studies show that OBEs can also occur from direct-brain stimulation. Out-of-body experiences are a part of near-death experiences. Some people that experienced an OBE proved it by describing details, previously unknown to them, that they had observed during the OBE. Other accounts state that some people that left their body realized it only after they saw their own bodies nearby. See **Enoch; Hughes, Marilynn; Near-Death Experience(s) (NDEs); Zoroaster.**

## Outer Darkness

Another name for the darker realms, referred to by some as the hell realms and lower realms.

## Over Soul

One's true self. It is the immortal part of an individual. The personality inhabiting a physical body is but one small portion of the soul of a person. The over soul is also referred to as the higher self. Souls have various levels of awareness, from the very basic, physical-level awareness all the way up to **God**-awareness and unity with the All That Is. A part of a soul's essence never leaves the spiritual world during an incarnation. Once the physical body dies and the incarnation is complete, the returning soul rejoins with the over soul in the spiritual world. The higher self has several personalities, which have formed through many incarnations. Once an incarnation is complete, that incarnation's personality returns to the over soul. Each "self" carries knowledge and wisdom accumulated from a particular lifetime. These selves maintain their individual personalities upon retuning to the over soul. The physical being that we are today is believed by some to have been created from our over soul and sent into the physical world to learn. The over soul has been likened to a probe made and sent to earth by its creator. This over soul is thought to later rejoin the original divine creator—a supreme being, often called God—who made each over soul from itself.

"He hoped and prayed that there wasn't an afterlife.
Then he realized there was a contradiction involved here
and merely hoped that there wasn't an afterlife."
—Douglas Adams, *Life, the Universe and Everything*

# P

## Palminota, Teresa

An Italian mystic famous for her psychic and supernatural abilities (1896–1934). She received the stigmata, and once fasted for three years. She was also able to manifest extraordinary phenomena; for example, a mysterious fire emanated from her breast and would burn anyone who came near her. She led a solitary life because of these abilities, but Palminota communicated regularly with the spiritual world. She received visitations from angels and communicated regularly with her guardian angel. Eventually, Palminota went deaf, and used her angel as an interpreter.

## Paradise

A word denoting heaven or the spiritual realm that, in some religions, the good go to after death.

## Partial Appearance

The visual appearance of a person that has passed. What is seen is only part of the person, such as the face, head, or torso. It can be the faint outline of the body or the entire body in a transparent form.

## Passageways

According to apocryphal lore, there are passageways or corridors within the spiritual world. These passageways are said to be patrolled on a regular basis by angels who belong to the order of angels called the powers. They patrol these heavenly passageways on the lookout for demons trying to enter. See **Portal(s); Power Spot(s); Transportal(s).**

## Past-Life Regression

A method of tapping into information that is stored in the subconscious mind, by the use of techniques such as hypnosis, in order to recall a past life or lives.

## Past Lives

The lives lived before one's present incarnation. The soul has an eternal life, and it takes on a variety of incarnations during its lifespan. The term "past lives" is generally referring to reincarnation.

## Perry, David

A soldier of the French and Revolutionary Wars (1741–1826). Perry had a near-death experience in 1762, which he recorded in his book *Recollections.* One of the only first-hand accounts of the wars written by a soldier during that time, the book (written in 1819 and published in 1822) is about Perry's life's experiences. Perry was on his way home from the hospital at Halifax, Nova Scotia, after fighting in the French and Indian War. During that period, he had contracted typhus. Perry writes of his soul separating from his body, after which he was "immediately conveyed to the gate of Heaven." He says that he was going to enter, but was told that he couldn't be admitted. He watched as others came and went and even came upon someone that he knew. He wrote of a being that spoke with him about entering later and about the Revolutionary War. He also talked of everything in heaven feeling solid and firm. He saw a "great gulph" and explained that many of the people went through there. Some, though, entered the gate into what he called the "Holy City."

## Persia
See **Zoroaster.**

## Personality
The complex combination of characteristics (e.g., mannerisms, temperament, emotions, mentality) that differentiates one individual from the next. Upon death, when one transitions to the spiritual world, one's personality is kept intact. A person takes their mind, personality, and experiences with them. After the death of the physical body, one has a spiritual body, which is a duplicate of the earth body, and they have the same personality and character that they had in life on earth.

## Pets
See **Animals.**

## Pharaohs
See **Egypt.**

## Physical Body
The physical body is a temporary home to the soul (also referred to as the spirit and the astral body). At birth we take on a physical body. At death we discard it and move on. The physical body is animated by our soul. We take on a physical body in order to come into physical life,

experience it, and learn lessons and/ or fulfill missions. The physical body is not our true self and cannot last forever. It can be likened to a space suit worn by an astronaut to fit the environment to which he or she travels. The saying "we are spiritual beings having a human experience" applies here. Our spirit self, the one that dwelled in the spiritual world, currently inhabits the body in which we find ourselves. When that body wears out, grows old, and finally dies, our spirit self is released and free to return to the spiritual world.

**Detachment of the Physical Body.** One does not have to wait until death to leave the physical body. This detachment can be achieved during the sleep state. During sleep, it is not uncommon for the soul to leave the physical body and travel in various realms. Some have learned to leave the body this way during relaxation and meditation by applying various techniques. There are also those that can come out of their body at will without any special techniques. When the physical body is at the point of death, the soul of the individual will detach from the body. The person will observe being outside of the physical body and will be able to perceive the spiritual world.

## Physical Dimension

The realm in which physical beings dwell. It is the place that provides an environment for our physical bodies and lives.

## Physical World

The physical world is our temporary home away from home. All people are light beings from another realm or world. All have chosen to come into the physical to live in and experience it before returning to the spiritual world. The physical world is an actual manifestation of the spiritual world. Only the frequency of vibration is lower. Here the spirit can experience love as well as pain. The journey that is life in the physical world begins when one awakens to find oneself as a baby. The journey is short, as all spirits must detach at some point, return home to the other side, and continue on their spiritual path of enlightenment.

## Piper, Leonora

Popular trance medium (1857–1950). Born Leonore Simonds, she was considered the best trance medium in the history of spiritualism, although she also displayed other clairvoyant abilities, such as channeling and the hearing and seeing of spirits. In fact, it was Piper who allegedly provided, through cross correspondences, the most complete proof of life after death.

At an early age, Piper displayed her clairvoyant abilities. One of her earliest experiences was hearing her recently-deceased aunt whisper in her ear, "Aunt Sara, not dead, but with you still." Piper also had a series of episodes in which she would see faces of people in her room. These episodes terrified her as a child, because she did not realize that the faces were those of people that had crossed over and who wished to communicate with her. In her early twenties, Piper's skills were even more apparent after she visited Dr. J.R. Cocke (a popular blind psychic who was well known for his medical analysis and treatments), where she joined his clairvoyant circle. Dr. Cocke's circles were designed to find medical treatments and to also help others develop their mediumship abilities. During her second visit to Dr. Cocke, he put his hand on Piper and she fell

into a trance and began writing on a piece of paper. She recorded an amazing message for another of the sitters in the circle, one Judge Frost. It was a message from his son, who had previously crossed over. After this circle session, word spread about Piper's abilities, and her popularity grew. Her psychic gifts also expanded as a direct result of her work with Dr. Cocke and put her on a path to professional mediumship, which she embraced a short while later.

Piper received many requests for readings, most which she refused (with the exception of her family). She did not enjoy the attention she was receiving. However, there was one request, from a Mrs. Gibbins, that she felt compelled to answer. Mrs. Gibbins and her daughter (Mrs. James), were so impressed by Piper that they brought her to the attention of Professor William James (known today as one of Americas greatest psychologists and philosophers. He was also one of the founders of the American Society for Psychical Research). James was Mrs. Gibbins' son-in-law. Because of Piper's accuracy during her sitting with his wife and mother-in-law, the professor decided to run scientific experiments on her clairvoyant and mediumship abilities. As he did, there was a control from the other side in charge of the readings. He was known as Phinuit, who, during his last earthly incarnation, was a French doctor. Professor James and a number of other scientists ran tests on Piper to test her abilities, and she never ceased to amaze and fascinate them.

Piper continued her mediumship career and held sittings for readings regularly. Many famous people from the unseen world also came through Piper. Some notable names included Cornelius "Commodore" Vanderbilt, Henry Wadsworth Longfellow and J. S. Bach.

## Place-Bound Apparition

Apparitions that are seen at specific locations on a regular basis, often due to circumstances surrounding their life. They may also be attached to a certain locality because of events surrounding their demise, such as a murder or tragic accident.

## Plane(s)

See **Dimensions.**

## Plants

The plant life on the other side is often mentioned by people who have traveled there and returned to tell about their experience. These people are often awestruck by the beauty in the parks, gardens, meadows, and countryside there. It is said to be lush, with rich, vibrant colors. It resembles the physical plane, but the beauty is so spectacular that human words cannot describe it. The foliage has been called greener than anything seen on earth and is said to have a special glow to it. In Ranelle Wallace's near-death experience account, the flowers, grass, trees, and other plants seemed musical. In Jayne Smith's experience, the flowers had colors that she had never seen before. The **City of Light** is said to have lush gardens and meadows filled with indescribably beautiful plants and flowers and colors far superior than what is seen in the physical realm. In addition, all of the plants, trees, and flowers emanate a gentle glow. The plants emit an aroma that fills the senses—one that is distinct to the other side.

## Plato

A Greek philosopher (428–348 BC). The oldest account of a near-death experience in Western literature comes from Plato. He tells of such an event in his tenth book of his legendary work *The Republic,* a Socratic dialogue written in approximately 380 BC. A soldier by the name of Er, who had been killed in war, returns to life on the funeral pyre (a stack of wood for burning a dead body) and tells of his visit to the spiritual world. He tells of leaving his body and traveling with a large crowd to the location where souls are judged. The good ascended through an opening in heaven, while the bad descended to meet their punishment.

Plato believed that at death, the soul is finally released from the body. In *Phaedo* (the last of his great dialogues written during his middle period), Plato tries to show that there is an afterlife and that the soul is immortal. *Phaedo* details the final days of the philosopher **Socrates** and contains the scene of his death. The dialogue is told from the perspective of one of Socrates' students, Phaedo of Elis. Having been present at Socrates' deathbed, Phaedo relates the dialogue to Echecrates, a fellow philosopher. In the dialogue, Socrates presents four arguments for the immortality of the soul. The first, referred to as cyclical, says the body and soul are opposites, as are fire and cold; therefore, since the body perishes, the soul, being its opposite, does not. The second argument, called recollection, says that humans have some nonempirical knowledge at birth; therefore, the soul existed before birth to carry that knowledge. The third, the Form of Life argument, explains that the Forms—incorporeal and static entities—are the cause of all things in the world, and all things participate in Forms. The soul, by its very nature, participates in the Form of Life, which would mean the soul could never die.

The fourth argument has sparked hundreds of years' worth of conversation. Socrates says that because souls are indestructible, they must have existed before they inhabited bodies and must continue after death as well. The soul does not decompose as the body does; it doesn't die, but lives forever. The first three arguments were unconvincing to the two men listening to Socrates; however, the fourth argument was one they found acceptable.

**Beliefs in Spiritual Beings.** In his writings, Plato referenced mediating spirits that existed in both the physical and spiritual realms. He believed that there were many spirits of different kinds. One of these spirits was Eros. According to Plato, Eros (the god of love in Greek mythology) had the duties of translating and showing the gods the thoughts of humans. He also communicated to humans what the gods required. According to Plato, the gods would not communicate directly with humans. He held that mediators were necessary to converse between the two.

## Portal(s)

A passageway to another realm. Portals (which are sometimes referred to as transportals) are believed to be all around us. Through these passageways, a person can leave this realm and time and continue on to a new world and new life. These portals carry us to the other side. When a person dies and leaves the body, a passageway opens right before them as a crossway to the other side. Other names for portals are *gateways* and *passageways.*

## Power Spot(s)

The specific location of a portal, or gateway, between the earth plane and the unseen spiritual planes. See **Portals.**

## Powers

See **Angels.**

## Prana

In Indian mysticism, prana is the vital life force (also known as life energy or energy body) that activates the body and mind.

## Prayer for the Dead

It has been said that praying for people both as they are dying and after their death benefits them as they transition to the other side. All religions seem to have prayers for the dead. Praying for a loved one's safe passage to the spiritual world is a good way for a person to let go of grief over that loved one's passing. Grief, it has been theorized, prevents a loved one from progressing through the spiritual realms by actually pulling their attention back towards earth and keeping them attached to friends and family here.

## Prebirth

The state of existence before a person is born. Other terms for prebirth include *before life, pre-existence,* and *premortal existence.* Some people that have had near-death experiences have reported obtaining knowledge regarding their prebirth existence. Some remembered a time before they were born, a time in the spiritual world. There have been accounts of some who remembered a past life on earth. Some people recalled how they selected their various life situations, such as their parents, disabilities, and even deaths. Some also recalled the missions that they were sent to earth to perform. Others recognized that their spirit guides, who had come to assist them at death, were people they had known before coming into earthly life. In one case, a person that had died and crossed over to the spiritual world

knew where he was and was able to go directly to the place where he could request to return to earth to continue his life. Author **Betty J. Eadie**, in her best-selling book *Embraced by the Light,* wrote of seeing a place where many people were preparing for their earthly life.

It is not only through near-death experiences that people remember an existence before birth. Some incidences of prebirth memories occur during hypnosis, meditation, and dreams.

**Preparation for Life.** Before souls come into life in the physical world, they go through a process in which they spend time with others, arrange to be with them together on earth as family and friends, and establish what lessons are to be learned, what missions to be performed, who the parents are to be, where everyone is to live, and the appointed time of each soul's birth and death.

During the period before birth, spirits are attempting to put together a life for themselves in which they can learn and grow spiritually. Bodies are chosen for different reasons, depending upon what it is spirits come into life to learn. In some situations, a spirit may chose to come into the world in a difficult life situation, such as having a handicap, to aid their spiritual growth.

There are said to be many souls waiting in line for handicapped bodies. These are often preferred over the normal ones because more karma can be repaid through a handicapped body. In addition, the souls that choose these physical lives, as well as those who choose to be their caretakers (e.g., parents), are able to learn great lessons. A handicapped person is said to teach lessons to each individual he or she comes in contact with.

**On Their Way.** Just before souls are to be born into physical life, they are taken by their spirit guide to a special place in the spiritual world to prepare for their new life. There they are shown what the lives they are about to undertake will be like. The guides advise them and then send them into life in the physical—a

new incarnation, a new adventure. A soul generally joins its physical body sometime between the fourth month of gestation and birth.

**Forgetting Our Prebirth Lives.** It is believed that we forget our previous life in the spiritual world in order to live our current earth life more fully, and so that we may concentrate on our special lessons and or missions we may have come to accomplish.

One famous case of prebirth memories is that of Roy Mills. Mills has memories of events that happened before his birth, memories from his life in the spiritual world. These memories were as real and vivid as those of any experience in his earthly life. Most people forget these memories when coming into life; however, Mills still carries his. It wasn't until age ten that he realized most people don't have such memories. According to Mills, he was asked by enlightened beings not to share his memories with anyone until he was given permission. Permission was granted by a heavenly messenger in 1995. He was told to write down his memories of the spiritual world in a book. His book is titled *The Soul's Remembrance: Earth Is Not Our Home.* Roy Mills remembers events that occurred before his birth. In his book, Mills humbly shares the memories of a magnificent world.

**Prebirth Teachings of Different Religions.** Jewish rabbinical literature says that **God** made human souls during the six days in which he created the world. When each person is born, a pre-existing soul is put into a body.

The belief in prebirth can also be found in Sufism, which teaches that the soul exists prior to life on earth. The life of the soul on earth is thought to be only a short time in the long life of the eternal person or soul. The soul is believed to be born through a number of worlds and states of existence before it returns to its home that lies beyond the stars. In addition, Sufis hold that during their life on earth, they must forget where they came from.

Mormons hold that before this mortal life, the spirits of all humanity lived with God as his children. The first born of God's children is believed to be Jesus.

## Premortal World
See **Prebirth.**

## Price, Jan
Author of the popular book *The Other Side of Death.* The book reveals Price's experience of crossing over to the unseen world. On December 30, 1993, at 1:35 p.m., Price died. At 1:39 p.m., she returned to life, with an amazing story of a world beyond this one.

## Principalities
See **Angels.**

## Psychic
An individual that reacts to psychic energy. This person may be able to pick up impressions that others cannot. This can include, but is not limited to, the seeing and hearing of images and voices that are not within the normal range of human senses.

## Psychical Research Involving Selected Mediums (PRISM)
An organization that encourages, guides, and funds research work with mediums.

## Psychopomp

A being that escorts souls into the spiritual world after death. The term literally means "the guide of souls." A variation of the term *psychopomp* is *psychompoi*.

## Purgatory

An in-between state found within the spiritual realm, where souls go as they wait judgment, contemplate their previous life, and decide where they want to proceed next in their spiritual growth. A more modern term for purgatory is *the void*.

# Q

## Quran

See **Koran.**

"We shall remember, when our hair is white,
These clouded days revealed in radiant light."
—George Orwell, "Our minds are married but we are too young"

# R

## Randall, Edward C.

An attorney, businessman, and author from Buffalo, New York (1860–1935). In the 1890s, Randall became interested in the subject of life after death after attending a séance. His interest was so piqued that he became a spokesperson and advocate of spiritualism. There was a strong effort on his part to prove the validity of mediumship and in so doing, he authored such books as *Life's Progression, Research in Metaphysics, The Dead Have Never Died*, and *Frontiers of the After-life*. Randall held séances with **Emily French** (an American direct-voice medium from Buffalo) for twenty-two years. He meticulously documented the details of the sittings by stenographically recording the spirit voices. His work with French, as well as his books, made him a minor celebrity in spiritualist circles during that period.

## Raudive, Konstantin

Electronic voice phenomena (EVP) researcher and lecturer (1906–1974). Raudive was born in Latvia and later became a student of **Carl Jung.** He was a psychologist who taught at the University of Uppsala in Sweden. He studied parapsychology his entire life and was especially interested in the subject of life after death. He, along with German parapsychologist Hans Bender, investigated EVP. In 1964, Raudive read a book by **Friedrich Jürgenson** titled *Voices from Space*. Impressed, Raudive had a meeting with Jürgenson in 1965. Afterward, they collaborated on their EVP efforts and made some EVP recordings. On some of the recordings they could hear faint voices. However, after listening to one particular recording one night, Raudive found that he could clearly hear a number of voices. He played the tape back over and over and came to understand each of them. Some of the voices were in German, some in Latvian, and some in French. However, he was quite taken with the last voice, which said, "Go to sleep, Margaret." A woman named Margarete Petrautzki had recently died; her sickness and death had left a great impression on Raudive. After that experience, he spent the last ten years of his earthly life researching EVP on his own. Raudive's classic book on EVP research, published under the English title *Breakthrough* (1971), was based on thousands of spirit voices he tape-recorded. After the publication of his book, the voices were often referred to as Raudive voices.

**From the Spiritual World.** Since his death in 1974, Raudive has been actively communicating with researchers here on earth from the other side. There is a classic two-way, thirteen-minute tape-recorded conversation between Raudive and **Mark Macy** (Instrumental transcommunication [ITC] researcher and pioneer).

## Real-Time Projection

The act of a being out-of-body and moving through the physical world invisibly.

## Realms

See **Dimensions.**

## Rebirth

The act of being born into another incarnation in the physical world after having experienced one or more previous lives and deaths. A soul can be born into many incarnations.

## Reincarnation

The belief that one has lived before in another lifetime (or other lifetimes), and that one will live again after physical death. Belief in reincarnation dates back as far as the ancient Egyptians. It is an idea that some argue was believed in by **Jesus** and the Essenes of his time. Reincarnation can also be found in the philosophies of Buddhism, Greek mythology, **Hinduism, Jainism,** and **Taoism.** According to ancient Hindu teachings, after death, the soul of an individual temporarily goes into the spiritual world and then reincarnates into a different form of life, such as a plant, insect, animal, or human being.

The basic belief about reincarnation, from a metaphysical standpoint, is that through multiple lifetimes, the soul gains experience and learns and grows spiritually. Each of these lifetimes is said to be a contract with **God.** We are born, grow, age, and die as physical beings multiple times to gain life experience from various points of view. As we do so, we purposely forget about our past incarnations. It is believed that if we did remember, the memories would cause a distraction and possibly interrupt the lessons we are in the present lifetime to learn. Forgetting who we are helps us to concentrate on the present life. Souls grow in knowledge and wisdom through this basic process. When we leave the physical body and return to the other side, we then review the lifetime we just lived, as well as any other past lives, and examine our lessons and our progress. We do this with the assistance of those that love us on the other side as well as our spiritual guides and with wise and experienced teachers and counselors like the **Council of Elders.**

## Republic, The
See **Plato.**

## Ring, Kenneth
A professor emeritus of psychology at the University of Connecticut and co-founder and past president of the International Association for Near-Death Studies (IANDS) (1936–). He is one of the world's foremost authorities of near-death experiences (NDEs). Early in his research, Ring surveyed 102 NDE survivors, and half of them reported experiences containing NDE elements. He also surveyed seventeen suicide survivors who reported that they had experienced all of the various elements commonly found in NDE accounts. His data suggested that the core experience of an NDE consisted of five distinct stages: peace, body separation, entering the darkness, seeing the light, and entering the light. Ring was also the first to offer scientific validation to near-death experiences. He has authored several books on NDEs, including *Life at Death, Heading Toward Omega, The Omega Project, Lessons from the Light,* and *Mindsight: Near-Death and Out-of-Body Experiences in the Blind.* Ring has been retired from the NDE field since 1998.

## Ritchie, George
American author who had a near-death experience (1923–2007). In his books *Return from Tomorrow* and *Ordered to Return: My Life After Dying,* he recounts his amazing near-death experience and the revelations and

divine truths given to him during his time out of his body. In 1943 Ritchie died from double lobar pneumonia while he was undergoing basic army training in Texas. After meeting a "being of light," which he believed to have been **Jesus,** Ritchie was shown his life in just a few seconds of time. Afterward, Jesus took him on a spirit trip through the spiritual regions of the earth, where he witnessed millions of the lost dead continuing on in an endless life in spiritual form only, with no way to hide their private thoughts and intentions from each other. After that, Jesus took him toward a city. Ritchie later revived in a morgue. After his experience, Ritchie devoted the rest of his life to helping people. Ritchie passed into spirit permanently on October 29, 2007.

## River Styx

The River Styx, of Greek mythology, was a junction where the physical world met the spiritual world. There the living met the dead, and eternal gods and mortal men, kings and ordinary people, all made their way across on a one-way journey to the spiritual world.

## Roberts, Jane

A trance medium and author, best known for her work with the Seth Material (1929–1984). Born in Saratoga Springs, New York, Roberts had the ability to put herself into a light hypnotic trance and channel (see **Channeler**) a spiritual personality named **Seth.** The texts that were channeled were published and are known as the Seth Material. Her books on Seth have sold millions of copies.

## Rome (Ancient)

Ancient Rome was filled with beliefs about an unseen spiritual world. The Romans held that after death, they became immortal and were spirited off to paradise on a fiery, four-horse chariot. Spiritual deities can be found among the gods and goddesses of Rome. Two of the gods were the basis for the angels of the monotheistic religions that came later. There was the winged god Mercury, who carried messages between heaven and earth for Jupiter (the supreme being), and Eros, the winged god of love. Romans also held the belief that a guardian spirit was assigned to each person at his or her birth. This spirit was thought to protect the individual from harm. Proserpina, one of **Christianity**'s most notorious she-demons, was once a goddess of Rome. Romans also believed that each household had a lare (a guardian spirit) watching over the family. The lare was believed to be the spirit of the family's founder. The lare was credited as the source of the family's creativity and considered a part of its everyday life. Centuries later, Rome converted to Christianity and adopted the Christian beliefs in spiritual beings such as angels.

"The supernatural is only the natural of which
the laws are not yet understood."
—Agatha Christie, *The Hound of Death*

# S

## Sabom, Michael B.

A cardiologist and near-death experience researcher. In his research, conducted with partner Sara Kreutiziger, he found that of 100 hospital patients who had been unconscious and near death, 61 had had near-death experiences. Sabom has written *Recollections of Death: A Medical Investigation,* a book about his research. His book is hailed as the first to seriously explore the relationship of the near-death experience and traditional Christian experience. Sabom is also the author of *Light and Death: One Doctor's Fascinating Account of Near-Death Experiences.*

## Saved by the Light

A film based on the near-death experience of **Dannion Brinkley.** After suffering a sudden, severe electrical shock, Brinkley (played by Eric Roberts) has a near-death experience and is shown the future, which transforms him into a highly spiritual person.

## Schucman, Helen

The channeler of *A Course in Miracles* (1910–1981). *A Course in Miracles* is considered to be the most successful channeled work of the twentieth century. Schucman was the daughter of Sigmund Cohn, who was a chemist. Even though her mother studied Theosophy and Christian Science, and she herself had been baptized as a child into the Baptist facet of **Christianity,** Schucman professed herself to be atheist. She earned a Ph.D. in 1958 and afterward landed a job at Colombia-Presbyterian Medical Center. There she worked with William N. Tetford, who was in charge of the psychology department. The two had a rocky relationship. Eventually, as a solution to their interpersonal problems, Tetford suggested they meditate together, as he had been recently studying the subject. On October 21, 1965, Schucman heard an inner voice that said, "This is a course in miracles. Please take notes." Tetford advised her to write down what she was hearing. She did so. During the following seven years, she took shorthand notes of what she received, and Tetford transcribed them. In the end, some

1,200 pages were received. Those pages are what is known now, the world over, as *A Course in Miracles,* which, according to Schucman, was dictated by **Jesus.**

## Scientology

A religion founded in the United States in 1954 by L. Ron Hubbard. Scientology focuses on the soul and spiritual awareness. Its goal is to help people reach true spiritual freedom. Scientologists also adhere to a belief in reincarnation and believe that humans consist of three parts: body, mind, and *thetan* (the soul). The word *thetan* was coined by Hubbard, who took it from the Greek letter *theta,* the eighth letter of the Greek alphabet. Scientologists believe that the thetan is the real person that occupies the body and it is the true nature of an individual. One does not have a soul, as so many of the religions teach, but one *is* the thetan and not the body. The thetan can exist outside of the physical body. In addition, Sci-entologists believe that through a process called exteriorization, a thetan can leave its body, but still control it. A person that is capable of practicing exteriorization is referred to as an operating thetan (OT). Scientologists have no defined belief in life after death, except that of reincarnation.

## Séance

A meeting in which several people convene to try and reach loved ones, friends and relatives that have passed on from the physical realm into the spiritual world. There is usually a medium present to communicate messages received back from the other side. See **Mediums.**

## Senses (Spiritual)

It has been said by some that have crossed over to the spiritual world and come back that they experienced heightened senses on the other side. On earth, human beings have five senses. In the spiritual realms, people have increased sensory abilities.

Sight. In the spiritual world, sight is more keen and, according to one near-death experience account, more powerful than earthly sight. One person reported having the ability to see in all directions at once. Blind near-death experiencers have reported having perfect sight in the spiritual world. Some have been disappointed to find that, upon returning to their body, they were blind once more.

Smell. Different individuals that have visited the other side have said that the air is clear. They also say that it is difficult to describe the aromas and fragrances of the gardens and parks, which are filled with trees, flowers, and grasses that have much more luxurious and vibrant scents than those in the physical world.

Taste. Food is not required for the spiritual body. However, it is present in the spiritual world for the pleasure of its taste. The fruits and vegetables, according to near-death accounts, are more delectable and enjoyable in the spiritual world. However, most souls do not eat. The desire for food wanes the longer one is there and is generally utilized only by spirits newly returned from earth.

Touch. The sense of touch is alive and well on the other side. Much of the experience of touch is the same as in the physical world, but like everything else, is more heightened and pleasurable.

New Senses. In the afterlife, souls have an additional sense that most of us do not have on this side. There an individual has the ability to see into the very soul of each living thing, as well as the ability to communicate with them. Souls even know the other's thoughts and desires without having to communicate with them verbally.

## Sensory Communication
See **After-Death Communication.**

## Seraphim
See **Angels.**

## Seth
An internationally acclaimed non-physical teacher, who has dictated thousands of pages of literature through modern-day channeler **Jane Roberts.** Roberts's husband, Robert Butts, served as a stenographer, recording the messages in shorthand, although sometimes a tape recorder was used. In his channelings, Seth described himself as an "energy personality essence no longer focused

in physical reality." It was Seth who coined the phrase, "You create your own reality." Seth's messages are said to be the catalyst to the New Age philosophical movement. He has written over twenty-six books, which have been translated into numerous languages and have sold millions of copies around the world. His messages, consisting mainly of monologues on a wide variety of topics, are collectively known as the Seth Material. Seth very eloquently spoke on such topics as the eternal validity of the soul and the concept that we create our own reality according to our beliefs, as well as a host of other metaphysical ideas. His teachings have rippled out into the world to affect the lives of people in every corner of the globe.

## Shadow People

Mystical beings that appear as black, shadowy silhouettes that resemble human forms. At one time, reports of seeing shadows in one's peripheral vision were common. In recent years, however, there have been more and more reports from people claiming to have seen shadowy figures for longer periods of time. They are no longer just fleeting images in the corner of one's eyes, but are now seen so often that they have become a phenomenon. Shadow figures can range in size and shape. Some have reported to be as tall as seven feet, while others are as small as children. Some have a distinct human shape, and others are just a shadowy mass. Some are cloaked, some are hooded, and some have even been reported as having legs. But all are dark and resemble shadows. Often, these shadows are seen darting, running, and generally moving quickly across a room or even a wall. They are even said to be able to walk (or run) through walls. Most of these shadows are shy and do not like to be seen or scrutinized. They usually will run behind a piece of furniture or seem to either hide or disappear all together. They are most often seen at night, although many have witnessed them moving around during the day. Just like the shadow of a real person, they have no discernible facial features, although there have been reports of shadow beings with red eyes.

**History of the Shadow People.** The phenomenon of shadow people seems to be entirely modern. Even more interestingly, shadow people have been reported around the world. There are a number of theories as to who and what shadow people are. Some believe them to be ghosts. Researchers argue that although they appear to be some type of spiritual being, they do not follow the normal criteria of a ghostly apparition. They are thought by some to be spiritual guardians that are watching over us. Others believe them to be malevolent entities. Another hypothesis is that they are beings from another dimension. Although theories abound, who and what shadow people are is still unknown.

## Shamanism

A religion of the Native Americans, **Inuits,** and the peoples of northeast Asia. It is based on the belief in good and evil spirits who are influenced by the shamans (medicine man). In shamanism, belief in an unseen spiritual universe is predominate. There are reports from shamans of journeys to the spirit realms or realms of the dead. Shamans believe that the residents of this world are spirits that come into the physical realm to either help or harm. Some of the spirits are winged beings similar to angels.

## Shen

See **China.**

## Shinto

See **Shintoism.**

## Shintoism

Indigenous religion of Japan. A pantheistic religion, Shintoism, or "Way of the Gods," recognizes a spiritual world that includes a variety of ethereal beings and gods, which were created from the primordial coupling of a divine brother and sister named Izanagi and Izanami on the "floating bridge of heaven." The gods (also referred to as *kami*) of the Shinto religion are believed to have created Japan as their image of paradise on earth.

The Afterlife. In Shinto beliefs, a person becomes a kami after death. A kami is a being that exists in a different dimension. However, it continues to influence the lives of the family it left behind. If a person was good in life, he or she becomes a helpful kami. If however, the person was evil, then in the afterlife he or she would also be a cruel and harmful kami.

## Sibyl

A woman of ancient **Greece** and **Rome** that was regarded as an oracle or prophet. Such women would channel the teachings and predictions of ethereal beings and deities not of this world.

## Signs

A method of communication used by those in the spiritual realm to communicate with those on earth. Signs are also a way that loved ones that have crossed over connect with those left behind. Signs often come in the form of objects used or loved by the person that has passed. In some cases, people have made arrangements before death to send a still-living loved one a special sign to prove that the deceased is still alive in spirit. A sign can come in the form of a favorite flower, icon, totem, symbol, or even a special fragrance. The famous singer Patti Labelle once commented that her sister came to her as a butterfly. A grandmother whose granddaughter died in a car accident left behind an angel-shaped cookie for her to find. One child, whose father used to give her pennies before he died, started finding them in the oddest places after he'd passed. It is believed that by keeping a keen eye out, loved ones on this side can receive signs from those on the other side. Often they miss these signs simply because they lack the knowledge and belief that life continues on after death. Once people have trained themselves to look for signs, they often realize that their loved ones have been trying to make contact all along.

## Silver Cord

The cord that attaches the astral body to the physical body. It is invisible to normal vision. At death, the cord is severed. Once this cord is broken, re-entry into the physical body is impossible. The silver cord has been described as elastic. The closer the soul is to the body, the shorter and thicker the cord becomes. While the soul is away from the body, the cord becomes longer, thinner, and more elastic.

In his research on near-death experiences, **Robert Crookall** found numerous references to a kind of psychic umbilical cord that appears to connect the nonphysical soul body to the physical body. Citing such cases from his research, Crookall wrote: "With regard to form, several [experiencers] have described seeing merely a 'cord' and said that it was about half an inch wide." **Sylvan Muldoon** also mentioned the cord in his writings. He described being out of his body and the cord becoming smaller and pulling him back into his body. The cord is mentioned in the **Bible** in Ecclesiastes 12:6–7, which states, "Remember (your Creator)—before the silver cord is severed."

## Sloan, John Campbell

Independent direct-voice medium of Glasgow, Scotland (1870–1951). Through Sloan, those on the other side could easily reproduce their own voices and communicate with friends and loved ones left behind. Born in Dalbeattie, Scotland, Sloan worked as a packer in a warehouse and later ran a small shop for support as he performed free séances for people.

He was well known for not accepting money for his medium work. His spirit control was called White Feather and was Native American. White Feather was known to have a very friendly and pleasant personality and preferred to be called Whitey. White Feather spoke through Sloan's vocal organs. Sloan participated in experiments with the British College of Psychic Science, as well as with **Arthur Findlay,** who wrote extensively about Sloan.

## Smell

See **After-Death Communication; Clairscent.**

## Smith, Gordon

Scottish medium (1962–). Known as the "Psychic Barber," he is renowned for bringing powerful messages to people from their loved ones on the other side. The seventh son of a seventh son, Smith has been called the United Kingdom's most accurate medium and is famous for his amazing accuracy of details in his readings. He has proven his psychic skills to scientists and amazed them by stating the exact names of people, addresses, events—

even specific streets—of a deceased person's life. Today Smith travels the world, displaying his abilities and helping others cope with the grief of losing loved ones. He is the author of such titles as *Developing Mediumship, The Amazing Power of Animals, Life Changing Messages, Through My Eyes, Stories from the Other Side, The Unbelievable Truth, Spirit Messenger,* and *The Times of Our Lives.*

## Socrates

Greek philosopher (469–399 BC). Born in Athens, Socrates is often regarded as one of the wisest men of all time. He is credited with laying the foundation for Western philosophical thought. His "Socratic method" involved asking probing questions in a give-and-take manner, which would eventually lead to the truth. Socrates' iconoclastic attitude didn't sit well with everyone, and at age seventy, he was charged with heresy and the corruption of local youth. Convicted, he carried out the death sentence by drinking hemlock, and so became one of history's earliest martyrs of conscience. Socrates most famous pupil was **Plato,** who in turn instructed the philosopher **Aristotle.**

"The hour of departure has arrived, and we go our own ways—I to die, and you to live. Which is better **God** only knows." These dramatic lines, spoken by Socrates at the end of Plato's *Apology*, are among the most memorable in the history of Western philosophy. *Apology* recounts Socrates unjust condemnation to death by a court in Athens. Before leaving the court, Socrates requests to speak to his friends on the subject of his impending execution. He reasons that death is not an evil; in fact, he argues, "There is much reason to hope for a good result . . . Death is one of two things. Either it is annihilation, and the dead have no consciousness of anything or, as we are told, it is really a change—a migration of the soul from this place to another." If death is a state of nothingness, he argues, it will be like an eternal sleep, and therefore will be a gain and nothing to fear. If death is migration of the soul into another world—a spiritual world of true judges—then there is also nothing to fear because no evil can await a good and just person. So,

Socrates concludes, the good person can be of good cheer about death, and know for "certain—that nothing can harm a good man either in life or after death."

## Soul(s)

The immaterial part of an individual. Most ideas and beliefs about who and what the soul is are consistent around the world, no matter what culture, religion, or time in history. The soul is generally viewed as the invisible spiritual part of humans, that lives on after the death of the physical body. In most of the world's religious beliefs, the soul is eternal and after death will travel to either a good place or a bad place, depending upon the deeds in one's life. In some metaphysical beliefs the soul is made up of intelligent energy. Metaphysicians also believe that one's earthly incarnation is just a short time in the long and eternal journey of the soul, and may return to have many different lifetimes on earth or on other worlds in the universe.

Once the individual finishes their journey on the earth and experiences death, the soul travels home to the spiritual world, only to decide whether or not it wants to come back into another lifetime on earth. It is believed that removing itself from a perfect home (the spiritual world) and being born into the not-so-perfect earth allows the soul to grow spiritually. The earth is believed to be the learning ground for the soul, where the soul experiences all of the delights of being in the physical and learns the difference between good and evil.

**The Soul's Place in the Body.** Through the centuries, there have been many ideas about where the soul resides within the physical body. People in ancient Babylon, for instance, thought that soul lived in the ears. Ancient Jews believed it could be found in human blood. Interestingly, the Russian language connects the idea of a soul with the word *breath*. Since ancient times, Russians observed the dead and the living and concluded that there must be something within the human that is connected to the breath. They called that something *dusha*, which means "soul" in Russian.

**Old Souls vs. Young Souls.** The term *old souls* is often used when referring to souls that have incarnated into physical life many times. Young souls are the ones that are new to incarnating. But all souls are believed to be the same age and came into being at the same time.

See **Binary Soul Doctrine.** See also **Birds.**

## Soul Contract

A contract with **God** made before an incarnation on earth. It is a soul's solemn agreement with God to come to the earth to fulfill missions, learn lessons, or serve in the betterment of the earth and/or humankind. The contract gives the soul goals to meet and lessons to learn in a particular incarnation. It also incorporates such life conditions as where a person will live, his or her economic status, where he or she will be born, what events will happen during the person's life, and who will be the significant people in his or her life. It is written with the help of a spirit guide on the other side. The guide is usually someone who knows the person well and who agrees to be with the person during their incarnation on earth.

Missions, lessons, or purposes vary from soul to soul. Each and every soul has its own purpose that will be fulfilled in due time. This purpose or mission is stated in the soul contract. Once a soul's mission is fulfilled, its purpose is served, and its lessons have become available, it leaves the earth and returns to its former home and to God with the knowledge and experience it has just gained, and its contract is fulfilled.

**Forgetting the Soul Contract.** After death, the soul must be reminded of its true identity. Those that have incarnated are living in a constant state of amnesia; they have forgotten who they are. This is because when a person incarnates into a life on earth, they agree to forget that they are a soul that has taken on a body to experience life in the physical. It is believed that souls agree to this amnesia because if people remembered their real home, they would not want to live out their lives here, fulfill the missions they came here to perform, or learn the lessons they intended to learn.

## Soul of the World

A pure ethereal spirit that is found throughout nature. It is the divine essence that brings energy to all life found in the universe. In Latin it is translated as *anima mundi*.

## Soul Sleep

1. The state that a person in spirit is put in after crossing over, to rejuvenate them after an extremely trying life on earth. Those souls that have had extensive illnesses, a particularly abusive life, a violent death, or souls that are simply worn out, are put into a soul sleep. This sleep has also been referred to as cocooning.

2. The state a person waits in while between physical death and resurrection, according to some religious dogma.

## Soul Spark

Another name for soul or spirit. Generally, the soul spark is thought to be a part of **God** or the divine sent out to experience life in the physical. We are each considered to be sparks, or soul sparks, of the divine. This idea was a great part of ancient Gnostic beliefs.

## Specter

A term sometimes used when referring to a roaming and haunting spirit. A specter is usually a person who is restless because he or she is troubled.

## Spirit(s)

The eternal part of an individual. In most of the world's religions, as well as in spiritualism and much metaphysical thought, a human being is a twofold entity: part spirit and part physical. The physical element (the body) disintegrates at death. However, the spiritual part (also referred to as the soul) continues exactly as it was before the physical incarnation, only in another form of existence.

The word *spirit* has various meanings. However, two particular definitions of the term are often used in reference to the unseen world: (1) The English word *spirit* comes from the Latin word *spiritus,* which means "breath." To some, the spirit is the breath of a person, given for life. To others, it is the consciousness that lives on long after a person passes on. Still others define it the same as the human soul. It is most commonly believed to be the intelligent, immaterial, and immortal part of a human. (2) Some use the word *spirit* in the same context as the word *ghost*. In fact, when people see a person that has crossed over to the other side, they usually refer to what they see as the spirit of the person and not the soul. It is this spirit that is believed to be sometimes caught between the physical and spiritual dimension, and that is sometimes seen by unsuspecting individuals on the earth plane.

Trapped Spirits. A spirit that is trapped on the physical plane is not the same as a soul that has fully crossed over into the spiritual world. If trapped here in the physical plane for whatever reason—be it to look after loved ones, wrap up unfinished business, or to stay close to a home and material possessions—the spirits cannot call up the memories and knowledge of the other side that they had prior to the physical incarnation. The spirits are essentially the same individuals they were when they passed, and having not returned to the other side, they still exist in this world, even though they are in a different form. It is during the complete crossing over that spirits regain the full knowledge of their soul's journey, their true life's path. It is only then that they can remember prior incarnations, and eventually reach a higher plane or incarnate again.

Another definition of the term is often used in reference to the unseen world.

The Nonphysical Part of a Human Being. Also called the spiritual body, the spirit is the duplicate of the physical body and the eternal part of an individual. It is the part of a human that survives death. It is most commonly believed to be the intelligent, immaterial, and immortal part of a human—the consciousness that lives on long after a person passes on. Some define the spirit as the same thing as the human soul.

In most of the world's religions, as well as in spiritualism and much metaphysical thought, a human being is a twofold entity: part spirit and part physical. The physical element (the body) disintegrates at death. However, the spiritual part (also referred to as the soul or spiritual body) continues exactly as it was before the physical incarnation, only in another form of existence. The spirit carries with it all of the personality, character traits, and memories held during the physical life on earth. The spirit is attached to the physical body via a silver cord. At death the silver cord is severed.

Other terms for the spiritual body include *linga-sharira* (Hindus), *ka* (ancient Egyptians), and *pneuma* (ancient Greeks).

## Spirit Guide(s)

An invisible helper from the spiritual world, assigned to guide an individual throughout his or her physical incarnation. When incarnating, each individual is assigned a being from the other side who will go with them and help steer them through that life. These beings are referred to as guides or spirit guides. They act as personal instructors to humans on earth. Spirit guides are highly advanced beings. They are often people who once lived on earth and who desire to help others in similar life situations or in certain circumstances that they were once in. One's guides are always with them, throughout all of the learning and ordeals in life. It is the work of the spirit guides to give silent counsel and aid without interrupting the life path of the individual. Although invisible, the guides are able to communicate their help through various means, including telepathy, dreams, signs, intuition, and other ways that may get their charge's attention. These spirits act as bodyguards and protectors. Some people are quietly aware that someone (their guide) is with them their whole life.

**Temporary Spirit Guides.** Additional guides may also come into a person's life as he or she grows, changes, and needs to learn different lessons while on earth. Some guides come to teach, others to encourage. Others may have an expertise in a certain area the person on earth needs help with. Often when a person has a new idea or takes on a new subject to learn, a guide may be sent to assist. These guides are temporary. They are there to help the individual for a short period of time. In her book *Messengers of Light*, angel expert and author Terry Lynn Taylor says, "Spiritual guides come in and out of our lives according to need. They usually represent the essence of a particular culture, race, or religion, or they can represent a career or avenue of life. They are teachers."

**Spirit Guides' Role at Death.** In addition, guides come at the moment of a person's death. The guide that arrives at death may be the one that was with the person their entire life, or it may be a loved one from the spiritual world. In either case, the guide comes to assist the person as they transition to a spiritual body and their new surroundings. This guide, or sometimes more than one, will make an appearance when the person that just crossed over feels confused and even desperate about their situation. The guide may appear right away at death or after the person crosses over to the spiritual world. In some cases loved ones that have crossed over also become guides to family and friends left behind.

## Spirit Intervention(s)

The act of a person from the other side intervening or mediating in some unfinished business surrounding their death. The unfinished business may involve such cases as wills, hidden money, secret or hidden documents, or the resolution of the person's murder or some mystery surrounding

their death. From the other side, they may send messages, via some form of after-death communication, to reach the individuals seeking to resolve the situation. The intervention is often done to bring some relief to grieving families that may be seeking to locate the individual's physical remains or find the perpetrator behind a crime.

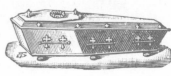

## Spirit Painting

Paintings created, through a medium, by a person existing on the other side.

## Spirit Photography

See **Hope, William.**

## Spiritism

The belief that the spirits of those who have passed on return to the physical plane to communicate with individuals existing on this side. Spiritists differ from the spiritualists in that they do not accept the idea of reincarnation. Spiritism is generally associated with **Allan Kardec.**

## Spiritual Body
See **Spirit.**

## Spiritualism
The belief that the spirits of those who have passed on return to the physical plane to communicate with individuals existing on this side. Spiritualism also embraces the concept of reincarnation, unlike **Spiritism.**

Spiritualism is a religious movement that began in 1848 by the activities of Catharine and Margaret Fox, known as the Fox sisters. They were natural-born mediums whose skills were unknown even to themselves until one fateful day when an unseen person came calling. This spirit person, in order to make them aware of their presence, would rap and knock to get their attention. In an attempt to alleviate their sheer terror, the girls made an attempt to communicate with the spirit. It was a successful attempt—and one that put the girls on the path of their own life's journey. The girls took their mediumship skills on the road, and became a sensation during their time, prompting others to follow in their footsteps. Other mediums began springing up throughout the United States, and the practice of spiritualism continues to this day (although not all mediums claim to be part of the religion of Spiritualism).

Spiritualism advocates that contact with loved ones on the other side is possible—through gifted mediums. Spiritualists believe and have proven that through talented mediums, people who have died are still able to speak, write, and even levitate or materialize objects. Spiritualism was most popular between the 1840s and the 1920s. It eventually spread to Europe. It is said that around the late 1800s, it had more than eight million followers in the United States and United Kingdom. It later became recognized as a religion. Today, one can find Spiritualist churches in the United States, as well as the United Kingdom.

## Spirituality
An attempt to find the good within and to battle negativity. It is what people, in their original spiritual state, are striving for. All are on a spiritual journey.

It is important for people here on earth to gain knowledge of the spirit while they're here. This knowledge is important because the more people know and understand, the faster they will grow on the other side. Often, due to a lack of information and knowledge, some people, after death, become trapped on this plane. They become what is termed earthbound spirits. Some examples of behaviors that would leave a person earthbound after death are materialism, addictions, and greed. Many times these individuals, at death, do not have the faith or knowledge to recognize the light and energy that pulls them towards the higher realm. Therefore, these spirits simply stay on the earth until they can let go of this world. More spiritually oriented people, who study and examine spiritual topics and strive to live their lives according to what they learn, have a better future ahead of them on the other side, as they often know what to expect at death. The kind of life people lead now, their thoughts and desires, affects where they will go and what they will do in the spiritual world. It may even determine if they leave the earth for good or must continue to reincarnate in order to learn more.

There is also plenty of opportunity for spiritual growth on the other side. Just as coming to the earth gives people various ways to learn lessons to grow spiritually, so there are also various ways to do so on the other side, thus allowing the person to continue progressing to even higher and more beautiful realms.

## Spiritual World

The natural world of human spirits and of other spiritual beings. It is the invisible counterpart to the physical world. It is also the next level of existence above the physical, where living beings that are still involved with the cycle of reincarnation and evolution study, rest, and learn in preparation for their next incarnation. Other names for the spiritual world are the other side, the afterlife, and the other world. Inhabitants of the spiritual world are called spirits.

The spiritual world is where souls exist after death. It is a place of emotional, spiritual, and physical well-being and happiness. Any sadness, depression, or sickness—or anything else that is negative and against a harmonious state of love and perfection—that people experienced during their last incarnation on earth is gone when their souls, or spirits, return to the spiritual world. The spiritual world is also where people visit when their souls are astral traveling during the sleep state.

The spiritual world is a dimension that interpenetrates the physical world. On earth, we are living in both dimensions at the same time, although we cannot see the spiritual world from our physical world. It is a far vaster dimension than the earth plane. There the soul can experience love unconditionally and receive help from higher spiritual beings such as angels. It is from this plane that beings are working together in an effort to bring spiritual progression and advancement to the earth.

Often people confuse the term *heaven* with *spiritual world* thinking that the two are one and the same. They are not. Unlike heaven, the spiritual world is made up of many dimensions, including some that we cannot begin to comprehend. In fact, heaven is but one area of the spiritual world. The astral realms are the same as the seven heavens (see **Afterlife; Books of Enoch**).

Time. In the spiritual world, time is distorted. While it may seem like only minutes have passed while one is astral traveling in the spiritual world, in actuality, several hours of earth time have usually passed.

Size. No one knows precisely how large the spiritual world is. However, in trying to answer the question, the Christians have recorded a number in the **Bible** book of Revelation. Revelation 21:16 states that heaven is a perfect cube, 12,000 stadia (approximately 1,400 stadia on each side). However, many believe these measurements are symbolic.

Evidence of a Spiritual World. Modern evidence shows that there is indeed an unseen world teaming with life. That evidences includes: (1) accounts of out-of-body experiences, (2) accounts of near-death experiences, (3) after-death communication, (4) electronic voice phenomena, (5) communications from the other side, (7) revelations through channels.

Hierarchy in the Spiritual World. According to ancient Hebrew tradition, there is a hierarchy to the spiritual world. The early Christians accepted this hierarchy as well. According to tradition, **God** is located both at the center of the universe and at the highest point of the hierarchy. Angels radiate outward from his presence; some are close to the center, while others move further and further away from it.

## Spirit Control
See **Control.**

## Spirit World
See **Spiritual World.**

## Steiner, Rudolph
German philosophic genius and clairvoyant (1861–1925). From a very young age, Steiner could see, hear, and communicate with angels. At the age of forty, he began teaching about what had been communicated to him by the angels regarding the spiritual world. Steiner believed that all people had a companion angel that stays with them through each of their incarnations. He held that during childhood, each individual had an angel who guided them. The angel worked with the individual, assisting them in the development of the soul. During the person's middle years, the angel would leave the person temporarily as the person developed themselves. Later in life, the angel would return to help that person to develop their spirituality. The angel also keeps track of all of that person's former lives. At a certain point in their spiritual development, the individual may ask their angel to reveal their former incarnations. At the end of that person's earthly incarnation, the angel leaves. It is at that point that the individual has evolved to the consciousness of an angel and to a higher spiritual plateau.

Steiner wrote extensively about the orders of angels and their functions. He ranked the angels as follows: (1) seraphim, (2) cherubim, (3) thrones, (4) dominions, (5) mights, (6) powers, (7) archai, (8) archangels, and (9) angels. He believed that mankind and the angels were constantly evolving to higher states of being, until they reached the pinnacle in the evolutionary process.

## Stevenson, Ian Pretyman

A Canadian-American psychiatrist known for his research on afterlife phenomena related to children (1918–2007). He performed a number of studies and reported his findings in academic journals, in over two hundred articles, and in several books. His case studies involved children who had memories of past lives, memories of near-death experiences, and deathbed-vision experiences. Popular books by Stevenson include *Twenty Cases Suggestive of Reincarnation; Cases of the Reincarnation Type, Volume I: Ten Cases in India; Cases of the Reincarnation Type, Volume II: Ten Cases in Sri Lanka; Cases of the Reincarnation Type, Volume III: Twelve Cases in Lebanon and Turkey; Cases of the Reincarnation Type, Volume IV: Twelve Cases in Thailand and Burma; Reincarnation and Biology: A Contribution to the Etiology of Birthmarks and Birth Defects; Where Reincarnation and Biology Intersect; Children Who Remember Previous Lives: A Question of Reincarnation; Ordered to Return: My Life After Dying* (with **George Ritchie),** and *European Cases of the Reincarnation Type.*

## Styx

See **River Styx.**

## Succubus

A mythical spirit that is believed to have relations with sleeping men. The plural of the word *succubus* is *succubi.* In medieval times succubi were believed to take on the form of beautiful women, who would then seduce men. They later became thought of as invisible spirits who would climb into bed with men to have sexual intercourse. They are said to especially enjoy (but are not limited to) pursuing those who are dedicated to a life of celibacy, such as priests and monks.

## Suicide

The act of taking one's own life. Through the centuries, there have been various beliefs about what happens to the soul of a person who has committed suicide when it crosses over into the spiritual world. Ancient Japanese warriors and also the ancient Roman upper class viewed suicide as an honorable way to die. Later, the Christians taught that suicide was a sinful act that **God** would not forgive. This teaching is not **Bible** based. In fact, the Bible says virtually nothing on the subject of suicide. There were several people in the Bible, in both the **Old and New Testaments,** who took their own lives (Judas Iscariot, Samson, Saul); however, the Bible makes no comment on this act, not saying whether it was right or wrong in God's eyes. The position of most Christians, however, is that humans' lives are not their own to take and that only God has the right to take life. They believe that humans are required, therefore, to continue their lives on earth until they reach the end. Christian theologian and philosopher Thomas Aquinas wrote that no one had the right to reject God's gift of life. In fact, some churches banned the bodies of suicides from being buried in church cemeteries. Since suicides were forbidden, it was taught that there would be a harsh punishment in the spiritual world for those that indulged in it. That punishment was going to hell and, in some beliefs, burning in an eternal fire. Even in **Dante**'s *Divine Comedy*, there is a special area of hell especially for souls that committed suicide. In modern times, such spiritual

teachings about suicide are less common. The unforgiving, severe God of yesterday has been toned down.

Among the various metaphysical ideas of what happens to the souls of suicides once they enter the spiritual world is grossly different than the staunch religions of old. Metaphysicians believe that when a person commits suicide, they break their soul contract with **God.** This contract is one that was made before the soul incarnated to come to the earth to learn, grow, and experience. This contract is said to be a spiritual agreement between God and each individual soul and is not to be entered into lightly or broken. The soul is to live out its life on the earth until the time allotted for a physical death. When a person commits suicide and the contract is broken, it is believed that that soul is immediately sent back into another life to fulfill their contract.

What a person faces on the other side after committing suicide depends on a number of factors. One's motivation in the suicide is significant. If one has purposefully taken their own life for reasons involving unavoidable death (such as a terminal diagnosis), the consequences would be different than they are for those who kill themselves because of life's difficulties. Therefore, life on the other side may not be easier for the individual who has hastened to bring an end to their time in the physical life. According to some near-death-experience reports and channeled communications with spirit guides, the souls of nearly all people who committed suicide regret it. See **Fenimore, Angie.**

## Sumeria

Sumeria was an ancient country of western Asia, corresponding approximately to **Babylonia** of biblical times. Like most of the ancient cultures, Sumerians believed in an unseen world filled with a pantheon of gods and spiritual beings that were immortal, had supernatural abilities, and were unseen by humans. These beings were believed to rule the heavens and the earth. The four principal deities were An (god of heaven), Ki (goddess of earth),

Enlil (god of air), and Enki (god of water). To the Sumerians, heaven, earth, air, and water were the four key components of the cosmos, so it's no wonder that to them there would be four major gods associated with these elements. It was believed that the gods created the heavens, the earth, and humanity by simply speaking. Like Jews, Christians, and Muslims, they believed that the gods fashioned humans from clay.

## Summerland

Another name for the afterlife. The term is often used in earth-based beliefs. Summerland is the name for the heavenly realm in some beliefs. It is thought also to be the next, more advanced level of existence.

## Swedenborg, Emanuel

A Swedish scientist, religious teacher, mystic, visionary, and philosopher (1688–1772). From his writings, a religious system by the name of Swedenborgianism was developed. Swedenborg published widely in the fields of chemistry, geology, cosmology, physiology, religion, and philosophy. At the age of fifty-six, Swedenborg had a spiritual awakening and wrote numerous books on his theological views and related topics. He was especially interested in the spiritual world. Swedenborg derived inspiration from dreams and visions, and he claimed to be able to visit heaven and hell at will. Swedenborg's revelations about the harmonious ordering of marriage, friendship, work, leisure, and education in the spiritual world were a source of conversation and amazement among the eighteenth- and nineteenth-century social critics. His works were widely read after his death and highly regarded by poets, writers, and mystics. Books about the spiritual world written by Swedenborg include *Spiritual Diary* (the personal notebooks kept by Swedenborg of his experiences in and reflections on the spiritual world), *Heaven and Hell* (a description of the structure and phenomena of the spiritual world), and *Inter-relationship of the Soul and Body* (a brief description of the relationship and interaction between the spiritual and natural planes). In his later years, Swedenborg gave himself fully to the contemplation of spiritual matters.

Throughout his life, he regularly communicated with angels. He held that angels, like humans, have bodies, but are in the spiritual form. He believed that humans cannot see angels through their physical eyes, but only through their spiritual eyes. About angels Swedenborg once wrote, "I am well aware that many will say that no one can possibly speak with spirits and angels so long as he is living in the body. Many say it is all fancy, others that I recount such things to win credence, while others will make other kinds of objection. But I am deterred by none of these: for I have seen, I have heard, I have felt."

He believed that **God** had revealed the true inner doctrines of the divine word to him alone. And these doctrines were communicated to him by angels. Swedenborg incorporated the information revealed to him from the angels in his many writings. The book that speaks most about the spiritual world is *Heaven and Hell*. It is recognized as his greatest work.

See also **Time and Space.**

# T

## Taoism

A Chinese religion and philosophy based on the teachings of Lao-tse. The term *Tao* is not easily understood and cannot be easily translated. In one sense it means "the way," as in "the way to enlightenment" or "the way to live." Some sections of the Tao-te Ching (the centerpiece of scripture and inspiration to Taoism) suggest that the Tao is the all-ness of the universe and possibly even a synonym for **God.**

Taoists believe in ministering spirits. These spirits are classified as gods *(shen)*, but perform all of the angelic functions of some of the main religions. These functions include traveling between the spiritual and physical realms, performing miracles, curing the sick, exorcising demons, and instructing humans.

## Tartarus

See **Greece; Underworld.**

## Taylor, Elizabeth

One of America's great legendary actresses (1932–). A two-time Academy Award winner, she is known throughout the world for her beauty and performances. Taylor was also named by the American Film Institute as the seventh among the greatest female stars of all time.

In the late 1950s, Taylor died on an operating table. She was clinically dead for five minutes. In her accounts of this experience, which she has spoken of to such media outlets as the *Oprah Winfrey Show*, CNN's *Larry King Live,* and *America's AIDS Magazine,* Taylor speaks of going through a tunnel, seeing figures that she recognized, and seeing and feeling a white light, like warm sunlight. She described the light as being in liquid mercury and feeling weightless. She also saw Mike Todd, her third husband, who was killed in a plane crash in 1958. In an interview with *A&E Magazine*, she said, "I believe that the soul does not die. I went to that tunnel, saw the white light, and Mike [Todd]. I said, 'Oh Mike, you're where I want to be.' And he said, 'No, Baby, you can't come over, you have to go back.'" Taylor said that it was Todd's strength and love that brought her back. She has also said that as a result of this near-death experience, she has no fear of dying.

## Telepathy

The word *telepathy* is taken from the Greek *tele*, meaning "distant," and *patheia*, which means "feeling." It is the ability to communicate information, thoughts, and messages from one mind to another through means other than the senses. It is, simply put, mind reading or mental communication. It is the method of communication in the spiritual world. It is also a means by which loved ones from the other side can communicate with those on earth. See **After-Death Communication.**

## Telephone Calls

Telephone calls from the other side are rare, but do happen. Calling on the phone is one of the most fascinating and intriguing ways that those from the spiritual world have used to try to reach their loved one. Understandably, those receiving the call are usually so stunned they can't speak. The call is said to be rather short and lets the receiver know the deceased is alive and well in spirit. The caller may even

have a message of some sort to pass on. People are sometimes nervous to admit that they have had this type of communication for fear of ridicule or that they will not be believed. See **After-Death Communication.**

## Terry, Dame Ellen

English actress (1848–1928). Terry came from a prominent theatrical family. She made her debut at the tender age of eight as Mamillius in Charles Kean's production of *The Winter's Tale*. She played juvenile roles until her unsuccessful marriage, at sixteen, to G. F. Watts, the painter. She retired from the stage for six years, during which time she had two children, Edith Craig and Edward Gordon Craig, by E. W. Godwin. In 1878 she joined Sir Henry Irving at the Lyceum Theatre as his leading lady. With him she toured the United States, under the management of Charles Frohman. After 1902, she left Irving for an unsuccessful stint as manager of the Imperial Theatre, where her son, Edward, designed the sets. She also lectured on Shakespeare in England and in the United States. An actress of great beauty, she invested her verse-speaking with spontaneity in such Shakespeare roles as Portia, Olivia, and especially Beatrice. In 1925 she was made dame of the British Empire.

In a séance given by direct-voice medium **Leslie Flint** in 1965, Terry came through. She explained what the afterlife is like, how the people there live, and that there is no hell, only each person's evaluation of his or her life. She encouraged people to look forward to that afterlife, saying that it is the most wonderful part of their eternal life.

## Thanatologist

A person who studies the process of death and dying. They often work closely with people that are dying or bereaved and sometimes with those that have had near-death experiences.

## Thanatos

The angel of death and rebirth. In Greek mythology, Thanatos was the personification of the god of death. He came to humans when their life span was completed. Spreading his wings over the newly departed, he would cut off a lock of their hair and dedicate them to the underworld. He would then carry them away. In Roman mythology, he was called **Mors.**

## Thrones

See **Angels.**

## Tibet

See **Tibetan Book of the Dead.**

## Tibetan Book of the Dead

The Tibetans believed in a spiritual world where people traveled to after death. In fact, they wrote extensively about traveling to the spiritual world and what lies beyond death. These writings were incorporated into what is known as the Tibetan Book of the Dead. It is essentially a guide to the death and dying process, designed to help people to be more knowledgeable about what is happening to them and how to proceed through the transition. The following excerpt explains to the reader what to expect after the death of the physical body and how one's spiritual body will look.

*O Child of noble family, when your body and mind separate, the dharmata (light being) will appear, pure*

*and clear, yet hard to discern, lumi-*
*nous and brilliant, with terrifying*
*brightness, shimmering like a mirage*
*on a plain in spring. Do not be afraid*
*of it, do not be bewildered. This is the*
*natural radiance of your own dhar-*
*mata, therefore recognize it . . . . You*
*have what is called a mental body*
*of unconscious tendencies, you have*
*no physical body of flesh and blood,*
*so whatever sounds, colors and ray of*
*light occur, they cannot hurt you and*
*you cannot die. It is enough to recog-*
*nize them as your projections. Know*
*this to be the bardo state.*

## Time and Space

There is no time and space outside
of the material universe. Time and
space, as we know them, exist
only on the earth plane.
When we leave the earth
plane (or material uni-
verse), we leave all of
our physical and earthly
limitations, including
that of keeping time.
Therefore, the life we lead
in spirit, in regard to time, is
far different than what we experience
while living on earth. Once a person

crosses over to the spiritual world,
the time on earth seems brief.

According to Swedish mystic
**Emanuel Swedenborg,** who wrote
extensively about the spiritual world,
the "angels have no idea or concept
of time." In his book *Heaven and Hell,*
Swedenborg says, "The reason for the
existence of time in the world is the
sun's sequential progression from one
degree to another, producing the times
called 'seasons of the year.' Heaven's
sun is different. It does not produce
days and years by sequential progression or orbital motion, but causes
changes of state. This does not happen
at fixed intervals. This is why angels
are incapable of any concept of time,
thinking instead in terms of state."

## Trance

A temporary suspended state of
awareness in which a person that is
acting as a channel or medium enters into, in order to allow a spiritual
person speak through them from the
spiritual world.

## Transportals

Another name for portal.
See **Portals.**

## Travel (in the Spiritual world)

Travel within the spiritual world is done through thought and is instantaneous. The spiritual mind is very powerful. In order to journey from one place to the next, one simply must think about doing so. This information has been made available from those on the other side who have spoken to the living in channeled communications from mediums and from those that have had near-death experiences and know firsthand what it is to move at the speed of thought. One such example can be found in **Betty J. Eadie**'s best-selling book *Embraced by the Light*. There, Eadie tells of leaving her body after death and desiring to go home. A moment later she found herself moving quickly and arriving at her house, where she could see her children.

In the afterlife, we travel with weightless freedom. This concept also applies to the angels and other enlightened beings existing in the spiritual world. According to the ancient book of **Ezekiel,** angels travel at the speed of lightening (Ezekiel 1:14).

## Tunnel

A passageway from the physical world to the other side. People that have had a near-death experience often report seeing a tunnel open up before them, and they are rushed through it toward a bright light. The descriptions of this tunnel vary. Some report it to be dark; some describe it as having spirals of light. Others say it is a dark tube with a light at the end. In some cases, people have seen a starry tunnel or a starry universe.

The vast spiritual world has many tunnels, portals (or transportals), and passageways, which lead to and from the spiritual realms and dimensions. These corridors are said to be spherical in shape and often there is light radiating from them. It is believed that angels, beings of light, and other heavenly beings move back and forth from the spiritual world to earth through these openings.

Fortunately, **God,** or the divine, has provided an easy way for souls to go home to the spiritual world via one of these portals. When a soul leaves the body at death, a tunnel opens. Usually, the tunnel is perceived as going upward, although some have suggested that it extends outward from the spiritual body.

After reaching the end of the tunnel, the person enters the light. It is then that they see friends or relatives that have already crossed over, or an angel or being of light, ready to assist them.

Says **Dannion Brinkley** in his best-selling book *Saved by the Light:*

*A tunnel was forming, opening like the eye of a hurricane and coming toward me. I actually didn't move at all; the tunnel came to me. There was the sound of chimes as the tunnel spiraled toward and then around me. Soon there was nothing to be seen—no crying Sandy, no ambulance attendants trying to jump-start my dead body, no desperate chatter with the hospital over the radio—only a tunnel that engulfed me completely and the intensely beautiful sound of seven chimes ringing in rhythmic succession. I looked ahead into the darkness. There was a light up there, and I began to move toward it as quickly as possible. I was moving without legs at a high rate of speed. Ahead the light became brighter and brighter until it overtook the darkness and left me standing in a paradise of brilliant light.*

Best-selling author **Betty J. Eadie** relays her personal account of the tunnel in her book *Embraced by the Light*: "I saw a pinpoint of light in the distance. The black mass around me began to take on more of the shape of a tunnel, and I felt myself traveling through it at an even greater speed, rushing toward the light."

# U

## Underworld, The

In traditional mythology, the universe was often divided into the heavens, earth, and the underworld. A god usually ruled the last. It was the nether pole of the cosmic hierarchy and often thought of as the land of the shadows. It was a place where, in order to arrive, one would have to undergo difficult ordeals, such as hazardous river crossing, the weighing of one's deeds on a scale, and other obstacles.

In ancient **Egypt** the underworld was the dangerous realm through which a boat carrying the sun god and his companions, including the deceased, must travel each night.

The Greek and Roman underworld was named **Hades.** It was, essentially, the kingdom of the souls of the dead. The entrance to the underworld was believed to be located at Avernus, a crater near Cumae. Three judges, Minos, Rhadamanthys (also Rhadamanthus), and Aeacus (also Aiakos), passed sentence on the righteous and unrighteous souls. In addition, five rivers ran through the underworld: **Styx** (the river of hate), **Acheron** (the river of woe), Lethe (the river of forgetfulness), Cocytus (the river of wailing), and Pyriphlegethon (the river of fire). **Charon,** the ferryman of the dead, transported souls across the River Styx or Acheron. In order to take this essential ride, the deceased would have to pay a fare (a coin) and have had a proper burial. Hermes Psychopompus, who was the leader of the souls, escorted souls of the dead to Charon. There was a guard dog to the underworld as well. It was a three-headed, ferocious dog named Cerberus. To the Greeks, Proserpina was the queen of the underworld.

In the Testament of Solomon (an Old Testament pseudepigraphical work), Abezethibou is ruler of the underworld. In other sources, Abbaton is a guardian angel of the underworld, and the archangel Raphael is the guide of the underworld. Other names for the underworld are *Atala, Amenti, Dis, hell, the infernal region, limbo, the netherworld, Orcus, Sheol,* and *Tartarus.*

## Unintentional Dream Incubation

A spiritual dream received by a person sleeping in a holy place, but who has made no effort to contact any supernatural entity.

## Unseen World

A term used when referring the spiritual world. The phrase "unseen world" can be loosely used to encompass all things found in the spiritual realm, which is made up of many dimensions. It is the realm of angels, spirits, souls, otherworldly and ethereal beings, and worlds unseen by the human eye. It is the place that we journey to when we astral travel. It is where we find ourselves, for better or worse, after death. There, in this unseen world, our loved ones await us as we finish our time on earth before returning home. It is a place filled with wonder and great beauty. However, dark places, such as the void, are said to be for those who are not ready to ascend to the higher dimensions of beauty, light, and spiritual enlightenment, also exist in the unseen world. It is where many believe the divine creator of all things **(God)** originated and dwells. It is the place in which all beings on this planet will one day return, to wherever their soul's journey is taking them.

# V

## Valhalla
See **Norsemen.**

## Van Praagh, James
World-renowned medium and author (1958–). In April of 2002, CBS aired a miniseries, *Living With the Dead,* based on his writings and starring actor Ted Danson as Van Praagh. A TV series, *Beyond With James Van Praagh,* debuted in the fall of 2002. Van Praagh has penned a number of books on being a medium and on the spiritual world. They are *Talking to Heaven; Reaching to Heaven; Healing Grief; Heaven and Earth: Making the Psychic Connection; Looking Beyond: A Teen's Guide to the Spiritual World;* and *Meditations with James Van Praagh.*

## Vedas, The
Sacred scriptures of **Hinduism;** also known as the Books of Knowledge. They are a collection of manuscripts that were recorded in Sanskrit from about 1200 BC to 100 AD. The Vedas are amongst the most ancient, revered, and sacred of the world's holy books. The four Vedas—Rig Veda, Atharva Veda, Sama Veda, and Yajur Veda—are regarded as divinely revealed and filled with other-worldly eternal wisdom. Individual immortality is a large part of what is taught by the Vedas. They discuss a kingdom of the dead, ruled by Yama, with distinct spiritual realms for the good and the evil. The good dwell in a realm of beautiful light and share in the feasts of the gods. The wicked, however, are exiled to a place of "nethermost darkness."

## Vibration(s)
Energy in motion. Everything that exists vibrates. The only difference between earth's dimension and the spiritual world is the rate of vibration. This vibration determines which spiritual realm the soul will reside in after death and the amount of light the soul will emanate. Vibration also controls the rate of thought communication and travel in the spiritual and physical realms.

Beings of light, angels, spirit guides, and spirits residing within the spiritual world work on a higher vibration than people on earth. In the spiritual world thoughts are pure energy and vibrate at a much faster rate. In addition, beings vibrate at different frequencies depending upon their consciousness. The higher the vibration, the brighter and more intense the light around a being is. The higher the vibration, the closer a being is to heaven and the nearer it is to **God.** The lower the vibration, the further away from God that being is. Some of the lower vibratory rates found within the spiritual world propel spirits into dark places. In addition, a person's vibratory rate is based upon their spiritual status (or spirituality). One reason spirits incarnate is to learn lessons and improve their spirituality, so that in the afterlife their vibration (or spiritual level) will be raised. It is the only way to gain access into the higher realms and be nearer to God.

On earth, humans vibrate at a much lower rate than they do in the spiritual world. In order for spirits to talk to us on the physical plane, they must slow down their vibrations, which is not an easy process. If we were to meet spirits in their natural state, we would not be able to see them. Their movements would be much faster than our conscious mind could comprehend.

When transitioning to the spiritual world after death, people find themselves with others that are at their same rate of vibration and in a realm that supports that vibration. Therefore, in the afterlife, each person is destined to live in a world that they made for themselves while on earth. That world can be either a high spiritual realm or a low one.

## Virtue, Doreen

A spiritual psychologist who works with the angelic realms (1958–). An extremely prolific writer, Virtue is the author of numerous books about angels, as well as about health, diet, and other mind-body issues. As a child, Virtue could see and hear angels. This unique ability has allowed her to help others throughout the world. Virtue holds B.A., M.A, and Ph.D. degrees in counseling psychology. She has worked in the psychiatric field and specialized in treating women's psychological issues. Virtue's Angel Therapy practice is a combination of her background in psychology and her clairvoyant work with the angels. Today, she is known the world over for her work with the realm of angels. It has become her life's mission to show others how to listen, hear, and apply their own messages from the angels in their lives. Virtue does this through her literature, workshops, and a call-in online radio show on Hay House Radio. Some of Virtue's books include *How to Hear Your Angels, Archangels and Ascended Masters, Healing with The Angels, Messages from Your Angels, Angel Numbers, Angel Medicine,* and *The Miracles of Archangel Michael.* Virtue has also created a number of Angel Therapy tools, such as oracle cards and guidebooks, that were inspired by the angels and Virtue's vast storehouse of knowledge. Her schedule of workshops for learning how to commu-

nicate with angels can be found on her website: *www.angeltherapy.com*

## Virtues
See **Angels.**

## Vision of Adamnan, The
An Irish-Gaelic other world experience had by Saint Adamnan. Adamnan was a renowned scholar-abbot of Iona who traveled to the spiritual world and visited heaven, a purifying realm and a realm of retribution. The vision dates back to the tenth century and is preserved in *The Book of the Dun Cow* (c. 1100). The Vision of Adamnan describes the journey of Adamnan's soul, which is guided by an angel. He first travels through a fragrance-filled realm. He next goes through the seven stages through which an aberrant soul passes to reach perfection. Next, he passes through the land of torment, which is filled with fiends. Historically, this account is very important because it is one of the first medieval Irish out-of-body experiences to be recorded.

## Visions
See **Deathbed Visions.**

# V

## Visions of God
See **God.**

## Visions of Unborn Children
On occasion, people that travel out of their body to the other side and those that have had a near-death experience have seen their unborn children before these children came into earthly life. One person that traveled through the astral realms about a year before her marriage found herself in a place where she saw a boy that she never forgot. Years later she recognized that boy in her then five-year-old son. There have been cases of near-death experiences in which people that have crossed over interact with others in the spiritual realm, only to recognize the others in their children who are born sometime later. In **Raymond Moody Jr.'s** book *Life Before Life*, there are accounts of parents who saw and spoke with the children that would be born to them in the future.

## Visitation
See **Afterlife Visitations.**

## Visits to the Afterlife
Journeying to the afterlife is not only done via death. Those still existing in the physical world are able to journey there as well. There have been numerous accounts of those who traveled to the spiritual world after being proclaimed clinically dead, only to be revived and return to life (often under protest on the other side) to complete their mission or their time on earth. Others travel there during sleep, while under hypnosis, while critically ill, or by using induction techniques that allow the soul to journey outside of the physical body.

In addition, instead of incarnating back into a life in the physical world, a spirit may wait in the spiritual world for loved ones who are still in the physical world. Others move back and forth between the physical world and the afterlife, checking on their loved ones left behind. This is one reason why people report seeing ghosts.

## Visual Communication
A communication by sight, usually given by a loved one that has died, in an effort to communicate that they

are alive and well on the other side. In a visual communication, the experiencer may see a picture or images of the deceased in the form of a vision. The vision is spontaneous and can occur anywhere at anytime. Usually, the deceased person appears younger and in better health than before they crossed over. See also **After-Death Communication.**

## Voices
See **After-Death Communication; Auditory Communication.**

## Void
In the unseen world, a great void is said to be located in the lower realms. References to this void first appear in ancient legends and scriptures, where the void is referred to as the abyss. The word *abyss* is derived from the Greek word *abyssos,* which means "the bottomless pit." In the biblical book of Revelation (20:1–3), the abyss is where the archangel **Michael** will

lock Satan away for a thousand years. In ancient Babylonian lore, there is a female spirit of the abyss named Apsu. In ancient Hebrew beliefs, Abaddon, another spirit being, was the guardian over the abyss.

Reference to a great void can also be found in some of today's near-death-experience accounts, such as that of **Ned Dougherty,** who shares his journey to the other side and back in his book *Fast Lane to Heaven.* Dougherty speaks of falling slowly into a dark and what seemed like an endless, empty space. He felt that reaching the bottom would have meant the end to his existence. In another experience, **Angie Fenimore,** in her book *Beyond the Darkness*, writes of committing suicide and, after crossing over, finding herself in a vast space of darkness and desolation. This great void is believed by many to be the same realm that religions are speaking of when they teach about hell and purgatory.

"I saw Eternity the other night
Like a great ring of pure and endless light,
All calm as it was bright."
—Henry Vaughan, "The World (1)"

# W

## Walk-Ins

A term that is used for a highly developed entity from the spiritual world who, with the permission of a soul inhabiting a physical body, enters that body to begin its mission on earth. The soul occupying the body leaves and enters the spiritual world. By walking into an adult body, the being can right away get started in its work on earth while avoiding childhood. The two individual souls have agreed in advance to switch places. The first soul, the one in the body, has reached its limit and gone as far as it can in its spiritual development on earth. This does not prevent the soul from incarnating back into life in the future. The soul that is taking over will learn different lessons than the one before and will live out the remaining lifespan in an entirely different capacity. Another term for this walk-in phenomenon is *soul transference*. Author and channeler **Ruth Montgomery** first brought walk-ins to public attention.

## Wandering Spirits

Another term for **Lost Souls.**

## Welcoming, The

Our welcome into the afterlife can be any number of ways. Near-death experiencers have reported seeing angels, spirit guides, and, most often, relatives come to greet them. Apparently, there is a great celebration when a spirit that's newly departed from earth returns home to the spiritual world. The person, whose memory of the spiritual world is very foggy at this point, is greeted by a relative or close friend (depending on one's life circumstances) and is then led to an area for a review of their life. At that point, they see higher beings, such as elders or important religious figures (if that is what is expected). In some instances, people are welcomed by religious figures such as **Jesus** (if one was Christian) in order to make the transition easier and the welcoming warmer. The welcoming takes place immediately after one has passed through the tunnel and is entering the light.

## White Sounds

Sometimes referred to as "white noise," these sounds are believed to be distortions that are captured on tape when endeavoring to record the voice of a person existing in the spiritual world.

## Whitfield, Barbara Harris

Thanatologist, author, near-death experiencer, and therapist (1943–). She has been on the board of directors for the Kundalini Research Network and was on the faculty of Rutgers University's Institute on Alcohol and Drug Studies for twelve years. Whitfield spent six years at the University of Connecticut medical school studying the aftereffects of near-death experiences. She has also sat on the executive board of the International Association for Near-Death Studies. She is a consulting editor as well as contributor for the *Journal of Near-Death Studies*. She is the author of many published articles and several enlightening books, including *The Power of Humility; Full Circle: The Near-Death Experience and Beyond; Spiritual Awakenings: Insights of the Near Death Experience; Other Doorways to Our Soul; Final Passage: Sharing the Journey as This Life Ends; The Natural Soul;* and *Kundalini Rising: Exploring the Energy of Awakening*. Whitfield's website is *www.barbarawhitfield.com*.

## Williams, Kevin

Near-death experience researcher. Williams is the creator and webmaster of the popular near-death experience website Near Death Experience and the Afterlife and author of the book *Nothing Better Than Death*. A computer scientist, Williams first became interested in the subject of near-death experiences in the 1970s after reading **Raymond Moody Jr.**'s book *Life After Life*. Since then, Williams has devoted himself to informing others of the important messages found in near-death experience accounts. Some of the topics found on his website include near-death research conclusions, notable near-death experiences, and near-death experiences of the religious. William's website can be found at *www.near-death.com*.

# Y

## Yensen, Arthur E.

A geologist and nationally syndicated cartoonist. In August of 1932 Yensen was in a fatal car accident, which propelled him into the spiritual world. When first entering, he found himself looking at what he called "a bright, new, beautiful world, beyond imagination." For a moment he was able to see both the spiritual world and the physical world together. Then the physical world disappeared. Yensen described seeing people that were so glorious that he was filled with "awe." One of the most interesting points taken from his experience was what he termed the "Master-Vibration," which, in his view, explained why heaven was eternal. It was due to the Master-Vibration that things in the spirit world didn't break down, get old, dirty, or decay as they do on earth. The Master-Vibration, Yensen believes, emanates from **God.**

## Young Soul

See **Children; Soul(s).**

"Death is a door life opens."
—Adela Rogers St. Johns, *Love, Laughter and Tears*

# Z

## Zaleski, Carol

Historian of religion. She is the author of *Otherworldly Journeys: Accounts of Near-Death Experience in Medieval and Modern Times* and *The Life of the World to Come,* and coauthor, with Philip Zaleski, of *Prayer: A History; The Book of Heaven;* and *The Book of Hell.* In *Otherworldly Journeys,* Zaleski compared a variety of near-death experience accounts of post-mortem journeys of the soul with modern-day writings of near-death experiences, showing that visions of the afterlife are based on experience, not speculation.

## Zammit, Victor J.

Afterlife researcher and author of the book *A Lawyer Presents the Case for the Afterlife: Irrefutable Objective Evidence.* Zammit had a number of psychic as well as spiritual experiences, which led to his searching for answers and proof of life after death. It was this questioning and research that led to the publishing of his book. In it, Zammit provides twenty-three different areas of proof that there is, without a doubt, an afterlife. Many experts from around the world have examined Zammit's evidence in an effort to refute it. As of yet, no one has been able to do so. More information about Zammit and his book can be found at *www.victorzammit.com.*

## Zoroaster

Ancient Persian prophet who founded the first world religion—Zoroastrianism (630–550 BC). He was born in Medea and was active in Bactria. He was a man known for his devotion and obedience to **God.** According to the Zend Avesta, the sacred book of Zoroastrianism, Zoroaster was born in Azerbaijan, in northern **Persia.** He is said to have received a vision from Ahura Mazda, **(God),** the god of light, who called on him to preach the truth. Zoroaster began preaching his message of cosmic strife between Ahura Mazda and Ahriman, the principle of evil. He taught that the world is polarized in a perpetual battle between good and evil and that we are supposed to choose between them. Zoroaster emphasized good thoughts, good words, and good deeds. The end of the world would come when the forces of light would triumph and the saved souls would rejoice in their victory. Zoroaster's teaching became the guiding light of Persian civilization and was called Zoroastrianism.

Zoroastrians had keen ideas about the spiritual world, God, and the spiritual beings that dwell there. Followers of Zoroaster believed in a god that created all things and oversaw the heavens and earth. There were also powerful spiritual beings that are the equivalent of the angels of **Christianity.** Zoroaster learned of these beings and more in what seems to be out-of body experiences to the spiritual realm, as it is said that he made numerous trips to the spiritual world. In fact, the Zend Avesta is filled with references to the spiritual world.

In Zoroastrianism, every thought and action of an individual is seen as contributing to his or her existence after death. It is believed that the earthly life is connected with the afterlife, which is perceived as a state of being where God will reward good conduct and punish bad. In addition, Zoroastrians believe that the soul of the departed remains near the body for three days. On the fourth day, the soul crosses over the **Chinvat Bridge.** Afterward, there is a weighing of good and evil deeds. If the good actions outweigh the bad, the soul ascends to heaven, which is viewed as a place of eternal happiness and light. If, however, the bad deeds outweigh the good, that person goes to hell, a place of darkness and terror. Unlike the hell of other beliefs, the Zoroastrian hell is not everlasting. There is a final judgment that occurs at the end of time. During this period, the bodies of the dead are resurrected and reunited with their souls. Afterward, there is a final purgation and cleansing of all souls, and all will be allowed to enter into heaven.

Zoroaster held that angels dwelled within the unseen spiritual world and worked very closely with God. He believed that the angels emanated from God and were a part of the divine. Zoroaster wrote that there are both male and female angels. He portrayed them as large and human-like. According to Zoroaster, there are six archangels that assisted God. These six angels represented six fundamental moral ideas: wisdom, truth, devotion, desirable dominion, wholeness, and immortality. In addition, from the spiritual world, each was a protector of one of six aspects of creation: cattle, fire, earth, the sky, water, and plants. Other spiritual beings included the angel of fertility and fruitfulness; the angel of fire; the angel of blessings; the angel of truth, justice, holiness, and virtue; the angel of divine intuition; the angel of justice; and the angel of light and mercy. There were also angelic beings that guarded the interests of humankind, although God himself was regarded as the protector of humankind. Finally, there was the spirit of darkness, God's adversary.

# SOURCES AND
# RECOMMENDED READING

━━━◆━━━

## *Books*

Altea, Rosemary. *The Eagle and the Rose.* New York: Warner Books, 1995.

———. *Proud Spirit: Lessons, Insights and Healing from "The Voice of the Spirit World."* New York: Eagle Brook, 1997.

Anderson, George, and Andrew Barone. *George Anderson's Lessons from the Light.* New York: G.P. Putnam's Sons, 1999.

Atwater, P. M. H. *The Big Book of Near-Death Experiences.* Charlottesville, VA: Hampton Roads Publishing Company, 2007.

———. *Coming Back to Life: The After-Effects of the Near-Death Experience.* New York: Ballantine Books, 1988.

———. *The Complete Idiot's Guide to Near Death Experiences.* Indianapolis: Alpha Books, 2000.

Bartlett, John, and Justin Kaplan. *Bartlett's Familiar Quotations.* New York: Little, Brown & Co., 1992.

Barrett, William. *Death-Bed Visions.* Northamptonshire, England: The Aquarian Press, 1986.

Bongard, Gerald. *The Near-Birth Experience: A Journey to the Center of Self.* New York: Marlowe & Company, 2000.

Briggs, Constance Victoria. *The Encyclopedia of Angels*. New York: Plume, 1997.

Brinkley, Dannion. *Saved by the Light*. New York: Villard Books, 1994.

Browne, Sylvia. *Conversations with the Other Side*. Carlsbad, CA: Hay House, 2002.

————. *Life on the Other Side: A Psychic's Tour of the Afterlife*. New York: New American Library, 2000.

————. *The Other Side and Back*. New York: Dutton, 1999.

————. *Visits from the Afterlife: The Truth about Hauntings, Spirits, and Reunions with Lost Loved Ones*. New York: New American Library, 2004.

Cannon, Dolores. *Between Death & Life*. Huntsville, AR: Ozark Mountain Publishers, 1993.

Dougherty, Ned. *Fast Lane to Heaven*. Charlottesville, VA: Hampton Roads Publishing Company, 2001.

Eadie, Betty J. *Embraced by the Light*. Placerville, CA: Gold Leaf Press, 1992.

Edward, John. *One Last Time: A Psychic Medium Speaks to Those We Have Loved and Lost*. New York: Berkley Publishing Group, 1998.

Fenimore, Angie. *Beyond the Darkness*. New York: Bantam Books, 1995.

Fuller, John G. *Ghost of Flight 401*. New York: Berkley Publishing, 1976.

Guggenheim, Bill, and Judy Guggenheim. *Hello From Heaven*. New York: Bantam Books, 1995.

Guiley, Rosemary Ellen. *Harper's Encyclopedia of Mystical and Paranormal Experience*. New York: Harper Collins, 1991.

Guetebier, Amber, and Brenda Knight. *The Poetry Oracle*. San Francisco, CA: CCC Publishing, 2008.

Hamilton-Parker, Craig. *What to Do When You Are Dead*. New York: Sterling Publishing Company, 2001.

Langley, Noel. *Edgar Cayce on Reincarnation*. New York: Warner Books, 1967.

Lewis, James R. *The Death and Afterlife Book*. Canton, MI: Visible Ink Press, 1995.

Lundahl, Craig R., and Harold A. Widdison, *The Eternal Journey*. New York: Warner Books, 1997.

Maggio, Rosalie. *The New Beacon Book of Quotations by Women*. Boston: Beacon Press, 1996.

Martin, Joel, and Patricia Romanowski. *We Are Not Forgotten: George Anderson's Messages of Love*. New York: Berkley Publishing, 1991.

———. *We Don't Die: George Anderson's Conversations With the Other Side*. New York: Berkley Publishing, 1998.

Mitchell, Janet Lee. *Out-of-Body Experiences: A Handbook*. New York: Ballantine Books, 1981.

Monroe, Robert. *Journeys Out of the Body*. New York: Main Street Books, 1971

Montgomery, Ruth. *Here and Hereafter*. Brooklyn, NY: Fawcett Crest Books, 1968.

Moody, Raymond. *Life After Life*. Covington, GA: Mockingbird Books, 1975.

Morrissey, Dianne. *You Can See the Light*. Walpole, NH: Stillpoint Publishing, 1997.

Newton, Michael. *Destiny of Souls: New Case Studies of Life Between Lives*. St. Paul, MN: Llewellyn Publications, 2001.

———. *Journey of Souls: Case Studies of Life Between Lives*. St. Paul, MN: Llewellyn, 1994.

Novak, Peter. *The Lost Secret of Death: Our Divided Souls and the Afterlife*. Charlottesville, VA: Hampton Roads Publishing, 2003.

Price, Jan. *The Other Side of Death*. New York: Fawcett Columbine, 1996.

Ritchie, George G., and Elizabeth Sherrill. *Return from Tomorrow*. Old Tappan, NJ: Spire Books, 1978.

Schwartz, Gary, with William L. Simon. *Afterlife Experiments*. New York: Atria Books, 2003.

Springer, Rebecca. *Within Heaven's Gate*. New Kensington, PA: Whitaker House, 1984.

Taylor, Ruth Mattson. *Witness From Beyond*. New York: Hawthorn Books, 1975.

Van Praagh, James. *Talking to Heaven: A Medium's Message of Life After Death*. New York: Signet, 1997.

Wills-Brandon, Carla. *One Last Hug Before I Go: The Mystery and Meaning of Deathbed Visions*. Deerfield Beach, FL: Health Communications, 2000.

## *Websites*

Afterlife Knowledge, *www.afterlife-knowledge.com*

All About Spirituality, *www.allaboutspirituality.org*

American Association Electronic Voice Phenomena, *www.aaevp.com /index.htm*

American Society for Psychical Research, *www.aspr.com*

Astral Journeys, *www.reconnections.net/astral_journeys.htm*

Australian Institute of Parapsychological Research, Inc., *www.aiprinc.org*

Biographies of Classical Mediums and Spiritualists, *www.spiritwriting .com/mediumbiographies.html*

Edward, John, *www.johnedward.net/learnmore_crossingover.htm*

Ellie Crystal's Metaphysicaland Science Website, *www.crystalinks.com*

Encyclopedia of the Unusual and Unexplained: Afterlife Mysteries, *www.unexplainedstuff.com/Afterlife-Mysteries/Individual-Human-Experience-with-Death-and-the-Afterlife.html*

*Evidence for the Afterlife,* Victor J. Zammit, *www.victorzammit.com*

First Spiritual Temple, *www.fst.org*

Fortune City, *www.fortunecity.com/roswell/seance/78/ind2.htm*

George Anderson Grief Support Programs, *www.georgeanderson.com*

Global Oneness, *www.experiencefestival.com*

Haunt Masters Club, *www.hauntmastersclub.com*

Haunted Museum, *www.prairieghosts.com/museum.html*

International Association for Near-Death Studies, Inc., *www.iands.org*

Life After Death, *www.fatheralexander.org/booklets/english/life_after_death.htm*

Lites of Heaven, *www.litesofheaven.com/life-after-death.html*

Meta-Religion, *www.meta-religion.com/contact.htm*

Muldoon, Sylvan, *www.psychwww.com/asc/obe/whois_mu.html*

Near Death Experience Research Foundation, *www.nderf.org*

Near-Death Experience of David Perry, *homepages.rootsweb.ancestry.com/~dagjones/docs/neardeath.html*

Near-Death Experiences and the Afterlife, *www.near-death.com*

Ozark Mountain Publishing Inc., *www.ozarkmt.com*

South of Heaven, *www.southofheaven.smartemail.co.uk*

Spirit Daily, *www.spiritdaily.org*

Stephen O'Brien, Messenger for Another world, *website.lineone.net/~enlightenment/index.htm*

SurvivalAfterDeath.org.uk, *www.survivalafterdeath.org.uk*

The New Institute of Life Between Lives Hypnotherapy, *www .spiritualregression.org*

Website of P. M. H. Atwater, *www.cinemind.com/atwater/bio.html*

Word Gems, *www.word-gems.com/death.html*

World ITC, *www.worlditc.org*

# ACKNOWLEDGMENTS

I would like to thank my husband Ghobad and my children Kion and Shireen for their unyielding support and patience as I researched and wrote this book. A special debt of gratitude is also owed to Amber Guetebier, Rachel Leach, and the editorial and artistic staff at Red Wheel Weiser. Without all of these people this book would not have been possible.

# ABOUT THE AUTHOR

Constance Victoria Briggs is a researcher and writer on metaphysical, spiritual, and paranormal subjects. Her interest in these subjects began early in life, stimulated by her own personal experiences in these areas. She has had mystical experiences, out-of-body experiences, and communication with the other side. Constance's goal is to give everyone the opportunity to question and learn, while answering intriguing questions about subjects that lie beyond the surface of life.

Constance is the author of two books, *The Encyclopedia of Angels* and *The Encyclopedia of God*. She and her family make their home in Southern California. Visit her website at: *www.starseedmission.com*

## TO OUR READERS

Weiser Books, an imprint of Red Wheel/Weiser, publishes books across the entire spectrum of occult and esoteric subjects. Our mission is to publish quality books that will make a difference in people's lives without advocating any one particular path or field of study. We value the integrity, originality, and depth of knowledge of our authors.

Our readers are our most important resource, and we appreciate your input, suggestions, and ideas about what you would like to see published. Please feel free to contact us to request our latest book catalog, or to be added to our mailing list.

Red Wheel/Weiser, LLC
500 Third Street, Suite 230
San Francisco, CA  94107
*www.redwheelweiser.com*